Poland to Pearl Harbor

Poland to Pearl Harbor

The Making of the Second World War

William Carr

Edward Arnold

First published in Great Britain 1985 by
Edward Arnold (Publishers) Ltd, 41 Bedford Square, London WC1B 3DQ

Edward Arnold (Australia) Pty Ltd, 80 Waverley Road, Caulfield East, Victoria
3145, Australia

Edward Arnold, 300 North Charles Street, Baltimore, Maryland 21201, USA

British Library Cataloguing in Publication Data

Carr, William
   Poland to Pearl Harbor: the making of the
   Second World War.
   1. World War, 1939–1945—Causes
   I. Title
   940.53'11   D741

   ISBN 0–7131–6438–7

To Kathleen and Mary Louise

Text set in 10/11pt Baskerville
by Colset Private Limited, Singapore
Printed in Great Britain by The Camelot Press Ltd, Southampton

Contents

Abbreviations Used in the Footnotes

AHR	*American Historical Review*
DDF	*Documents diplomatiques français*
FRUS	*Foreign Relations of the United States*
GDFP	*Documents on German Foreign Policy*
HZ	*Historische Zeitschrift*
IMT	*International Military Tribunal*
JMH	*Journal of Modern History*
KTB	*Kriegstagebuch*
KTB/OKW	*Kriegstagebuch des Oberkommandos der Wehrmacht*
MGM	*Militärgeschichtliche Mitteilungen*
ZfG	*Zeitschrift für Geschichtswissenschaft*

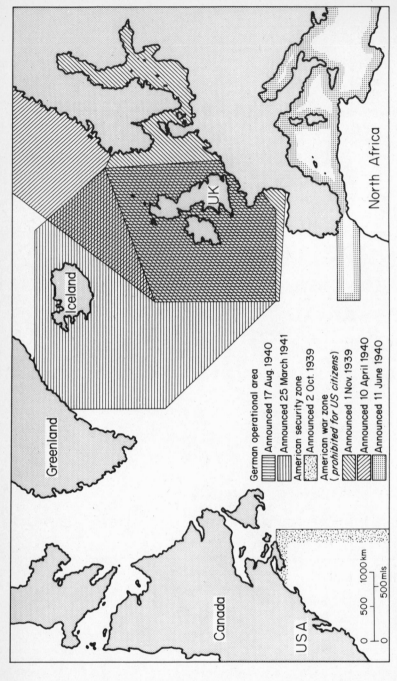

The Battle of the Atlantic

German operational area
Announced 17 Aug. 1940
Announced 25 March 1941

American security zone
Announced 2 Oct. 1939

American war zone
(*prohibited for US citizens*)
Announced 1 Nov. 1939
Announced 10 April 1940
Announced 11 June 1940

Greenland

Iceland

UK

North Africa

Canada

USA

0   500   1000 km
0   500 mls

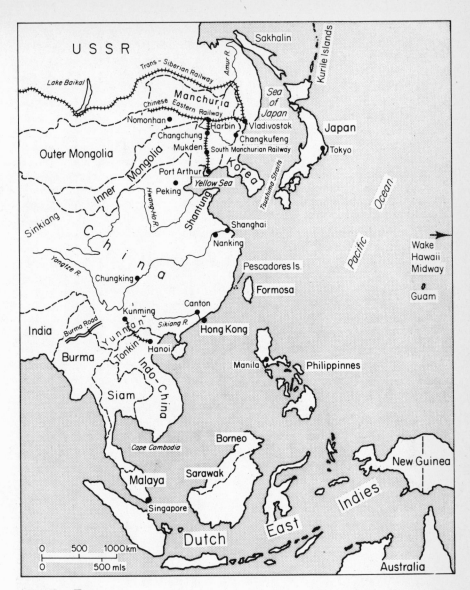

The Far East

Preface

Much has been written about the origins of the Second World War and about the military campaigns during that conflict. This study on the making of the war is concerned with a rather different problem: how did it come about that the attack on Poland, which ended in a matter of days in a total German victory, followed by some months of relative military inactivity, led in 1941 to a truly global war when the Soviet Union and the United States of America entered the conflict within six months of each other? This question cannot be answered satisfactorily if the war is conceived of as a wholly European phenomenon. A broader scenario is called for, one which takes account of the collapse of international order in the Far East where Japan was seeking to make herself the dominant power in east Asia. The militarization of Japanese policy in the 1930s and the American response to it are as important for understanding the escalation of the war in 1941 as Hitler's fateful decision to attack the Soviet Union in a bid to make Nazi Germany the dominant power in Europe from the Atlantic to the Urals.

It would be sheer presumption to claim that I have mastered in its entirety the formidable mass of material: primary printed sources and secondary works – to say nothing of unprinted archival material – appertaining to the policies of half a dozen major powers. What is offered here is in the nature of an interpretative essay which examines the interrelationship between the fears, conflicting ambitions and misconceptions of the policy-makers: primarily those in Washington, Berlin and Tokyo and to a lesser extent those in London and Moscow. Of course, it is no longer possible to conceive of international relations exclusively in terms of diplomatic correspondence and foreign office memoranda. The conflicting forces which determine the broad thrust of a country's foreign policy – economic interests, military strategies and ideological fixations of ruling groups – figure prominently in this study.

I am indebted to many scholars both in Europe and in the United States for helpful suggestions and for encouraging me to perservere with this work. A special word of thanks is due to the Department of History at the University of Utah for inviting me to teach in Salt Lake City in the summer of 1983. Without the splendid facilities of the university library this book would have taken much longer to complete.

Finally, I owe, as always, an immense debt of gratitude to my wife for her patience and understanding during the long absences and periods of mental withdrawal which seem to be inseparable from the writing of any book.

Sheffield
September 1984

1

The *Dramatis Personae*: America, Germany and Japan

The history of the twentieth century has been moulded in large measure by a titanic clash between two secular forces which emerged out of the carnage and upheaval of the First World War. In eastern Europe, as the 600-year-old Romanov Empire collapsed in chaos, the followers of Lenin came to power and laid the foundations of the new Soviet state, the nucleus today of a world-wide socialist order embracing one-third of humanity. Simultaneously, as the world supremacy of Europe crumbled under the strain of four years of bloody warfare, the United States of America emerged phoenix-like out of the ashes as a world power of the first magnitude and the linch-pin of the liberal–capitalist order.

As the old balance of power established in Europe in 1871 disintegrated under the strain of war and the old industrial powers Britain and Germany tore each other apart, the United States entering the war in 1917 exerted immense influence over the post-war settlement. Not only was her military contribution decisive in the closing stages of the fighting; behind the respect paid to Woodrow Wilson, one-time professor of political science and twice-elected president of the United States, lay a growing and grudging recognition that the state of which he was head had at last emerged on the international scene as a major political and economic force.

Statistics reveal the extent of the dramatic transformation in America's fortunes. Although she had lent and invested abroad before 1914, the United States remained on balance a debtor nation owing Europe approximately $1,000 million. The war turned her into a creditor nation to the tune of $12,000 million, of which $10,350 million represented allied war debts. Under the stimulus of orders from the belligerent powers, particularly Britain and France, for raw materials and munitions the productive capacity of the United States increased by about 15 per cent during the First World War. In 1914 she exported $6 million worth of explosives; by 1916 the figure was $467 million. American prosperity did not end abruptly in 1918. Throughout the 1920s American productive capacity continued to grow. By 1929 American industry was producing 70 per cent more goods with the same labour force as she had done 10 years previously. In the same year American industrial production represented 40 per cent of the world total and world indebtedness to the United States reached a staggering total of $20,000 million.

While it would be grossly misleading to interpret American foreign policy in the interwar years in terms of a facile economic determinism, there can be little doubt that the search for markets to dispose of surplus production remained a dominant theme of American commercial policy in the 1920s and 1930s. In

1929 when the American share of world trade was 15.6 per cent, 14 million Americans depended for their livelihood on this trade; copper, tobacco and tyres were very heavily dependent on foreign markets.[1] The active interest the United States showed in the removal of trade barriers in the 1930s cannot be explained simply as an axiomatic corollary of the liberal political philosophy in which American policy-makers were steeped; it was quite simply a matter of economic necessity. Similarly, America's commitment to the preservation of world peace, a theme constantly reiterated by successive secretaries of state, was not just a matter of ethical attitudes; it reflected concern about the negative effects of war on America's world trade as well as anxiety about the threat civil disturbances in Europe and Asia posed to the security of America's vast over-seas investments both public and private. Economic, strategic and ethical threads were inseparably interwoven in the pattern of American foreign policy.

So, although isolationism became a formidable and emotive force in the interwar years handled by administrations with great circumspection, for com-pelling economic reasons the United States could not afford to turn her back on the wider world. When the United States refused to join the League of Nations she may well have dealt that organization a body blow from which it never fully recovered. But that decision did not represent a head-long flight from internationalism. Indeed, had Wilson compromised on Article X, which com-mitted League members to uphold the territorial status quo, the Senate might well have accepted the Covenant – for many of Wilson's opponents accepted the general proposition that the United States must now play a leading role in world affairs.

Far from ignoring the rest of the world, successive administrations played an active role in the search for peace. For example, Secretary of State Charles Evans Hughes's intervention during the impasse over reparations in 1923-4, when Franco-German relations plummeted to an extremely low level, proved crucial in defusing that situation and bringing about the Dawes settlement. Continuing American interest in Europe was hardly surprising in view of the massive economic stake the United States had in the continent. In 1929 45 per cent of all American agricultural exports were sold in Europe; there were over 1,300 American or American-controlled firms operating in Europe; and American investment in Europe totalled $4,300 million. To protect American economic interests peace was essential and peace in its turn was expected to provide optimum conditions for the expansion of America's stake in world markets.

A dynamic foreign commercial policy was one major ingredient in American policy in the 1920s and 1930s. Another was the defence of the western hemi-sphere and of American imperial interests in the Far East. During the 1890s the American eagle was stirring its wings conscious of its growing power. But it was the Spanish–American War of 1898, in the course of which the United States acquired the Philippines as well as the islands of Guam, Hawaii, Midway,

---

[1]Although under 10 per cent of American trade was conducted with the outside world, in key sections of the economy dependence on export markets was crucially important; in 1929, for example, 49.2 per cent of cotton, 50 per cent of cycle and 41.5 per cent of typewriter production was exported: H.J. Schröder, *Deutschland und die Vereinigten Staaten 1933-1939. Wirtschaft und Politik in der Entwicklung des deutsch-amerikanischen Gegensatzes* (Wiesbaden, 1970), p. 54.

Samoa and Wake, that really conferred on her the status of a world power, bringing with it the problems of global defence. President Theodore Roosevelt, determined that the United States should play in world affairs a role commensurate with her new status, commenced the construction of a large navy. By 1914 the United States had become one of the leading naval powers in the world.

Other areas of importance to the United States in the twentieth century were Central and South America. The acquisition of the Panama Canal Zone in 1903 and the building by American engineers of the canal linking the two oceans drew the United States inexorably into the affairs of Central America. In the decade before the First World War the United States intervened constantly in the internal affairs of one Central American state after another. She established virtual protectorates over Cuba, Haiti, Nicaragua, Panama and Santo Domingo. In Cuba and Nicaragua she acquired bases to complete her control of the Caribbean. Successive presidents – Theodore Roosevelt, William Howard Taft and Woodrow Wilson – regardless of their political complexion, landed the marines in these republics as and when required to restore order and ensure that debts were paid – for by 1914 over one quarter of America's foreign investments were in Central America. And while the great powers were locked in mortal combat in Europe, the United States was engaged in a running battle in Mexico; it was Wilson, the great apostle of internationalism in 1919, who landed troops at Vera Cruz in 1914 to overthrow President Victoriano Huerta and sent General John Pershing into Mexico again in 1916 to subdue the forces of Pancho Villa.

After the First World War the United States, painfully conscious of growing resentment in Central and South America, gradually abandoned these crude methods. President Warren Harding laid the foundations of a policy continued by President Calvin Coolidge, greatly accelerated under President Herbert Hoover and brought to fruition under President Franklin Delano Roosevelt as the 'Good Neighbour' policy. In response to the new mood the United States began to withdraw her military presence from Central America. In 1922 the marines were withdrawn from Santo Domingo, in 1925 from Nicaragua (although they returned in 1926 and remained there until 1933 to prevent the spread of revolutionary contagion from Mexico), and in 1934 from Haiti, leaving no American forces south of the Rio Grande. Already in 1928 the State Department repudiated the so-called Roosevelt Corollary to the Monroe Doctrine in which President Theodore Roosevelt attempted to justify intervention in the area. But the gradual transition to more sophisticated methods for controlling an area vital to American security did not signify any diminution of interest as the 1930s were to prove.

Finally, ideological considerations. Diffused through American society was a profound distaste for European autocracy on which so many immigrants turned their backs in the nineteenth and twentieth centuries. This was allied to a firm belief in liberal democracy as the form of government not only best suited for Americans but the model for all mankind. The notion of a universal mission to reform the Old World, of which Woodrow Wilson was the most impressive and articulate exponent, persisted – albeit in diminished form – after the First World War despite the Senate's refusal to endorse the

Treaty of Versailles in 1920. This idealistic spirit, which looked forward to the day when swords were beaten into ploughshares, goes a long way towards explaining the constant interest the United States displayed in disarmament between the wars. American delegates participated in the negotiations at Geneva; in the Three-Power Conference of 1927, in the Preparatory Commission drawing up a draft convention for a full conference, and finally in the Disarmament Conference in 1932. Roosevelt and Cordell Hull were ardent supporters of Wilson and both sympathized with his international outlook.[2] During the Second World War Roosevelt, freed from the restraint of isolationism, reverted to the idealism of his younger days, to the dream of one world wedded to democracy, self-determination and capitalism, a new order which would be brought into being by the moral authority and political muscle of the United States.

Although the inhumanity of the Nazis deeply offended most Americans including leading members of the administration, it did not automatically align all Americans with the democracies of the Old World. The isolationist ideology exerted as much if not more influence on American policy, especially in the late 1930s. Isolationists came from many different groups in American society: ethnic minorities, conservative opponents of Roosevelt, liberal reformers, socialists and out-and-out pacificists. What held them together was disillusionment with the internationalism of Wilson and a deep conviction that war was an abomination to be avoided at all costs. America must steer clear of all foreign entanglements certain to end in conflict, and retire into herself in a storm-tossed world confident that she was strong enough to repel any invader. That was the isolationist message. How the power conflict in the Atlantic and Pacific eventually destroyed isolationism as a political force is one of the themes of this book. Of course, it must not be supposed that Americans can be neatly divided into isolationists and internationalists. Those who took up these positions were political activists; the vast majority of ordinary citizens, as elsewhere in the world, were pretty indifferent to foreign policy and primarily concerned with bread-and-butter issues.

Few would deny that a huge gulf separated the political tradition of George Washington and Thomas Jefferson from that of Germany which, though ostensibly republican after the First World War, remained deeply authoritarian in outlook. Yet confronted by the world economic crisis beginning in October 1929, which sent shock tremors through the capitalist system, the Americans, like the Germans, gave their support to men of outstanding ability prepared to adopt extra-ordinary measures to cope with mass unemployment. Between 13 million and 15 million Americans were out of work when Franklin Roosevelt delivered his Inaugural Address on 4 March 1933, while in Germany when Adolf Hitler was appointed chancellor on 30 January the

---

[2]Roosevelt's internationalism was frequently coloured by political ambition; he abandoned his bellicose nationalist stance after the First World War in favour of the politically fashionable Wilsonism only to abandon that in the late 1920s as it waned in popularity.

unemployed had reached a total of six million.[3]

While neither leader had any expert knowledge of economics, both had an acute ear for the political effects of economic policy. And to cope with the crisis of capitalism both adopted broadly interventionist methods. In February 1933 Hitler announced a state-sponsored Four Year Plan to save German farmers and workers. In May and June Roosevelt secured the consent of Congress to the National Industrial Recovery Act, the Agricultural Adjustment Act and the Tennessee Valley Authority. Under the auspices of the Tennessee Valley Authority a remarkable piece of regional planning was carried out which caught the imagination of the world and seemed to epitomize the essence of the New Deal.

In Germany economic recovery was made possible through a deliberate policy of deficit financing. Already in 1932 the Nazis had taken over the ideas of the 'German Keynesians', i.e. those economists working along the same lines as John Maynard Keynes, who believed that countries should spend their way out of deflationary situations. With the appointment of Hjalmar Schacht as president of the Reichsbank in March 1933 Hitler found a financier willing to place unlimited credit at the government's disposal to make Germany a great power once more. With the willing co-operation of key sectors of heavy industry – converted to the Nazi cause in the winter of 1932–3 by the promise to destroy the free trade unions and 'Marxist' parties and hand out lucrative arms orders – the recovery got under way quickly.[4]

The Reinhardt Plan in June 1933 set the pattern with substantial tax concessions to industry, the reduction of social contributions and the placing of government orders for road construction and house improvements worth 1,000 Reichsmarks (RM). By the end of 1934 with the help of massive credits totalling 5,000 million RM, the economy had pulled out of crisis. Only in 1935 did armament orders replace work procurement as the pacemaker in the growth of the economy; military expenditure rose from 4 per cent of all public expenditure in 1933 to 39 per cent by 1936 and to 50 per cent by 1938. While other west European countries had pools of unemployment throughout the 1930s, by the end of 1936 Nazi Germany had attained full employment and shortages of skilled labour manifested themselves in certain key industries. And despite Nazi attempts to keep wage rates low, by 1938 real wages (weekly) exceeded the 1929 level while real GNP rose by an average 10.4 per cent from 1933 to 1938. Quite apart from the heavy price the German people paid in terms of the loss of political liberty and exposure to the Nazis' terroristic methods, the 'German economic miracle' rested on insecure foundations; the Nazis ignored 'demand management', i.e. no serious attempt was made to prevent 'overheating' after

[3]In some respects the American crisis was more severe than the German; since 1928 industrial production had fallen 44 per cent compared with 26 per cent in Germany, and the gross income of farmers by 60 per cent compared with 37 per cent in Germany. Since 1929 exports had fallen by 73 per cent compared with 70 per cent in Germany.

[4]In America commercial interests and light industry supported Roosevelt but the great industrial corporations were hostile. The General Consul in New York reported in August 1933 that there was much understanding for Germany in Wall Street where German economic policy was compared favourably with Roosevelt's 'socialization measures': P. Schäfer, 'Franklin D. Roosevelt und das New Deal', *ZfG* 4 (1965), p. 605.

the attainment of full employment so that inflationary pressures – to be referred to later – built up in the economy on the eve of war.

Roosevelt was much less successful with his New Deal. Ideologically it was an uneasy amalgam of mutually exclusive intellectual traditions: Progressivism which sought to reform society and curb Big Business – but not at the expense of rugged individualism – blended with the views of the institutional school of economics which advocated the regulation of the economy. The New Deal sought, first, to alleviate the hardship consequent upon the crisis; second, to rejuvenate the economy in the long-term; and, third, to introduce long-delayed reforms to bring the United States into line with other advanced countries. But this is *post-hoc* rationalization. There was no overall strategy; merely a series of measures very largely improvised by the president with the help of a group of advisers known as the 'Brain Trust'. Roosevelt was rightly compared with a man 'who, having no time for a deliberate aim, chooses a shot gun rather than a rifle for his weapon in the hope that one or more of a heavy charge of pellets may take effect in a snapshot which a simple bullet would probably miss'.[5]

Long-term recovery was, in fact, retarded by some of the short-term measures. For example, paying farmers to restrict production certainly alleviated their immediate plight and helped stabilize prices but did little to stimulate a general recovery. And the codes worked out by the National Recovery Administration which fixed minimum wage levels and maximum hours of work and regulated competition by fixing sale prices were slow in boosting production and did little to encourage badly-needed investment. What might have done the trick was a bold policy of deficit financing as in Germany. But the new administration, which had attacked Hoover for excessive public expenditure, attached overriding importance to a balanced budget. Among the first acts of the president were reductions in civil service pay and ex-servicemen's pensions. Yet, as so often with Roosevelt, he wanted the best of both worlds, and embarked on modest relief measures the cost of which he hoped would be covered by increased tax receipts; in other words, budget deficits were not planned during the First and Second New Deals but represented a casual by-product of policies designed for other purposes.

The First New Deal was followed by a Second New Deal in 1935 centred on a gigantic Works Progress Administration to take charge of all relief funds and provide work rather than dole relief to the unemployed. Other prominent features were a Social Security Act laying the foundations of old-age, unemployment and sickness insurance, and the National Labor Relations, or Wagner, Act reaffirming the right of working people to bargain collectively through their own elected representatives. By 1936 the economy was showing definite signs of recovery. But unemployment fell only once below five million in the 1930s and was back at 10 million by 1939. Furthermore, once industry had recovered from the shock of the crisis, opposition soon mounted to 'government

[5]G.M. Gathorne Hardy, *A Short History of International Affairs 1920–1939* (London, 1952), p. 279. Roosevelt remarked in 1936: 'As regards economic questions our theory is very simple: we have no theory': J.A. Garraty, 'The New Deal, National Socialism and the Great Depression', *AHR* (1973), p. 917.

interference' and 'creeping socialism'. So effective was the opposition that in 1935–6 the Supreme Court declared the National Recovery Act and the Agricultural Adjustment Act unconstitutional. In 1937, worried by criticism of mounting deficits, Roosevelt tightened credit and slashed the budget. Once government credit was withdrawn and in the absence of private investment expansion quickly collapsed. During the so-called 'Roosevelt Depression' production fell by 33 per cent and unemployment rose from 6 million to 11½ million. In an attempt to deal with this new crisis Roosevelt went back in a fit of pragmatism to unbalanced budgets; he increased expenditure on relief and public works, introduced a new Agricultural Adjustment Act to raise farm incomes, and a Fair Labor Standards Act to establish minimum wages and maximum hours of work.

But after the defeat of the Democrats in the mid-term elections in November 1938 a coalition of Republicans and Southern Democrats blocked further reform legislation. Roosevelt conceded defeat in January 1939 by declaring the New Deal at an end. Subsequently he refused to support schemes for sickness benefits and for a national medical-care service.

Summing up on the New Deals, one can say without fear of contradiction that they made a lasting impact on the United States. Federal intervention became an accepted part of the American political scene as an instrument for mitigating the harshness of *laissez-faire* capitalism. But in the short-term the New Deals were a failure compared with Nazi manipulation of the German economy. Only after war broke out in Europe generating a demand for raw materials and armaments did American unemployment fall substantially, and that only in 1941.

When the war was at its height in the 1940s Hitler and Roosevelt were deadly rivals epitomizing the conflict to the death between Totalitarianism and Democracy. This was emphatically not the case in 1933. The Nazi press commented favourably on Roosevelt's energetic measures as a welcome sign that authoritarianism was on the march even in the world's greatest democracy, and parallels were frequently drawn between the New Deal and the Four Year Plan.

Not that Hitler was ever well-disposed towards the United States. His views were from beginning to end negative and grossly distorted. On entering politics in 1919 he declared that New York's banks, industry and press were controlled by two million Jews who brought her into the First World War purely for financial gain. In a fleeting reference in *Mein Kampf* he repeated his belief that Jewish control of the stock exchanges was the most significant feature of the United States. True, in the *Secret Book* he showed some awareness of the economic power of the United States which, he declared, would enable her to defeat Europe in the struggle for markets. But, being an incorrigible racist, he attributed American economic power not to her enormous productive capacity but to the presence of racially pure emigrants from Europe who had exploited her material advantages. His conclusion in 1928 was that only a German-dominated Europe would be capable of preventing the 'threatening world hegemony of the North American continent'.[6] This phase was short-lived. By

[6]G.L. Weinberg, ed., *Hitler's Secret Book* (New York, 1962), p. 103.

1932 Hitler was referring contemptuously to America as 'a conglomerate of disparate elements' controlled by gangsters, corrupt politicians, Jews and negroes, on the brink of social revolution – for he seems to have been deeply impressed by the economic collapse of the United States – and doomed to inevitable decline.[7] He was clearly worse informed about the United States than any other country. Nor did he make the slightest effort to correct this state of affairs, ignoring the sober advice of diplomatic representatives such as Hans Dieckhoff, German ambassador in Washington from 1937 to 1938, and clinging stubbornly to his delusion that Freemasons, Jews and communists ran America, and that she could be discounted as a military factor. He did not even mention her in his calculations when addressing his top advisers on 5 November 1937.

Underestimation of American military potential remained characteristic of his outlook throughout his life. In the early months of 1933, uncertain of his footing on the international ladder, he did go out of his way to welcome the American initiative for an all-round arms reduction. But by April 1939, when he contemptuously rejected Roosevelt's appeal for peace, the need for caution was long past. On the other hand, once war broke out his desire to keep her out of the fighting as long as possible suggests that, despite a constant stream of denigratory comments about America, he still retained deep down some dim awareness of her potential as an adversary.

Although the American press was divided in its attitude to Hitler, Roosevelt did not at first anticipate any major difficulty in dealing with the new regime. He was anxious for an early meeting of the World Economic Conference at which the nations could discuss the possibility of international co-operation to overcome a crisis distinguished from previous ones by its duration and severity. Hitler, too, insisted on an early meeting and overruled Alfred Hugenberg, the minister of economics, who advocated an immediate retreat into autarky. Not that Hitler hoped for any economic benefits for Germany through international co-operation. Uppermost in his mind was the need to allay widespread fears about the new regime's intentions.

When Schacht, president of the Reichsbank, talked to Roosevelt on 6 May during a visit to Washington no fundamental differences surfaced. Hitler, sceptical about the chances of the World Economic Conference succeeding, kept a low profile and waited on events. In fact it was Roosevelt, not Hitler, who effectively sabotaged the conference. While Secretary of State Cordell Hull was in London roundly condemning the pernicious doctrine of economic nationalism and calling for free-trade agreements to stimulate the world economy, the president suddenly dropped a bombshell. On 3 July he rejected as premature the attempts being made in London to stabilize currencies. Not that he was less concerned than Hull to restore world trade by 'international economic readjustment'. But he was clear on assuming office that 'the economy at home cannot await on that accomplishment'.[8] Until other countries had raised their own prices by government action through balanced budgets he refused to

[7]H. Rauschning, *Hitler Speaks* (London, 1939), p. 77.

[8]S. Rosenman, ed., *The Public Papers and Private Addresses of Franklin D. Roosevelt* (New York, 1938–50) II, p. 14.

stabilize the dollar at too high a level. The decision to take the United States off the gold standard in April and let the dollar float was an attempt to appease American farmers; as long as the dollar continued to fall and the United States won new markets, their earnings would remain high.[9] However intelligible the president's decision appears in a domestic context, the fact remains that the conference was so angered that it quickly came to an end. The Nazis were jubilant but took care not to blame Roosevelt for the breakdown. Instead they went out of their way to praise his 'nationalistic' policy as eminently sensible and worthy of emulation.

The honeymoon in American–German relations was of limited duration. By 1934–5 deep differences both political and commercial had emerged. The brutal treatment of political opponents, especially Jews, in the new Germany aroused deep anger in the United States; that, as Hull bluntly informed the German ambassador in March 1934, was the most outstanding cause of ill-feeling between them. If in what follows more attention is devoted to financial issues this is simply to remind readers that these, too, played a substantial role in the alienation of the two countries. The first clash occurred over the repayment of German debts to America.

By 1933 Germany was unable to keep up repayments on her huge indebtedness of 24,000 RM, of which 5,000 RM were owed to the United States. The cause was a sharp decline in exports for which an overvalued mark was partly to blame.[10] Schacht, lulled into a false sense of security by his friendly reception in Washington, informed Hull two days later that Germany intended to reduce the interest rates payable on foreign debts. The next day Schacht was tartly informed by Hull that Roosevelt was 'profoundly shocked' by this suggestion. Schacht beat a hasty retreat and decided that serious negotiation with the creditor nations for a moratorium was unavoidable. At the end of May the principal creditors placed the problem in the lap of the World Economic Conference. Meanwhile on 9 June Schacht declared unilaterally that from 1 July foreign creditors would receive only 50 per cent of the interest due in foreign currency. Scrip notes for the other 50 per cent would be issued by the German government. These notes could be spent in Germany or converted into transferable currency by selling them at a 50 per cent discount. Although not an unreasonable settlement in view of Germany's difficulties, it still aroused adverse comment in the United States.

Further complications arose when Schacht threatened to make payment of interest dependent on the balance of trade between a bondholder's country and Germany. In November Schacht took fresh unilateral action when he signed treaties with Holland and Switzerland guaranteeing payment of 100 per cent of the interest due on German debts. New threats of reducing payments on bonds from 75 to 65 per cent led to American threats of retaliation. By January 1934 Schacht had agreed to redeem scrip payments at a slightly higher rate than

[9]In fact commodity prices sagged in the autumn of 1933. Roosevelt's attempt to boost them by government purchases of gold at prices above world levels – which depressed the dollar – had a very limited effect. In the end he gave way and in January 1934 the dollar was stabilized at 59 per cent of its pre-1913 gold value.

[10]The mark was overvalued by 40 per cent owing to the German wish to cling to the gold standard.

before and to work towards the ending of discriminatory payments on all foreign debts. Whereupon Britain, France, Italy, Holland, Sweden and Switzerland threatened to impound German balances. As she had favourable balances with these countries, Germany reluctantly signed treaties with them guaranteeing full payment of the Dawes and Young loans and a 40 per cent cash settlement on other loans. But because Germany was running an adverse balance with the United States, Schacht offered only 75 per cent of the interest due on the Dawes Loan. In 1935 a final settlement with the United States reduced the interest on all loans. Apart from a further protest there was nothing the United States could do about this discrimination which rankled all the more in Washington because it was felt that Germany could have continued full payment had Schacht not given priority to re-armament.

The transfer problem was no more than an irritant from which in time American–German relations would no doubt have recovered. A much more fundamental cause of friction was the clash between their respective commercial policies. Whilst the Reciprocal Trade Agreements Act of 1934 committed the United States (in theory) to the expansion of world trade, Nazi Germany under Schacht's New Plan was pursuing a policy of bilateralism with the intention of establishing a closed economy in central and south-eastern Europe.

Roosevelt's bombshell announcement on 3 July was not a retreat into economic nationalism. On the contrary, both president and secretary of state were absolutely convinced that the conquest of foreign markets was essential for long-term American recovery whatever short-term action might be necessary to alleviate poverty at home. Although previous administrations were well aware of this fundamental truth, in bursts of irrational nationalism they had raised tariff barriers first in 1921 (Fordney–McCumber Act) and again in 1930 (Smoot–Hawley Act) to appease small manufacturers and the powerful farming lobby. By 1931 some 25 countries had raised their tariffs in retaliation restricting American trade still further.

In asking Congress to support the bill which became the Reciprocal Trade Agreements Act Roosevelt described it as 'an essential step in the program of national economic recovery'.[11] Under it he was vested with plenary powers to negotiate without reference to Congress trade treaties embodying tariff cuts of up to 50 per cent. Roosevelt and Hull fully appreciated that further tariff increases would invite further retaliation and exacerbate the American position, already serious enough: American exports had fallen in value from $5,240 million in 1929 to $1,675 million in 1933. The answer, they were convinced, lay in a bold multilateral trading policy capable of winning markets to absorb American surpluses. However, as usual under New Deal legislation, a large

---

[11]Rosenman, *Public Papers* III, p. 115. Whether he was as enthusiastic as Hull initially is very doubtful. Significantly he was unwilling to oppose the efforts of George N. Peek, his special adviser on foreign trade, to negotiate a bilateral treaty with Germany in 1934. Probably not until 1935 was Roosevelt finally converted to Hull's policy: see Schröder, *Deutschland*, pp. 152–60. Interesting, too, that in 1934 Peek almost talked Roosevelt into a bilateral treaty with Germany: Lloyd C. Gardner, *Economic Aspects of New Deal Diplomacy* (Madison, 1964), pp. 101–3; A.A. Offner, *American Appeasement, United States foreign policy and Germany 1933–1938* (Cambridge, Mass., 1969), pp. 99–102.

dose of pragmatism entered into the arrangements; in order to win support in Congress it was agreed that concessions to foreigners would be selective. Industry and commerce worked hand in glove with the State Department to ensure that foreign imports were only allowed in if they represented no serious threat to American producers. In essence the treaties were almost exclusively bilateral, so minimal were the concessions the United States made to her trading partners.[12]

In theory bilateralism was, of course, the great enemy; Britain, France and Germany had all won markets at American expense by entering into bilateral agreements with former American customers. Therefore the United States insisted on the inclusion of a clause embodying most-favoured-nation treatment in all the agreements negotiated in the 1930s. This meant that concessions made by the Americans were extended to all other countries provided they did not discriminate against American goods; and concessions offered by America's partners to third countries were automatically extended to the United States. From a position of commercial equality the United States supposed that she could win new markets in the face of stiff international competition thereby solving her problem of unsold surpluses. And it should be noted that the battle against bilateralism and economic nationalism was seen, certainly by Cordell Hull, as a positive contribution to world peace: 'unhampered trade', he said, 'dovetailed with peace. High tariffs, trade barriers and unfair economic competition with war'.[13] In practice the new policy did not lead to any great increase in exports because of the limited nature of American trading concessions as well as the disturbed state of world trade. But the Reciprocal Trade Agreements did at least prevent further trade losses through possible foreign discrimination.[14]

Nevertheless, because the Reciprocal Trade Agreements Act represented a fundamental shift away from protectionism – to which the United States has never returned – any challenge to its liberal principles was bound to arouse concern in Washington. Just such a challenge was presented by the autarkical commercial policies of the Axis powers in the 1930s.

That different economic problems call for different solutions seems obvious enough, reluctant though Washington was to recognize this unpalatable fact. The German problem was not to find markets for raw materials and food surpluses but to acquire raw materials when export markets were difficult, foreign reserves dangerously low and (by 1934) Germany was running a deficit on her balance of payments. The position was further exacerbated by the tendency for raw materials to rise steadily in price in the mid 1930s whilst the

[12]D. Junker, 'Nationalstaat und Weltmacht. Die USA 1938–1941', in O. Hauser, ed., *Weltpolitik II 1939–45 14 Vorträge* (Göttingen, 1975), p. 25; cf. R. Dallek, *Franklin D. Roosevelt and American Foreign Policy 1932–1945* (New York, 1979), pp. 92–3.

[13]Quoted in A. Gardner, *Sterling–Dollar Diplomacy in Anglo-American Collaboration in the Reconstruction of Multilateral Trade* (Oxford, 1956), p. 6.

[14]Harold L. Ickes, a critic of the Reciprocal Trade Agreements, said that they 'might have led to something in ordinary times when peace was the principal preoccupation of the nations of the world but as I remarked to the President on one occasion, with the world in a turmoil they were like hunting an elephant in the jungle with a fly swatter'. Quoted in F. Wells, *The Ordeal of World Power. American Diplomacy since 1900* (Boston, 1973), p. 176.

price of manufactured goods stagnated up to 1937. In purely economic terms a policy of import controls, quotas and blocked accounts was forced on Germany. She could no longer afford to trade with the world on a most-favoured-nation basis. In September 1934 Schacht's New Plan formally recognized the facts of life; the government started to make extensive use of exchange controls introduced by previous administrations to stop the outflow of gold and foreign exchange and to regulate imports and exports. Henceforth Germany would buy no more abroad than she could pay for, and spend foreign exchange on vital imports only. A month later Schacht gave notice of Germany's intention to terminate the 1923 trade treaty with the United States – not because Schacht was uninterested in purchasing American cotton, copper and mineral oils – but because he wanted a new bilateral agreement. That the State Department would not entertain either in 1934 or later in 1937 when the Germans evinced renewed interest in negotiations. Washington feared that discrimination in favour of Germany would result in retaliation against American goods undermining the strategy on which the Trade Agreements rested. Furthermore, as Germany had been unable to build up her exports to the United States, a bilateral agreement would simply enable her to rearm at American expense.

The Americans were right in supposing that German commercial policy was closely interwoven with political and strategic objectives. The Nazis, like their predecessors, sought to transform central and south-eastern Europe into a German sphere of influence, probably as a preliminary stage in the drive for *Lebensraum* in the east. Secondly, they were determined to reduce to a minimum German dependence on imported food and raw materials so vulnerable to blockade in wartime. As the countries of south-eastern Europe had large food and raw-material surpluses they were unable to dispose of in world markets, they were only too pleased to trade with Germany and put up with the disadvantage of having in return to purchase dearer German goods. The pattern of Germany's foreign trade altered significantly. In 1932 3.5 per cent of German imports came from south-eastern Europe and 5 per cent of her exports went to that area. By 1938 the figures were 9.8 per cent and 10.3 per cent respectively. By 1938 five south-east European states – Bulgaria, Greece, Hungary, Rumania and Yugoslavia – together with Turkey exported roughly 50 per cent of their produce to Germany.[15]

Recent research suggests that these countries were in practice much less dependent on Germany than Nazi propagandists gleefully proclaimed. Nevertheless, the Americans were worried by the adverse effects of German bilateralism. For example, in 1932 the United States supplied 13.8 per cent of all Greek imports; this fell to 7 per cent in 1939 whilst Germany, which supplied only 9.6 per cent in 1932, was by 1939 supplying 29.9 per cent. This was a matter of simple economics: Greece could not afford to squander foreign exchange on high-quality American goods; she had to make do with inferior-

---

[15]In 1933 Germany took 15.35 per cent of all exports from south-eastern Europe and supplied 18.44 per cent of all imports. In 1939 the figures were 46.08 and 50.61 per cent respectively: H.E. Volkmann, 'Die NS Wirtschaft in Vorbereitung des Krieges', in W. Deist, M. Messerschmidt, W. Wette, *Das Deutsche Reich und der Zweite Weltkrieg* (Stuttgart, 1979) I, p. 257.

quality German products at higher prices purchased with her blocked marks.

The Americans did not see it that way. George S. Messersmith, who later became the most influential of the president's advisers on German affairs, commented bitterly in February 1938 on Germany's growing ambitions in south-eastern Europe: 'The developments have a very real interest to us for these countries . . . have been looking forward to trade agreements with us as part of a constructive movement towards economic peace. . . . Germany feared our trade agreement program in south-eastern Europe and now that she is embarking on this course of expansion, I see small prospect for our progress in south-eastern Europe. Even though we negotiated agreements they would have very little value for what is the use of our making arrangements between independent states when an international gangster at the point of a gun is forcing international subjection? I see the trade agreement program in general severely menaced for these events in south-eastern Europe will have a disturbing and upsetting influence generally.'[16]

Even more alarming from Washington's vantage point was German economic penetration of Latin America. For over half a century the United States had been extending her economic influence south of the Rio Grande. By 1914 nearly half her foreign investments were in Central and South America, and the Central American states had in effect become American satellites. During the First World War the United States made great inroads into the South American markets of Britain and France. Throughout the 1920s an increasing volume of American investment poured into South America; in 1913 she had a total of $170 million invested there; by 1929 the total reached a staggering $2,294 million. Some of her most important markets were located in that region; in 1935 53.5 per cent of her total steel production was exported to Latin America as well as 54.1 per cent of textile and 22 per cent of automobile production. Some countries, especially Cuba and Mexico, became very heavily dependent on the United States; in 1936 Mexico, for example, sold 61 per cent of her exports to the United States and bought from her 59 per cent of all imports.

The Roosevelt administration sought to expand this trade still further. In the mid 1930s the United States negotiated with several South American states to buy their food and raw materials in return for increased imports of American manufactured goods. And American interest in Latin American trade increased still further during the 1937–8 recession which shook the United States economy at a time when war between China and Japan was threatening American trade in the Far East and German expansionism her trade with Europe. But American success was strictly limited. By 1939 only Brazil, Colombia and Ecuador had signed treaties with the United States and that largely because they were aligned politically with her. Latin America as a whole simply could not afford the luxury of most-favoured-nation clauses. In any case powerful vested interests in the United States effectively restricted Latin American entry into their markets.

Latin America had obvious attractions for Germany. Many essential raw

[16]*FRUS* 1938 1 Memorandum 18 February 1938, p. 21.

materials – cotton, wool, coffee and mineral ores – could be purchased there. The Germans were undeterred by the competitive edge of American and British goods following the devaluation of the dollar and the pound sterling. For the Latin American states were obliged to restrict imports as foreign exchange was urgently required to service foreign loans, and could not be squandered on unlimited imports of automobiles, the price they would have to pay for an agreement with the United States. Secondly, the German trade delegation, which visited nearly all these states in 1934, offered special inducements: assured markets for their products; prices sometimes slightly higher than world levels; and in exchange manufactured goods at cut prices financed by export subsidies and astute trading techniques. On this basis bilateral treaties were signed with Argentina, Chile and Uruguay. The German share of these markets grew rapidly; in 1932 she supplied 7.3 per cent of all Latin American imports; by 1936 this rose to 14 per cent; although the American share of the market in 1932 was much greater at 28.8 per cent, it grew by a miniscule 0.6 per cent to 29.4 per cent in 1936. In some countries Germany even overtook the United States; for example, in 1934 the Germans supplied 14 per cent of all Brazilian imports compared with America's 23.6 per cent; by 1936 the figures were 23.5 and 22.1 per cent respectively despite the trade agreement with the United States. Similarly in Chile, Germany supplied 28 per cent of all imports in 1936 compared with 25.4 per cent for the United States. It may seem surprising that, although Germany was seeking with might and main to establish a *Grossraumwirtschaft* in south-eastern Europe in the 1930s, in fact in 1938 15 per cent of total German imports came from Latin America compared with 10 per cent from south-eastern Europe. The truth is that, contrary to popular belief, the Danubian basin simply could not supply all Germany's needs.[17]

American exporters and the National Foreign Trade Council constantly protested to the administration about unfair German trading practices. By 1936 the administration was taking the German threat seriously and doing what it could to counter German penetration. Though reluctant to impose discriminatory measures on Germany, the administration admitted in effect that the Reciprocal Trade Agreements had failed and resorted to more direct methods; in particular increasing use was made of the Export–Import Bank, established in 1934, to offer loans to South American states to finance their importation of American goods. By 1938 German diplomats were reporting that American representatives in Latin America were conducting a general propaganda offensive against 'totalitarian' states.[18] In effect a new element of ideological warfare was being superimposed by Washington upon a local campaign designed primarily to protect American markets. Without doubt the American experience of German economic and political penetration of Latin

[17] By 1938 it had dawned on high officials in Nazi Germany that Germany's needs could only be met fully through control of the resources of southern Russia: David E. Kaiser, *Economic Diplomacy and the Origins of Second World War* (Princeton, 1980), pp. 277–9.

[18] e.g. *GDFP*: D.I. Thomsen, chargé d'affaires in Washington to Berlin, 12 September 1938; *GDFP*: D.V. Ritter, ambassador in Brazil to Berlin, 30 March, 1938: 'Whereas last year they [the Americans] conducted the struggle against Germany primarily in the economic and commercial-political area, now they are attacking Germany politically'.

America contributed significantly to the growing belief in Washington that the Axis powers were actively conspiring together in Europe, Asia and Latin America to undermine the position of the United States.

Recent research into the Third Reich has destroyed the myth of monolithic unity in the corridors of power in Berlin, and has revealed a surprising degree of intrigue and confusion with rival groups competing for the ear of the Führer. The American situation was not so dissimilar. For the cumbersome and creaking machinery of government inherited from the eighteenth century effectively isolated the head of state and positively encouraged factionalism and rivalries between institutions. In Washington, as in Berlin, advisers with differing viewpoints were seeking through the head of state to influence the course of foreign policy. It is also abundantly clear that in this field Roosevelt and Hitler were no ciphers manipulated by selfish interest groups and without minds of their own. Though both were prone to disengage themselves from the battleground at crucial moments retreating into themselves and leaving advisers in an agony of suspense, nevertheless both retained final policy decisions in their own hands. For both had a profound sense of mission. Though Roosevelt did not refer overtly to it, as Hitler did, a contemproary observed of the president's career that 'a fierce flame [was] burning at its core'.[19]

Their style of government was uncannily alike. Both disliked career diplomats and being consummate politicians organized a command structure designed to keep final decisions in their own hands. 'His favourite technique', wrote Arthur Schlesinger of Franklin Roosevelt, 'was to keep grants of authority incomplete, jurisdictions uncertain, charters overlapping. The result of this competitive theory of administration was often confusion and exasperation at the operating level; but no other method could so reliably insure that in a large bureaucracy filled with ambitious men eager for power, the decisions and the power to make them, would remain with the President'.[20] This might have been written of Hitler so similar were the methods. Both were superb tacticians adept at twisting and weaving their way forward, improvising as they went along. Hitler was also a past master in the art of concealing his purposes from his advisers and only revealing to individuals as much information as he thought appropriate for the task in hand. So it was with Roosevelt of whom it has been said: '[He] deliberately concealed the processes of his mind. He would rather have posterity believe that for him everything was always plain and easy. . . . than ever admit to any agony of indecision'.[21]

Both were also notorious for their reluctance to make decisions, preferring instead to play for time until issues clarified themselves. And neither was strong

[19]R.G. Tugwell, *The Democratic Roosevelt. A Biography of Franklin D. Roosevelt* (Garden City, NJ, 1957), p. 12. Roosevelt's crushing retort to a subordinate vehemently advocating a certain policy was: 'I do not have to go your way and I will tell you the reason why. The reason is that although they may have made a mistake, the people of the United States have elected me President not you'. *Op. cit.*, p. 531.

[20]A.M. Schlesinger Jr, *The Coming of the New Deal* (Boston, 1959), p. 527. For perceptive comments on his style see pp. 533–44; cf. Dallek, *Foreign Policy*, pp. 532–3.

[21]Tugwell, *Democratic Roosevelt*, p. 15.

on rational analysis; both liked to externalize issues, listening to advisers arguing in front of them rather than wrestling alone with problems in the silence of the study. And both frequently by-passed official advisers preferring on occasion to seek advice from favoured outsiders, adding to the chaos endemic in the system, exacerbating rivalries between advisers and shrouding decision-making in obscurity and uncertainty until the last moment.[22] It is probably no exaggeration to say that in the case of the United States policy emerged from the clash between the views of rival departments or individuals which this personalized style encouraged, with the head of state playing the role of honest broker intervening first on one side then on the other. This was much less the case in Nazi Germany where Hitler had a firmer grip on areas which interested him such as foreign policy and military strategy but even there rival factions could and did exert some influence on policy.

Roosevelt's foreign policy, like Hitler's, has been the subject of considerable controversy over the last 30 years. In Roosevelt's case the rapid break-down of wartime unity between the United States and Soviet Russia led many to question his handling of Stalin during the Second World War. His stature has been diminished by the charge, which owes much to hindsight, that he failed to recognize the threat posed by Soviet expansionism and react promptly to it. And as Roosevelt was an unfathomable character who, like Hitler, left comparatively little by way of marginalia and no memoirs, his policy throughout his terms of office is open to more than one interpretation.

Many historians have interpreted American foreign policy in the 1930s in terms of an ideological tug-of-war between a far-seeing president who was fully aware of the danger of fascism and constantly seeking out opportunities to aid the western democracies, and a reactionary and isolationist-minded public opinion morbidly suspicious of all foreign entanglements. For purely tactical reasons Roosevelt was obliged to dissemble, move forward with infinite caution and avoid damaging confrontations with the isolationists. Some have argued that he was perfectly right to do so, biding his time until the American people were ready to fight.[23] Others accuse him of a lamentable lack of leadership because he chose to drift with the tide and suppress his own preferences.[24]

Whatever the emphasis, this broad interpretation posits a duality in his behaviour which probably did not exist. The evidence suggests that during his first term as president from 1933 to 1936 Roosevelt's distaste for Nazi and Japanese aggressors, a reaction which all decent Americans shared, was moderated by an equally strong determination, supported by an overwhelming

[22]The effects were described vividly by John Maynard Keynes: 'in a negotiation lasting weeks, the situation is entirely fluid up to the last minute. Everything you are told, even with the greatest appearance of authority and decision, is provisional, without commitment. . . . There is no orderly progression towards the final conclusion . . . . I liken them to bees who for weeks will fly around in all directions with no ascertainable destination, providing both the menace of stings and the hope of honey; and at last, perhaps because the queen in the White Hive has emitted some faint, indistinguishable odour, suddenly swarm to a single spot in a compact impenetrable bunch'. Quoted in C. Thorne, *Allies of a Kind. The United States, Britain and the War against Japan 1941–1945* (London, 1978), p. 115.

[23]e.g. B. Rauch, *Roosevelt. Munich to Pearl Harbor* (New York, 1962), pp. 5–7.

[24]J.M Burns, *Roosevelt: The Lion and the Fox* (New York, 1956), p. 262.

majority of his fellow-countrymen, to keep out of foreign entanglements at all costs. It took much longer for the president to admit reluctantly that in the modern world with its shrinking geography foreign entanglements could scarcely be avoided in the long run if American interests were to be defended effectively.

That was not the president's position in the mid 1930s during the passage of the neutrality legislation which it is necessary to explain here for an understanding of the course of events in the 1930s. Isolationism had become a much more powerful force in American politics for several reasons. Growing hostility to Roosevelt's mounting expenditure on the navy at a time of depression; suspicion of the growing power of the executive under the New Deals; the considerable impact on public opinion of the Nye Committee, set up by Senate to investigate the munitions industry, which concluded – quite erroneously – that Wilson took the United States into the First World War solely to please armaments manufacturers; Roosevelt's abortive attempt in January 1935 to persuade the United States to join the World Court, a manoeuvre which aroused latent suspicion of European entanglements; and most of all, the darkening international scene with war looming up over Abyssinia. Consequently there was an upsurge of public feeling in favour of legislation to prevent a repetition of 1917. Congress went along with the tide and the result was the First Neutrality Act of 1935. This measure, initially for six months, empowered the president in the event of war to impose a general embargo on the export of arms, ammunition and implements of war, and gave him discretionary power to warn American citizens that they travelled in belligerent ships at their own risk.

In 1936 the act was extended for a further period with the addition of clauses forbidding loans to belligerents. Finally, in 1937 the legislation was made permanent. It was strengthened by the addition of clauses, to last for two years, forbidding Americans to sell goods on credit to belligerents or use American ships to carry specified goods. The president was, however, given discretionary power under the so-called cash-and-carry clause to allow general trade with belligerents on condition they paid 'cash on the barrel-head' and used their own ships to transport the goods. This clause prompted a contemporary publication to comment sharply that 'the law of 1937 was not designed to eliminate war by rendering it profitless. On the contrary the "cash and carry" plan was plainly a device for making money with a minimum of risk'.[25] Understandably enough, Congress chose not to offend farmers and manufacturers dependent on foreign trade.

It has been argued that Roosevelt's acquiescence in the legislation was due not to conviction that this was the right policy but simply to the exigencies of the domestic scene. The New Deal had reached a critical stage, so the argument runs; in 1935 Roosevelt needed Congressional support for the Second New Deal; and in 1937, in an attempt to end opposition to his reforms in the Supreme Court, he commenced a battle (ultimately unsuccessful) to appoint additional judges and outflank his opponents. Success depended on preserving

---

[25]Whitney H. Shepardson and William O. Scroggs, *The United States in World Affairs, 1937* (New York, 1938), p. 51.

at all costs the New Deal alliance of Republicans and Democrats, and concessions over neutrality legislation was the price he had to pay.

The evidence suggests that it is at least – if not more – likely that Roosevelt was not greatly disturbed by the legislation. With war on the horizon in Europe, his major concern was to avoid a repetition of 1917 when the United States went to war in defence of the principles of neutral rights, an issue which then aroused deep emotional feeling. If these rights were restricted by legislation this would, it seemed to Roosevelt, prevent another 1917. So the president did not attempt to veto the legislation. Indeed, he had taken the initiative in 1935 in urging the Nye Committee to prepare neutrality legislation. He declared himself 'perfectly satisfied' with the first act. And he went out of his way in a campaign speech in 1936 to praise the legislation and to insist that the United States isolate itself completely from war. Significantly, his plea for discretionary power to impose an arms embargo, which Congress rejected, was due to fear that an impartial embargo might drag the United States into war instead of keeping it out, i.e. if victim and aggressor were equally penalized, the latter might win to the ultimate detriment of the United States which might then be forced to fight in its own defence against the aggressor.

Nevertheless, Roosevelt was no dyed-in-the-wool isolationist. He had by no means completely abandoned his early Wilsonian vision of the interdependence of nations. When international crises arose he tried to operate the legislation to the victim's advantage. For example, when Italy attacked Abyssinia in 1935 Roosevelt, against the advice of his diplomatic representatives and in advance of the League of Nations, promptly declared a state of war to exist between Italy and Abyssinia and imposed an arms embargo which he knew full well would affect Italy more than land-locked Abyssinia with neither cash nor ships to purchase war material in the United States. And even though he dare not align the United States openly with the League of Nations in applying sanctions, he and Cordell Hull urged businessmen not to trade with the belligerents. When Italian purchases of raw materials rose sharply Hull threatened to publish the names of exporters; the moral embargo was effective and trade fell back at the end of 1935 to 20 per cent of the 1934 level. It was not president or secretary of state who let the League of Nations down but Britain and France by their surrender to Mussolini's demands.

Despite this rebuff, when war broke out in the Far East Roosevelt still tried to do what he could for the victim of aggression. To help China, which lacked both the cash and the ships to buy supplies on a cash-and-carry basis, he did not impose an arms embargo, finding a technical excuse in the failure of China and Japan to declare war. True, once Japan blockaded the Chinese coastline in August 1937 Roosevelt became apprehensive. And when it was discovered that a government-owned ship was about to transport bomber aircraft to China Roosevelt promptly detained the ship and, much to the annoyance of China, forbad all government-owned ships from carrying arms to either side. Ships flying the American flag were warned that they supplied arms at their own risk. However, as the bulk of the arms trade with China was conducted by merchant ships, Roosevelt's ban had only symbolic significance; in the last three months of 1937 the State Department granted licences for $2,500,000 of arms exports to China.

Yet it has to be admitted that the neutrality legislation, however sympathetically applied by Roosevelt and Hull, was 'a policy of scuttle and run to the storm cellar'.[26] Fear of war had so mesmerized the United States that she had in effect served notice on potential aggressors that she was not going to try and influence the course of events; by surrendering the traditional rights of neutral powers to trade with belligerents she would, in the event of war, do everything possible to avoid being drawn in. All that can be said in its defence was that it was a popular policy in the United States and that the president went along with it most of the way sharing with his people a determination never to go to war again.

At the beginning of the twentieth century Japan had already become a major power. While the Chinese Empire was tottering towards collapse in the 1890s, Japan was catching up with the modern world. In the 30 years following the Meiji Restoration of 1868 the ruling oligarchy imposed an upper crust of western technology on what remained in essence a semi-feudal society deeply committed to traditional values. On the surface the results were spectacular. A successful war against China in 1894–5 and the defeat of Russia in 1905 demonstrated that the Japanese had arrived as a significant military power in the Pacific. The First World War was another landmark in the rise of Modern Japan, not because of her minimal military commitment but for economic and political reasons. Like the Americans, the Japanese benefitted commercially from the war. The demand for Japanese cotton goods grew; she broke into the markets of south-eastern Asia; and she became a creditor nation. Secondly, while the European powers were locked in struggle Japan attempted to impose her will on China in the Twenty-One Demands, a piece of maladroit diplomacy which had lasting effects on Japan's relations with both China and the United States.[27]

In the decade before the First World War the pattern of Japan's foreign policy in the first half of the twentieth century was already taking shape. Japan's longstanding interest in controlling the Tsushima Straits, the Sea of Japan and the Korean peninsula was reinforced at the turn of the century by economic and demographic pressures. Although Japan had become a major trading nation – the Britain of the Far East – she was heavily dependent on the outside world for a wide range of raw materials. Increasingly she began to look to the mainland, initially to Manchuria, for easy access to rich coal and iron-ore deposits and for new markets. Add to this the pressure on resources of a population which grew from 40 million to 50 million between 1890 and 1910 and was still growing by 5.6 per cent annually throughout the 1930s; a growing sense of injustice at a division of resources which favoured the white powers; and the warrior tradition of the samurai: the end product was a thrusting

[26]Quoted in Robert A. Divine, *The Reluctant Belligerent. American Entry into World War II* (New York, 1965), p. 38.
[27]The Twenty-One Demands obliged China to recognize Japanese acquisition of the former German rights in Shantung, extend the lease on southern Manchuria to 99 years and make extensive economic concessions to China. Most galling of all, Japanese advisers would be attached to the Chinese government emphasizing its satellite status.

expansionist policy which characterized Japanese foreign relations for half a century.

The Chinese Empire, which exerted nominal suzerainty over the kingdom of Korea, an area of vital strategic importance to Japan, was the first to feel the power of the new Japan. Out of the 1894–5 war Japan emerged as the victor. Her growing ambitions were revealed for all to see in the Treaty of Shimonoseki under which she gained Formosa, the Pescadores, Port Arthur and the Liaotung peninsula while China was forced to recognize the 'independence' of Korea. However, the European great powers – Russia, France and Germany – alarmed by the rapid rise of Japan and recognizing a potential threat to their own interests in the Far East, banded together and in an unusual display of unity forced her to hand back Port Arthur and the Liaotung peninsula to China. The 1894–5 war marked the beginning of a tradition of rivalry between Japan and China which has lasted into our own day and was punctuated twice in the 1930s by further periods of warfare.

The Sino-Japanese War also revealed for the first time a basic incompatibility between Japanese and Russian ambitions on the mainland of Asia. Since the mid nineteenth century Russia had been expanding in central Asia subduing the unruly tribesmen of Turkestan and pressing hard on the frontiers of the decaying empires of Persia and China. As early as 1860 Russia acquired the Maritime Provinces and established a port at Vladivostok. Fifteen years later Russia acquired Sakhalin island from Japan in return for the Kuriles. And in 1891 Russia commenced construction on the Trans-Siberian Railway linking up Vladivostok with European Russia. As the most direct route to Moscow lay through Manchuria the Russians pressurized the Chinese into building the Chinese Eastern Railway running through the province and terminating at Vladivostok. The realization that Russia was acquiring a substantial stake in the Chinese Empire may well have been a factor in the Japanese decision to attack China in 1894. Resentment of Russian intervention in 1895 was reinforced by anxiety at her growing power in China; in 1898 Russia acquired a lease on Port Arthur and the tip of the Liaotung peninsula giving her an ice-free port on the Yellow Sea, one of the traditional goals of Russian statesmen. Shortly afterwards the Southern Manchurian Railway was built linking Port Arthur through Mukden with Harbin, the junction for Vladivostok. In 1900 during the Boxer disturbances Russian troops occupied Manchuria, greatly increasing Japanese fears for the future of Korea.

The spectacular conflict between Japan and Russia in 1904–5 abruptly checked Russian ambitions. This time the European great powers refrained from intervention. Japan was able to acquire the lease on Port Arthur; occupy the southern half of Sakhalin; obtain control of the South Manchurian Railway as far north as Changchung; and win recognition of her 'paramount political and economic interests' in Korea which she subsequently annexed in 1910.

For 50 years after this defeat Russia ceased to be a military 'threat' to Japanese interests on the mainland. Nevertheless, relations between them remained uneasy at the best of times. In ideology the Russians found a potent substitute for their lack of military power. Their open commitment to the cause of world revolution and encouragement of the national aspirations of oppressed colonial peoples caused alarm in Tokyo. Japanese army units in 1917 occupied the whole of the Far Eastern region to the east of Lake Baikal to 'strangle bolshevism at birth' in Winston Churchill's graphic phrase, by setting up counter-revolutionary governments in this area. Even when Japan evacuated her forces from Siberia in 1922 and from north Sakhalin in 1925 relations still remained uneasy throughout the early 1920s because of Russian support for the Kuomintang, the Chinese nationalist movement. Only after Chiang Kai-shek expelled his Russian advisers in 1927 did relations improve somewhat. But after the attack on Manchuria in 1931, as the balance of power swung towards Japan and powerful elements in the Japanese army began to advocate expansion at Russia's expense, it was Moscow's turn to become concerned at the prospect of war.

Finally, Japanese relations with the United States. There was no intrinsic reason why the emergence of the United States as a Pacific power in 1898 should have led to conflict with an up-and-coming Asiatic power. The ocean was capacious enough for both navies. Commercially, they were not in competition. Nor did the United States oppose Japanese expansion on the Chinese mainland in the initial stages; on the contrary, the Japanese were much admired in Washington as the standard-bearers of civilization in east Asia. Even the onslaught on China was welcomed as a long overdue step calculated to shake the Manchus out of their obscurantism and lethargy.

Only after the Japanese victory over Russia in 1905 did relations begin to deteriorate. Subconscious fears of 'the yellow peril' began to surface in America compounded by racist opposition to Japanese immigration in California. In 1907 the American navy, at the instigation of President Roosevelt, first drew up Plan Orange to cover the eventuality of war with Japan, although it is true that the navy's first priority still remained the Atlantic where a clash with Imperial Germany was thought a much more likely scenario. The problem of China, to be discussed later, also contributed substantially to the continuing deterioration in relations.

The mounting tension came to a head during and immediately after the First World War. Japan, increasingly depressed by unexpected opposition from the United States in Manchuria and by a general decline in Japanese influence in China, determined to seize the opportunity presented by war in Europe to restore the balance in her favour. Under pressure from vociferous chauvinistic groups the government seized former German islands in the north Pacific and the province of Shantung. As mentioned earlier, she then pressurized China in 1915 into accepting the Twenty-One Demands, placing that country wholly at her mercy, a step which aroused grave misgivings amongst Japan's elder statesmen who had controlled foreign policy in the early years of the century but whose influence was now in decline.

There were indignant protests in the United States. Wilson denounced the Twenty-One Demands and asserted America's continuing commitment to the Open Door Policy and to the maintenance of the territorial integrity of China. Popular indignation reached Capitol Hill. In 1916, to prepare for a combined German–Japanese attack, Congress approved a three-year naval programme. By 1917 naval command was demanding a fleet twice the size of the Japanese to ensure American supremacy not only in the eastern but in the western Pacific as well. At the Peace Conference of 1919 Wilson concentrated his efforts on talking Japan out of Shantung. As the Italian delegation had just left Paris over the Fiume issue and Japan threatened to follow suit, an unhappy Wilson decided that discretion was the better part of valour and left her in possession of Shantung. American–Japanese relations now reached an alltime low. In America Japan was widely regarded as the 'new Prussia' which would have to be cut down to size probably by war in the near future; while Japan began to fear for the first time that war with the United States was inevitable, and the Japanese navy also embarked upon an expansionist programme.

But it did not come to war because of changing attitudes in Tokyo and Washington. In Japan a severe economic and financial crisis in 1920–1 absorbed the attention of the government. At a time when commercial interests were demanding cuts in military expenditure and when the new spirit of Wilsonian democracy was beginning to pervade world politics, military adventures seemed an anachronism to ruling circles in Tokyo. Although Japan's policy-makers were under no illusion about the reluctance of America, Russia and China to give Japan her rightful place in the world, still, in the new age they were entering they appreciated that they could only achieve their objectives by peaceful means; in particular they hoped against hope for an understanding with the United States.

In Washington there was still great concern about the potential threat Japan posed in the Pacific and a desire to restore a 'proper' balance of power in that area. At the same time American public opinion was clamouring for disarmament and an end to the naval race with Japan. Britain, too, was anxious to avoid conflict in the Far East and ready to abandon the 1902 alliance with Japan in response to Canadian and American pressure. Secretary of State Hughes was a singularly clear-minded politician who, whilst nominally subscribing to the China policy, was not prepared to fight Japan on that account. Instead he pinned his hopes for the future on naval concessions which would reduce tension with Japan, make her amenable to corresponding concessions on the Chinese mainland and induce her to co-operate with Britain and the United States in order to maintain a stable international order in the Pacific area.

At the Washington Conference in 1921–2 America achieved her objectives. The Anglo-Japanese alliance was terminated and replaced by a Four Power Pact pledging the United States, Britain, Japan and France to co-operation, consultation and mutual help in the Pacific. On the central issue of disarmament Britain, accommodating herself to the realities of diminished power, accepted naval parity with the United States whilst Japan accepted a 5:3 ratio with the Anglo-Saxon powers in respect of capital ships and aircraft carriers. Japan agreed to withdraw several of the Twenty-One Demands, made substantial concessions over Shantung and promised to withdraw her forces from Siberia, where the size of her intervention in 1918 had been another cause of tension with the United States. In the Nine Power Treaty in 1922 she agreed to respect the sovereignty and independence of China and the Open Door Policy. Whilst promising not to seek 'special privileges' in China at the expense of friendly states, it was tacitly assumed by Japan that she would retain her privileged position in southern Manchuria and in the eastern half of Inner Mongolia.

After the Washington Conference American–Japanese relations underwent a remarkable transformation. Only in naval circles did the old hostility persist. American naval command, nursing exaggerated fears of Japanese intentions, bitterly criticized decisions which denied them a fleet twice the size of Japan's and deprived them of supremacy in the western Pacific. Initially Japanese naval command was also highly critical of the 5:3 ratio. But as time passed it became clearer that the balance of advantage was now in Japan's favour, especially as the great powers promised not to build any new naval bases in the Pacific. Generally speaking a mood of confidence characterized the American attitude to Japan in the early 1920s, partly because of changes (more apparent than real) in Japan and also because growing doubts were being expressed in America about the viability of China, a country racked by internal convulsions in the 1920s and sharply critical of American policy into the bargain. Symptomatic of the changed attitude was the comment in 1923 by Franklin Roosevelt, so hostile to Japan in 1916 and again in the 1930s, that the two countries 'have not a single valid reason, and won't have as far as we can look ahead, for fighting each other'.[28]

Then came the world economic crisis of 1929–33 which shook the island economy to its foundations. It is not too much to say that it gave a decisive twist to Japanese foreign policy reviving old imperialist dreams and setting her on a road which ended in September 1945 with the formal surrender of the Japanese armed forces to General Douglas MacArthur on board the battleship *Missouri*.

The crisis seriously affected an economy as heavily dependent upon exports as the Japanese. Raw silk exports, which represented 36 per cent of Japan's total exports in 1929, fell by 50 per cent between April 1929 and October 1930, a catastrophic blow when 40 per cent of her farmers were engaged in sericulture as a subsidiary occupation. The price of rice, falling since 1927, reached a record low in the autumn of 1930. Severe hardship and mounting discontent occurred in rural areas where the gross income of farmers was cut by almost half between 1926 and 1931. As the Japanese army was solidly based on peasant recruits largely officered by the sons of small landowners, the mood of unrest spread to the armed forces. This was bound to have serious consequences in a land where feudal forces remained immensely powerful despite superficial progress towards parliamentary government. Exports mostly of cotton goods to India and China, which accounted for 33 per cent of all exports, suffered severely. The Ottawa Conference of 1932 imposed a 75 per cent tariff increase on Japanese goods entering British territories while France and Holland raised tariffs on exports to Indo-China and the Dutch East Indies respectively. Japanese exports to China fell more sharply than American so that by 1931 the United States had replaced Japan as the main supplier of China. Financially Japan was in a parlous state. Gold poured out of the country in expectation of the depreciation of the yen; the reserves fell in value from 1,072 million yen in 1929 to 470 million in 1931; and in December the government fell and Japan came off the gold standard.

The crisis gave the *coup de grâce* to what slim hopes existed of democratic change in Japan. The prosperity boom caused by the First World War and the

[28]F. Freidel, *Franklin D. Roosevelt: The Ordeal* (Boston, 1954), p. 135.

victory of 'democracy' over 'German militarism' had encouraged the modernization of the conservative–authoritarian constitution of 1889. The army, a
powerful force in Japanese society since the 1890s, seemed to be losing some
ground; and the Zaibatsu, the four great oligopolies which, in lieu of a thrusting
middle class, had been the *accoucheurs* of industrialization and which possessed
a virtual stranglehold over the economy, inclined in the 1920s towards the
liberalization of the political system, a reduction of arms expenditure –
because of current economic difficulties – and a cautious foreign policy.

Too much should not be made of these signs of change. Party politics were in
their infancy in Japan. Bribery and corruption were rampant. Violence at
election time and unruly scenes in the Diet were commonplace. Behind the
confused political scene the dictatorship of the Tokugawa continued as before,
i.e. the great offices of state were in the hands of the aristocratic clans and the
samurai. Feudalism had been abolished as a system in Japan but the centuries-
old social structure of the ruling class remained intact and its members, though
they feuded with each other in the various ministries, were united in defence of
feudal–absolutist standards.

Japan was, therefore, highly unlikely to resolve her serious economic situation
within a democratic context. A large group of young army officers, led by senior
staff officers, was stung into activity by government attempts to cut military
expenditure as a way out of the crisis gripping Japan in the summer of 1931; their
solution was the establishment of an authoritarian system at home coupled with
renewed expansion on the Chinese mainland. In 1930 these elements founded
the Cherry Blossom Society to plot the overthrow of parliamentary government
by force. Abroad they advocated expansion in Manchuria. Here they were only
articulating a belief widespread in ruling circles in the 1930s that by virtue of the
capital poured into Manchuria before 1914 Japan had established her right to
exploit the mineral resources there. If a nation could not obtain the raw materials
she needed by trade then she had every right to seize them by force and build up
protected markets in an increasingly autarky-minded world. National self-
sufficiency achieved by expansion seemed to be the message of the 1930s for
young nations. And the reluctance of the Anglo-Saxon powers to rectify the
maldistribution of resources was seen as sheer hypocrisy which must not be
allowed to deter Japan from achieving her objectives. All the same, what probably galvanized Japan into action in 1931 was a purely strategic consideration –
the knowledge that the Kuomintang now posed a major military threat to
Japan's privileged position in southern Manchuria.

By 1926 Chiang Kai-shek's authority was recognized in almost every
province in China. In 1927 his armies gained control of the Yangtze valley and
took Nanking and Shanghai. In 1929 the Manchurian warlord, Chang Hsüeh-
liang, recognized the nationalist government and began to obstruct Japan at
every turn. Already in 1928 disgruntled officers in Japan's Kwantung
army – which garrisoned southern Manchuria – had become deeply resentful
of what they regarded as the 'weak' policy of Prime Minister Shidehara Kijūrō
and decided to force the pace in China.[29] The first plot to seize Mukden

---

[29]Prime Minister Shidehara attempted to protect Japanese interests in southern Manchuria by
negotiating with the local Chinese war lord in 1927–8. The attempt ended abruptly with the latter's
assassination by Kwantung army officers.

misfired. But in September 1931 on the flimsy pretext that Chinese troops had sabotaged the Southern Manchurian Railway – and without informing Tokyo – Japanese troops seized Mukden, occupied the whole of Manchuria and precipitated a major international crisis.[30] The Mukden Incident and the Sino-Japanese War o. 1931–3 which followed had important consequences for Japanese relations with Russia and with the United States.

First, Russia. After the Kuomintang broke with the Communists in 1927 Russia was driven onto the defensive in China and watched unhappily while Chiang Kai-shek's advance threatened Russian rights over the East Chinese Railway. Stalin defended these rights with the tenacity of the tsars; in 1929 troops were sent in to compel the Chinese to hand back the railway which they had just seized. Japanese aggression in Manchuria posed a new and much greater threat. Russian fears of Japanese intentions increased still further when Japan declined in December 1932 to sign the standard non-aggression pact which Russia was busily negotiating with her neighbours, the Japanese reason being that she wanted a comprehensive settlement of all contentious issues between them. Russia's conciliatory policy was accompanied by sterner measures: the build-up of military forces in the Far East which heightened the tension between Russia and Japan. In a further protective move Russia, much to Japan's annoyance, re-established relations with the 'bourgeois' Kuomintang movement.

The United States was also disturbed by the Manchurian Crisis but not because the prospect of a powerful Japanese Empire based on the Chinese mainland was thought to be a direct challenge to America's position in the Pacific which must lead inevitably to war. Naval circles apart, few Americans seriously contemplated conflict with Japan in the early 1930s. All the same, Manchuria cast a dark shadow over the American dream of a stable international order in the Pacific based on Chinese independence.

China occupied a very special place in the American folk memory. In the late nineteenth century as the American economy expanded and high tariff barriers threatened her European exports, a large section of American business looked to China as the market of the future, a never-never land capable of absorbing America's surplus production, and this despite the fact that American trade with Japan was infinitely more important. For 50 years until Mao Tse-tung's Communists drove Chiang Kai-shek off the Chinese mainland the will o' the wisp of the 'China market' mesmerized generations of American entrepreneurs. Today when the Chinese People's Republic is welcoming the importation of western technology, American expectations of a vast market of 1,000 million are rising once more. Between 1899 and 1900, as the European powers closed in on the helpless Chinese Empire, Secretary of State John Hay's Open Door Policy formalized existing practice and invited the imperialist powers to pledge themselves to maintain the principle of equal trading rights for all

---

[30]Too much emphasis has been laid on the unilateral natural of this aggression. In fact, army general staff in Tokyo was already planning forward action in Manchuria. Despite opposition in the cabinet, foreign office and navy, powerful factions supported the action and swung public opinion into the militarist camp, dashing all hopes that restraint by the League of Nations might enable Shidehara to regain control of the situation.

nations in all parts of China including the spheres of influence they had already established there. In 1908 during a temporary improvement in American–Japanese relations the United States secured Japanese adherence to this principle in the Root–Takahari agreement. Japan also recognized the independence and integrity of the Chinese Empire, a convenient political framework within which the imperialist powers could exploit the wealth of China.[31]

To suppose that the Americans were concerned only to maximize their trade in China is a misunderstanding of the complexity of the imperialist phenomenon. During the presidencies of William Taft (1909–12) and Woodrow Wilson (1912–21) a high moral tone began to colour American views on China. This corresponded to the awakening of interest in China displayed by wide sections of the American public around the time of the Russo-Japanese War. Increasingly many Americans came to feel a moral commitment to promote the advancement of the Chinese people, a sentiment fostered by hundreds of Christian missionaries working devotedly in China. The fall of the Manchu dynasty in 1912 and the stirrings of independence were greeted ecstatically in the American press. Sun Yat-sen was lionized as a Chinese George Washington trying to do for his sprawling faction-ridden country what the American hero accomplished a century earlier. Because Japanese attempts to detach Manchuria from China retarded the historical evolution of China to nationhood – a view which completely ignored the tenuous ties between that province and the old Chinese Empire – sentimental attachment to China went hand-in-hand with mounting hostility to the 'amoral' Japanese. This high moral tone puzzled Japan's leaders more accustomed to the balance-of-power approach of President Theodore Roosevelt who had conceded (though only in private) the right of the Japanese as good imperialists to encroach on the Manchu Empire and to act as a counterpoise to Russian expansion in the Far East.

Good will towards China continued unabated after the First World War. The efforts of Chiang Kai-shek to impose one rule on warring China were applauded by all American liberals. They continued to dream of a free, independent sovereign China modelling herself on the pattern of liberal–capitalist America, a stabilizing force in the Far East, her territorial integrity respected by the great powers and her doors thrown open to the trade of all nations. On that foundation-stone would rest a just and stable international order in the Far East. This scenario was consistently propagated by the Far Eastern Affairs Division of the State Department, a section which exerted a disproportionately great influence on China policy because most secretaries of state simply did not display a continuing interest in that area.

If this highly romanticized view of the Far East could ever be turned into a concrete political reality – which one may well doubt – it implied a willingness on the part of the United States to act vigorously and unilaterally: first, to facilitate China's progress to nationhood; and, second, to prevent encroachments on

[31]What the American public did not realize was that Roosevelt saw this as a limited commitment. The president's emissary and the Japanese foreign minister had agreed privately that southern Manchuria was not to be regarded as part of the Chinese Empire. On this private understanding Roosevelt maintained a discreet silence.

Chinese territory by would-be aggressors. In fact there was, inevitably, a serious shortfall between the ideal and the practice of American policy, between the moral commitment to China and the general thrust of American interests in the Far East. Thus, while the United States remained more sympathetic to Chinese aspirations than other imperialist powers, there were clear limits to the lengths successive administrations were prepared to go in helping China. Wilson's failure to persuade Japan to withdraw from Shantung province was one example. The Chinese were also disappointed in the Washington Treaties which, though they committed the signatories to respect and uphold the territorial integrity of China, still preserved the extra-territorial rights and tariff controls of the imperialist powers. American promises to revise the treaties once China had a stable government did little to console ardent nationalists.[32] And in the 1920s when Chinese nationalism took on an increasingly aggressive and anti-colonial colouration, the United States was as ready as other powers to act in defence of economic interests; when Sun Yat-sen's government threatened to appropriate customs revenues in 1923 the United States collaborated with other imperialist powers and sent a naval task force to strengthen their protest; and in 1927 when the nationalists attacked foreign settlements in Nanking America intervened to protect her nationals.

During the Manchurian Crisis it became painfully apparent that the roseate picture of China painted by church leaders and newpaper editors did not – and never had – corresponded with harsh power realities. The United States was as reluctant as ever to defend China against aggression. Even if the administration had favoured such a step, public opinion was against it. Secondly, the United States lacked the military power to stop Japan dead in her tracks. Thirdly, economic realities pointed in the opposite direction. The inescapable fact was that the United States conducted a mere 2–3 per cent of her total trade with China. Her investments in China in 1931 totalled $200 million–250 million (i.e. 3 per cent of her total investment) compared with Britain's £244 million. With Japan, on the other hand, the United States was conducting 8.9 per cent of her external trade by 1935 and had investments totalling $466 million. By the end of the 1920s 40 per cent of Japanese loans came from the United States. Not an unusual development, as advanced nations invariably invest more in advanced regions where the chances of quick returns are greater. And for the prudent investor the contrast between the political stability of authoritarian Japan and chaos-ridden China where rival factions were struggling for mastery in the 1920s was a persuasive factor. To pick a quarrel with Japan and damage American trade in the midst of a world economic crisis seemed the height of folly; for it was now dawning on important sections of the American business world that their stake in Japan was greater than in China. Finally, it must not be forgotten that the improvement in American–Japanese relations dating from the Washington Conference had more or less continued throughout the 1920s. Several top officials including Under-secretary William R. Castle, Ambassador W. Cameron Forbes in Tokyo and Minister Nelson T. Johnson in

---

[32]The United States was, in fact, the first imperialist power to grant tariff autonomy to the Nationalist government in July 1928. In the agreement the most-favoured-nation clause was retained.

Peking emphasized the importance of staying on good terms with Japan, the only power capable of sharing with the United States the task of keeping law and order in the Far East.

The fundamental incompatibility between ideological commitment to a Chinese nation state and reluctance to use force to defend China because American interests did not require it, was soon revealed for all to see. Japanese breaches of treaty obligation disturbed Congress and administration alike and were universally condemned. But there was no desire for unilateral action to aid China nor even for concerted action with members of the League of Nations; public antipathy to Geneva ruled out all but the most grudging co-operation.

President Hoover's statement to the cabinet in October 1931 pointed up the fundamental dichotomy between theory and practice in American policy very clearly. Hoover's forthright denunciation of Japanese actions as an affront to America's moral conscience was no new departure but a reaffirmation of the moral standards Taft and Wilson had applied to Japanese expansionism before 1914. And Hoover persuaded himself that China was more than a match for Japan. Much as western Europe pretended for most of the nineteenth century that the crumbling Ottoman Empire would be a reliable bulwark against Russian imperialism, so Hoover supposed – and not unreasonably as it turned out – that China's history of resistance to foreign invaders rendered American intervention unnecessary. Moreover, intervention would make little sense at a time of economic depression and military weakness. Therefore, Hoover believed that the United States should not attempt to unhold world peace by force. The Nine Power Treaty and the Kellogg Pact were 'moral instruments based upon the hope that peace in the world can be. . . . enforced solely by the moral reprobation of the world'.[33] He concluded that 'neither our obligations to China, nor our own interest, nor our dignity require us to go to war over these questions. These acts do not imperil the freedom of the American people, the economic or moral fibre of our people. I do not propose to sacrifice American life for anything short of this. If that were not reason enough, to go to war means a long struggle at a time when civilization is already weak enough. . . . We will not go along on war or any of the sanctions either economic or military for those are the roads to war'.[34] Finally, Hoover, like most of the cabinet, believed firmly in Japan as a stabilizing force in the Far East and sympathized with the difficulties she experienced at the hands of Chiang Kai-shek's Nationalists. America was prepared to help mobilize world opinion against aggression, nothing more. In December 1931, returning to the theme, Hoover proposed to the cabinet that the United States invite the League of Nations to refuse to recognize any Japanese conquests, an initiative which led to a government declaration to this effect in January 1932.

To base a foreign policy on the upholding of contractual obligations and to condemn countries when they do not abide by these standards – because their national interests point in a different direction – is not necessarily the only or even the wisest way in which regard for moral principle can be expressed in international affairs. While this is no place for a discussion of the theology of

---

[33] *The Memoirs of Herbert Hoover. The Cabinet and the Presidency 1920–1933* (London, 1952), p. 368.
[34] *Op. cit.*, pp. 369–70.

international relations, it does seem extremely doubtful, to say the least, whether one can apply to relations between sovereign states the standards one applies to judge the actions of individuals. There is merit in the argument that it might have been better – and could have been no worse in the long run – to allot to moral principle 'the unobtrusive. . . . function of the gentle civilizer of national interest' in American policy: that is, within the framework of a national policy based on a realistic assessment of American interests and of the changing balance of power in Asia America should have used her moral influence to bring peace and stability to China acting not as a judge sentencing a guilty person but as an honest broker mediating between contestants.[35] It might even be argued by the standards of the old diplomacy that a peace settlement leaving a substantial Japanese presence on the mainland would have had the advantage of establishing a new balance of power capable of holding Russia in check and enabling China to develop in peace. But no re-appraisal of American policy took place. Instead Washington clung tenaciously to the Non-Recognition Doctrine which, because it blurred the proper relationship between morality and political power, retarded the evolution of a realistic policy in the Far East and in the long run fatally restricted America's freedom of manoeuvre.

The Non-Recognition Doctrine, though vigorously applauded by liberal opinion in America had, predictably, not the slightest deterrent effect on the Japanese. By the end of the summer of 1933 they had turned Manchuria into the puppet state of Manchukuo completely under their control. Britain, though as unwilling as America to go to war with Japan, observed the American failure with a degree of *Schadenfreude*; Stanley Baldwin, Lord President of the Council, commented acidly that out of Washington came nothing but words: 'big words but only words'.[36]

The advent to power of Franklin Roosevelt changed nothing in respect of China. The president-elect, who shared his fellow countrymen's sympathies for China and mistrusted the Japanese – whom he suspected of harbouring far-reaching imperialist ambitions – endorsed the Non-Recognition Doctrine. So did the new secretary of state, Cordell Hull, a high-principled politician from Tennessee. The fact that Japan was pursuing monopolistic trading policies in Manchuria strengthened Hull's resolve not to yield an inch to the Japanese. Beyond verbal hostility it did not go. At Roosevelt's first cabinet meeting when the feasibility of war with Japan was discussed, there was general agreement that the United States would be driven onto the defensive and would only win a war after three to five years. Even if Roosevelt had wished to stop the Japanese by force in 1933 – which was not the case – dependence on an isolationist Congress for the passage of New Deal legislation would have made a wait-and-see strategy mandatory. To the general relief of the new administration the cessation of hostilities in March 1933 removed the embarrassing item from the agenda. One important shift in the Washington power structure had, however, occurred: the influence of the Far Eastern Affairs

[35]George F. Kennan, *American Diplomacy 1900–1950* (Chicago, 1951), p. 54.
[36]T. Jones, *A Diary with Letters 1931–1950* (London, 1954), p. 30.

Division increased sharply after 1933. Not only was the president pro-Chinese but Hull, sadly lacking experience in foreign affairs, was heavily dependent on . his advisers and encouraged them to keep the president informed of their pro-Chinese and anti-Japanese stance.

But in another respect Roosevelt's election marked a turning-point. A naval enthusiast from his teens, as assistant secretary of state at the Navy Department during the First World War he acquired a knowledge of and taste for naval strategy. On discovering that the navy was lamentably deficient in light cruisers and destroyers he at once sought to remedy the situation in the interests of national security; for, as he commented to a critic: 'the whole scheme of things in Tokyo does not make for an assurance of non-aggression in the future'.[37]

In Carl Vinson, chairman of the powerful House Committee on Naval Affairs, Roosevelt found a man after his own heart. In 1932 Vinson had already introduced an unsuccessful bill to spend $616 million on a long-range naval build-up. This time Vinson's efforts were crowned with success. Events in the Far East in 1932–3 aroused some concern in Congress. And by persuading Congress to allocate money for rearmament from funds earmarked for relief spending, Roosevelt cleverly associated naval expansion with the fight against unemployment. The critics of military expansion were also mollified because he trimmed back the sums involved in a compromise dictated by the primacy of domestic politics.

Still, this was the beginning of the steady growth of the United States navy. The $238 million allocated in June 1933 authorized the construction of 32 vessels, the largest building programme since 1916. This was followed by the Vinson–Trammell Act in March 1934 providing for the construction of 102 new ships over the next three years and enabling the United States to reach the Washington and London treaty levels. Appropriations rose in each succeeding year and by 1937 had doubled. It would be quite wrong to explain the administration's increasingly rigid attitude towards Japan in terms of the growing power of the navy. Nevertheless, the existence of a powerful fleet, commanded by men who believed firmly in the nefarious intentions of the Japanese and were committed to an offensive strategy in the Pacific, strengthened the hands of those members of the administration who argued that a tough policy would necessarily bring the Japanese to their knees as it had done in 1895 and again in 1922.

In the decade before the attack on Pearl Harbor – 'the dark valley' as Japanese historians call this period – the basic authoritarianism of Japanese society re-asserted itself as the democratic façade crumbled away. In Germany opposition to the Young Plan, the last act of reconciliation with the western powers, brought the right wing out in force in 1929 in an unsuccessful attempt to persuade the Reichstag to repudiate the agreement. In Japan the signature of the London Naval Treaty in 1930 served the same function. Hamaguchi

---

[37]Quoted in S.E. Pelz, *Race to Pearl Habor. The failure of the Second London Naval Conference and the Onset of World War II* (Cambridge, Mass., 1974), p. 79.

Osachi, a tough and courageous politician, agreed to a ratio in cruisers and other craft which the chief of naval general staff considered dangerously favourable to the Americans. Behind the policy of Hamaguchi and Foreign Minister Shidehara lay deeper political considerations. As Japan had just burnt her fingers attempting to negotiate with a Chinese war lord, they hoped that concessions to Britain and the United States might open the way to joint co-operation with the imperialist powers and so safeguard Japanese interests in Manchuria. With the emperor's support Hamaguchi secured the ratification of the treaty in what was to be the last victory for the moderates.

On the right wing the treaty was bitterly denounced as a flagrant betrayal of Japan's vital interests. The attack widened to include liberal–democractic institutions, allegedly the root cause of Japan's decline as a Great Power. The call went out from the right wing to abandon western-style democracy, return to Japan's traditional values and realize her 'manifest destiny' in east Asia. Further to the right, radical nationalist elements, led by young army officers and students hostile to the orthodox Establishment, agitated for the destruction of the political parties, the curbing of the power of the Zaibatsu and the intro-duction of a 'national socialist' state run by the military – the so-called 'Showa Restoration'. While the parties continued their petty wrangling, nationalist organizations pledged to the destruction of the parliamentary system grew rapidly; numbering 40 in 1930, they totalled 196 in 1932.

The Mukden Incident acted as a catalyst releasing in Japan a wave of xenophobic nationalism which played into the hands of right-wing militarists. The war that followed and Japan's withdrawal from the League of Nations strengthened their position still further. The mass media started to exalt mar-tial values and glorify the deeds of the Kwantung Army. As the chauvinistic mood spread, teachers of liberal persuasions were driven out of schools and universities. In the autumn of 1934 Japan announced that she would not renew the Washington and London treaties. Finally, in January 1936 she withdrew from the London Naval Disarmament Conference. In December the two treaties were terminated and an era of unrestricted rearmament commenced on both sides of the Pacific.

Encouraged by the drift to authoritarianism, Japanese radicals staged a number of *coup d'états*. The most serious occurred on 26 February 1936 when disaffected army units took over the centre of Tokyo for three days. All were abortive because the army was, in fact, deeply divided about the desirability of open military dictatorship. One faction, the Kōdōha or Imperial Way School, supported mainly by young army officers in close contact with civilian terror-ists, was prepared to use force to bring about the overthrow of capitalism and war with Russia. Opposed to them was the Tosheiha or Control Group to which most of army command belonged. This group preferred to work through a façade of constitutionalism to achieve much the same objectives: the mod-ernization of the army and the mobilization of the economy either for war with Russia or for expansion southwards. Far from opposing capitalism, the Con-trol Group established links with the Zaibatsu to ensure the broad support of industry for its plans. After the defeat of the Imperial Way insurgents in February 1936 civilian politicians relied more and more on the Control Group which quickly established ascendancy over them.

The tragedy of democracy in Japan was that civilian governments completely failed to exploit these internal divisions in the army. When *coup d'états* failed, no effective action was ever taken against the army units involved. Consequently as early as 1932 constitutional government no longer functioned properly. Political parties declined steadily in power, and important decisions were no longer made in the cabinet but in the middle echelons of the army and navy. After 1932 governments gave the army most of what it demanded; military expenditure increased by two and a half times between 1931 and 1936, and the army grew from 250,000 men in 1930 to 400,000 in 1936. The grip of the military over the cabinet tightened in March 1936 when Premier Hirota Kōki agreed at once to the demand that only officers on active service be eligible for appointment as ministers of war and of the navy. This device enabled the military leaders to control the civilian cabinets by threatening the resignation of either minister and refusing to nominate a successor if the composition of the cabinet displeased them.

It is significant, too, that with the approval of the inner cabinet – which consisted of the prime minister, foreign, finance, war and navy ministers – army and navy staff drew up a confidential statement of Japan's 'national policy' emphasizing the need for more 'positive' tactics to establish Japanese dominance in east Asia. Army and navy, formerly at loggerheads over armament priorities, were at least agreed on the desirability of expansion: the army in order to deal with Russia when the time was ripe and the navy to dominate the western Pacific. It is true that these clear lines were blurred by references to the need for understandings with Britain and the United States to attain these national objectives. This was not sheer hypocrisy but a sign – of which there were many in the next few years – of a congenital refusal to face up to the likely international consequences of the militarization of Japanese foreign policy. The impact of this policy statement on the domestic economy was quickly apparent. Military expenditure escalated sharply; army expenditure alone rose from 500 million yen in 1936 to 2,750 million in 1937 and the army increased in size from 450,000 men to 950,000 in the same period.

Around the time the Japanese militarists, bent on rapid rearmament to realize their territorial ambitions in east Asia, had established their ascendancy over civilian governments, on the other side of the world in Germany rearmament was also gathering pace and Hitler and his associates were taking decisions in the summer of 1936 likely to lead to armed conflict in the not-too-distant future. The paths of the two countries had already begun to cross. In November 1936 they came together in the Anti-Comintern Pact, the first formal step on the road to the Tripartite Pact of September 1940.

German interests in the Far East were considerable – not, however, in Japan but in China. This for two reasons. After the expulsion of Russian advisers in 1927 *Reichswehr* officers took over the training of Chiang Kai-shek's troops; and, second, a considerable volume of trade developed between the two countries. After the *Machtübernahme* these ties deepened. Once the Russian connection was severed at Hitler's insistence in the summer of 1933, the *Reichswehr* turned more and more to China. Growing numbers of officers visited China to counsel Chiang Kai-shek including prestigious figures such as General Hans von Seeckt, founder of the *Reichswehr*. Commercially the Chinese market beckoned on German export firms as it did their American rivals. The decisive factor was Germany's need for raw materials for rearmament. This gave an enormous boost to Sino-German trade. German trade with China increased from 4 per cent in 1931 to 12 per cent in 1937; heavy industry supplied China with arms, machinery and chemicals (fertilizers) and in return Germany obtained soya beans, oil seed, wool, cotton, wolfram and antimony.

Some prominent Germans did, however, favour close ties with Japan. They included leading party officials such as Hermann Goering; Alfred Rosenberg, head of the *Aussenpolitisches Amt* of the Nazi Party; Herbert von Dirksen, the newly appointed ambassador in Tokyo; the Far Eastern businessman Ferdinand Heye; and the maverick industrialist Fritz Thyssen. It has been argued that Hitler belonged to that group and that his failure to impose his wish for a Japanese alliance on the *Reichswehr*, foreign office and heavy industry illustrates the pluralistic nature of foreign policy in the Third Reich.[38] An explanation which fits the facts rather better is that Hitler, despite his emotional predeliction for the 'dynamic' Japanese, was quite prepared to benefit from the pro-China policy with its obvious economic advantages for Germany. At the same time he encouraged extra-diplomatic contacts with Japan to keep alive the possibility of using her one day as a pawn on the diplomatic chessboard. Hitler, with a politician's instinct for keeping his options open, postponed a final choice between China and Japan as long as possible.

When Hitler finally opted for Japan foreign political considerations were decisive. During the winter of 1935–6 his high hopes of a British alliance began to falter. There is little doubt that the influence of Joachim von Ribbentrop was important in this context. Once it had dawned on Hitler's envoy extraordinary that Britain was unlikely to commit herself to a German alliance, he started to work for a wider understanding with France and Italy as well as with Japan with the object of constructing a great anti-British front to deter Britain from interfering with German expansion in central and eastern Europe. However, while Hitler encouraged Ribbentrop's approaches to Japan – the negotiations were conducted without the participation but with the knowledge of the foreign office – this does not necessarily mean that their views coincided exactly. Hitler still hoped that he might at the end of the day woo Britain over to the anti-bolshevik front. He may conceivably have seen in Japan a useful ally against Russia in the quest for *Lebensraum* one day. In 1936, however, he seems to have been seeking only an ideological agreement with her as a counter to growing Russian influence. The ratification of the Franco-Soviet Pact, the election of a Popular Front government in France, and particularly the outbreak of the Spanish Civil War convinced him that 'bolshevism' was on the march and must be contained. As Britain's weak policy during the Abyssinian Crisis was deepening his doubts about her as a potential ally, he turned to Japan for immediate ideological support.

[38]B. Martin, 'Die deutsch–japanischen Beziehungen während des Dritten Reiches', in M. Funke, ed., *Hitler, Deutschland und die Mächte. Materialien zur Aussenpolitik des Dritten Reiches* (Düsseldorf, 1976), pp. 459–60.

Why was Japan interested in an understanding with Germany? Again, foreign policy was decisive. Chinese resistance to the Japanese presence in their country was hardening. Initially the civil war between the Kuomintang and the Communists, raging since August 1930, facilitated Japanese expansion in Manchuria. But pressure was growing in China in the early 1930s for an end to internecine warfare and for all-out war against the Japanese. Finally in December 1936 Chiang Kai-shek yielded to pressure and agreed to join up with Mao Tse-tung in a united front against the Japanese. This dealt a body blow to Hirota's 'positive diplomacy', i.e. the attempt to secure Japanese objectives through negotiation with Nationalist China, a policy supported by influential army circles anxious to avoid further trouble in China in order to concentrate their attentions on Russia.

For by this time Japan was deeply suspicious of Soviet Russia. It was assumed – quite erroneously – that Mao Tse-tung's anti-Japanese policy was Moscow-made. In addition, no progress had been made towards the delineation of the frontier between Outer Mongolia and Manchukuo or towards a renewal of the Russo-Japanese fisheries agreement. And Russia's more positive role in world affairs worried Tokyo. In the past differences between Britain and France on the one hand and Russia on the other facilitated Japanese expansion in China. The entry of Russia into the League of Nations in 1934 and the signature of the Franco-Soviet Pact created a new situation which might conceivably lead to joint action by all three to force Japan out of China. The pact Russia signed with Outer Mongolia in April 1936 was another disturbing sign of a hardening attitude. Finally, in the event of a clash with Russia Japan could mobilize only 28 divisions to face 40 in the Soviet Far Eastern Army. In these circumstances it made good sense to have a European ally capable of holding Russia in check and forcing her at a moment of crisis to send troops from the Far East to guard interests threatened in the West.

That was the view taken by influential circles in the army general staff. The Japanese foreign office, on the other hand, like its German counterpart was critical of negotiations from which it was excluded. These were conducted in Berlin by Ōshima Hiroshi, the Germanophile military attaché, who reported directly to the Japanese general staff. The negotiations were protracted because both foreign offices counselled caution, because the German military were less than enthusiastic and because the 26 February incident temporarily obscured the power configuration in Japan.

The Anti-Comintern Pact signed in November 1936 was very much a turnip-ghost. Both parties declared their opposition to communism. In secret protocols they promised to consult together in the event of an unprovoked Russian attack on either of them – which would no doubt have occurred without any agreement. The partners also agreed to sign no agreement with Russia without the other's consent – which did not deter the Germans in August 1939. In fact, although the pact could have paved the way for close political co-operation between Germany and Japan, in practice considerable reservations existed on both sides from the outset. Far from abandoning their economic stake in China, the Germans increased it substantially in 1936–7 and, to appease China, refrained from recognizing Manchukuo. Nor did the Japanese show the slightest inclination to make an exception of the Germans in the drive to exclude all white economic influence from Asia. To avoid antagonizing

Russia, the Japanese carefully excluded the fisheries negotiations and border delineation questions from the pact while the Germans kept the ghost of a connection with Russia alive by maintaining that the pact did not affect the 1922 Treaty of Rapallo or the 1926 Treaty of Berlin. The Japanese had also resisted Ribbentrop's attempts to give the pact an anti-British rather than an anti-Russian bias. Whatever Japan's ultimate ambitions might be, for the time being she had no desire to offend either Britain or the United States, for, as the pace of Japanese industrialization quickened in the mid 1930s, she was far too dependent on the outside world for imports of raw cotton, timber, iron-ore, scrap metal, oil and machine tools.

Once the Sino-Japanese war recommenced in 1937 the Germans were forced off the fence. When a chance encounter on the Marco Polo Bridge near Peking in July 1937 escalated into more general fighting Prime Minister Prince Konoe Fumimaro, anxious to avoid complications in China, ordered the local Japanese commander to negotiate a truce with his opposite number. But four days later the talented but easy-going Konoe yielded to pressure from War Minister Sugiyama Hajime to send immediate reinforcements to China. Whereupon Chiang Kai-shek, swept forward on a tidal wave of anti-Japanese feeling and acting on the assumption that Japan planned to seize the whole of north China, also sent in reinforcements. And so the fighting grew in scope and intensity. Obviously it was not Konoe's intention to plunge Japan into eight years of weary fighting in China when he gave in so weakly to military pressure. It is one of the ironies of history that at a time when most of the government and the general staff were seeking to extricate their country from the Chinese quagmire – largely because of their fear of Russia – intransigence on the Chinese side and fire-eaters in the Japanese ministry of war egged on by a chauvinistic press combined to destroy all hopes of a peaceful solution.

Even so it was several months before Germany finally abandoned her China stake. Hitler, conscious of the economic advantage of the China connection, evaded a decision. Between October 1937 and January 1938 he supported mediation attempts between the belligerents conducted by the German ambassador in China, Oskar Trautmann. The Japanese general staff grasped eagerly at this straw and supported moderate peace terms fearing that a long war on the mainland would divert Japan from her real objectives. But the Kwantung Army, the bit firmly between its teeth, set its face against a peaceful settlement and launched a new offensive which led to the fall of Nanking. The extremists in the cabinet led by the ministers of war, railways and communications got the upper hand at the end of 1937. Determined to smash Chiang Kai-shek completely, they insisted on new and draconian peace terms which they knew the Chinese would refuse. All hope of peace vanished. Now at last Hitler began to think seriously of throwing in his lot with Japan. Foreign policy was uppermost in his mind. He had finally concluded, not without great reluctance, that Britain must be regarded as a potential enemy. By opting for Japan he could at least pin the British down in the Far East and minimize the chance of their interfering with German expansion in Europe, a view in which Ribbentrop encouraged him. The recognition of Manchukuo in May 1938 and the recall of all military advisers from China in June signified the end of a chapter. It was no accident that this coincided with a period of mounting tension in Europe as Hitler prepared for a local war against the Czechs.

2

The Road to War 1936–1939

It is a natural temptation for Europeans to assume that the Second World War, which has left permament scars on the continent and completely upset the old balance of power, was essentially 'Hitler's war'; that is, that the Second World War commenced in September 1939 with a premeditated attack on Poland and ended with the collapse of Hitler's Reich and the capitulation of the German forces in May 1945. Compared with the struggle in Europe, the war in the Far East appears to be a sideshow of secondary importance, the outcome of which would depend in large measure on the defeat of Germany, the mainstay of world fascism.

Once the war became world wide with the entry into it of the United States and the Soviet Union then it did indeed make good strategic sense for the allied powers to concentrate their main effort on the defeat of Germany. But in explaining the origins of the Second World War a different historical perspective is called for. Germany's attempt to dominate Europe by force from the Atlantic to the Urals was only one cause of the breakdown of international order in the 1930s. The attempts of Japan to dominate east Asia represented a disruptive force of equal importance. As indicated earlier, Japanese ambitions, limited though they were in respect of China, led to the outbreak of war in 1937, a war which continued until 1945 and ended, in fact, after the capitulation of Germany. Historically it makes better sense to think of two quite distinct developments: German expansionism in Europe and Japanese expansionism in Asia, each disruptive of the established order, each running along separate but adjoining tracks and eventually merging in 1941 in one global conflict.

Let us examine, first of all, the origins of the European war. For a decade and a half after the end of the war historians believed that the coming to power of Hitler set a chain of events in motion: the re-introduction of conscription, the re-occupation of the Rhineland, the rape of Austria and of Czechoslovakia, and the attack on Poland, each coup following inexorably upon the other in accordance with the grand strategy Hitler had allegedly adumbrated in *Mein Kampf*.

Not until 1961 was serious doubt cast on this interpretation by Alan Taylor. War over Poland was by no means inevitable in 1939 argued Taylor. Hitler was a feckless coffee-house dreamer and manipulator who stumbled into war 'through launching on 29 August a diplomatic manoeuvre which he ought to have launched on 28 August' – though, characteristically, Taylor admitted on the same page that Hitler 'may have projected a great war all along'.[1] Taylor

[1] A.J.P. Taylor, *The Origins of the Second World War* (London, 1961), p. 278.

triggered off a great debate forcing historians to reconsider their attitude. At the end of the day an impressive phalanx of historians disagreed with Taylor though the number of defectors from that camp has increased somewhat over the years. But although his book did not overturn the wisdom of the mandarins on the origins of the Second World War, it did most assuredly encourage a more critical evaluation of the assumptions made by Sir Alan Bullock, Lord Dacre and Sir Lewis Namier in the second half of the 1940s.

Pinpointing the origins of a war is a forbidding task and the European war of 1939 is no exception. The proximate cause of that war can be easily identified in the German–Polish dispute between April and August 1939. The long-term causes raise more difficult questions. Where should one commence the investigation? With Hitler's accession to power? Or should one go back to the Peace Settlement of 1919–23 which set the seals of approval on the new balance of power set up in Europe after the First World War? Yet for the causes of the new outburst of aggression which destroyed that balance one must go back much further to the Reich Bismarck helped to create in 1871. And if one is to understand the root causes of the animosity between Germans and Poles one must go back long before 1933 to the 1848–9 Revolution and the confrontation over the Grand Duchy of Posen.

However, for the purposes of a book concerned with the transformation of the European War of 1939 into the World War of 1941, it is unnecessary to go back beyond 1933. There is clearly much sense in the argument that the coming to power of the Nazis, seen retrospectively, signified the beginning of the break-up of the post-war international order which rested on the supremacy of Britain and France. But it will be argued below that the real point of no return in international affairs, after which the Third Reich was irretrievably committed to war – though not necessarily against Poland – occurred not in 1933 but in the 18 months between the summer of 1936 and the spring of 1938.

Although it would be foolish to deny that 1933 marked a turning-point in German history in respect of the style of the new government and the unprecedented brutality shown to all opponents of the regime, in foreign policy there was much more continuity than discontinuity. The Nazis were treading a well-worn path when they sought to set aside the Treaty of Versailles. It is well-known that Hitler's objectives went far beyond that. His rejection of the frontiers of 1914 and his dream of a racial empire extending to the Urals is fully documented in *Mein Kampf*. But it should not be forgotten that republican governments before Hitler did not believe in the destruction of the Versailles Treaty as an end in itself. Both Nazis and Weimar politicians were seeking to re-establish Germany as the dominant power in Europe, an objective which carried with it certain implications: the annexation of Austria, the neutralization of Czechoslovakia and the establishment of a sphere of influence extending into eastern and south-eastern Europe. *Grossmachtpolitik*, not revisionism, was the common ground between foreign office, army command, sections of German industry and the Nazi leadership in the early 1930s.

Such differences as did exist between the Nazis and their predecessors – in the initial stages at any rate – concerned means not ends. Chancellor Gustav Stresemann and Chancellor Heinrich Bruening, for example, relied primarily on economic weapons to make Germany a great power again. The former's cultivation of the Russian connection was intended to pave the way for German economic domination of the east, while Bruening's Austro-German Customs Union in 1931 (frustrated by French opposition) and his trading policies towards Hungary and Rumania were steps on the road to German political domination of south-eastern Europe reminiscent of the 'Middle Europe' policy so popular in Germany during the First World War. Under the Nazis Schacht pursued a similar objective seeking with the support of heavy industry to absorb south-eastern Europe into a *Grossraumwirtschaft* centred on Berlin. Economic expansion coupled with the return of Germany's former colonies represented for Schacht and other imperialists of Wilhelmian vintage an alternative to racial imperialism in the east.

Economic imperialism did not go far enough for leading figures in army command and in the foreign office. They favoured outright territorial expansion in respect of Austria, Czechoslovakia and Poland. Hitler was himself well aware that *Grossmachtpolitik* in one form or another was an alternative to *Lebensraumpolitik*, as his remarks on 3 February 1933 to the commanding generals reveal. Historians, anxious to prove that *Lebensraumpolitik* was always uppermost in his mind, have laid great emphasis on Hitler's comment that a rearmed Germany should aim at 'the conquest of new living space in the east and its ruthless Germanization'. But it should not be overlooked that, though Hitler agreed that this was 'probably better' as an objective, he also admitted that it was 'impossible to say yet' how Germany should use her power when she had regained it. But he suggested that 'fighting for export possibilities' was a viable alternative, i.e. military power might be used in an act of *Machtpolitik* to intimidate Germany's neighbours into economic co-operation.[2] It would be pedantic to try to separate out with clinical precision the several strands in German policy in the 1930s. Clearly there was much overlap between *Grossmachtpolitik, Grossraumwirtschaft* and *Lebensraumpolitik* and all merged imperceptibly into each other in the end. At the same time one should not ignore the qualitative difference between the traditional *Grossmacht/ Grossraumwirtschaftpolitik* and the new aggressive racial undertones of Hitler's *Lebensraumpolitik*.

Between 1933 and 1937–8 – in contrast to the 18 months before the attack on Poland – the Nazis moved cautiously towards their policy objectives, and remained well within the limits of the coercive power at their disposal. At no time did Germany expose herself to the risk of a war which she could not conceivably have won. For example, during the Rhineland re-occupation when Hitler momentarily feared French intervention, his instinct was to withdraw at once; he was only talked out of it by Foreign Minister Konstantin von Neurath who realized that the French had no intention of taking military action. Similarly during the Austrian Crisis in March 1938; only when he was quite certain that neither Britain nor France nor Italy would lift a finger to help Austria and that the government of Chancellor Kurt Schuschnigg would not resist invasion – by carefully arranged invitation – did Hitler give the order for the German army to march across the frontier into Austria.

It is quite possible that had Hitler adopted a more conciliatory posture on

[2]J. Noakes and G. Pridham, *Documents on Nazism 1919–1945* (London, 1974), pp. 508–9.

rearmament, this would have done much to allay growing fears of Nazi intentions, and might well have enabled Germany to dismantle more of the
Versailles Treaty by agreement with Britain and France. The Germans did not
explore these possibilities. Instead, in response to the changing balance of
power in Germany, Hitler indicated to close associates in the summer of 1936
that rearmament must have the highest priority so that Germany could have an
offensive army ready for action as early as 1940. This was a decisive moment in
the history of the Third Reich. In effect Hitler had opted for a course of action
which quickly robbed Germany of her room for manoeuvre both economically
and diplomatically.

For by the end of 1936 Germany had reached an economic crossroads with
the attainment of full employment. Mounting expenditure on armaments and
on public works together with investment in the Four Year Plan and the
relatively unrestricted growth of consumer goods industries placed an intolerable strain on the economy. To accelerate rearmament still further after 1936
without adjusting their economic priorities – which is basically what the Nazis
did – was the high road to inflation and to serious overheating of the economy.
Whether the Nazis failed to exert effective control over the economy in the late
1930s because they were unable to do so or because they were unaware that
remedial action was necessary is a point for later discussion. So, too, is the
crucial question whether the deterioration in Germany's economic condition
exerted any significant influence on her decision to go to war in 1939.

One does not have to rely on economic arguments to make out the case for
1936–8 as the real turning-point in the history of the Third Reich. Strategic and
diplomatic considerations weighed heavily with the Nazi leadership at this
time. At the Hossbach meeting in November 1937 when Hitler addressed his
top advisers about his future objectives, he expressed concern about the nar-
rowing gap between German military strength and that of Britain and France.
Discussing the outlook in 1943–5 he remarked that 'After this date only a
change for the worse, from our point of view, could be expected. . . . Our
relative strength would decrease in relation to the rearmament which would by
then have been carried out by the rest of the world. . . . the world was
expecting our attack and was increasing its counter-measures from year to
year. It was while the rest of the world was still fencing itself off that we were
obliged to take the offensive. Nobody knew today what the situation would be
in the years 1943–5. One thing was certain, that we could wait no longer'.[3] To
this theme Hitler returned on several occasions in the next few months. A
historical parallel springs to mind at once: the German decision to go to war in
1914. At the height of the Sarajevo Crisis the knowledge that the massive
rearmament planned by Russia would tip the balance decisively against Germany by 1917 was a background factor of immense significance for the decision-
makers in Berlin in the summer of 1914. Similarly in the late 1930s; Hitler's
realization that Britain and France, alarmed by the general thrust of Nazi
policy, were beginning to rearm and that they possessed the potential to over-
take Germany once again infused an element of urgency into the situation.

Secondly, the deteriorating international situation had serious implications

[3]*Op. cit.*, p. 526.

for the pace of German foreign policy. In *Mein Kampf* Hitler had argued that Imperial Germany's bid for world mastery failed because she foolishly antagonized Britain and Russia simultaneously. The blunder must be studiously avoided by National Socialist Germany; if she was to succeed in her bid for European domination at the expense of France and Russia, she had to have both Britain and Italy as allies.

It did not work out as planned. Within six months of the signature of the Anglo-German Naval Convention Ribbentrop, its chief architect, realized that there was little likelihood of a British alliance. By the summer of 1936 Hitler, too, was so disillusioned by what he regarded as British weakness over Abyssinia and Spain, that he was talking of war with Britain should Ribbentrop's mission to London finally end in failure. Reluctantly he began to allocate to the Italians a larger place in his scheme of things than originally intended. There was another problem; if it came to war, then it seemed likely that the United States would come to Britain's aid against Germany. That, at any rate, was the interpretation the German ambassador in Washington placed on Roosevelt's celebrated Quarantine Speech in Chicago in October 1937. And even though Hitler was obstinate and hopelessly opinionated about America, that does not exclude the possibility that he had some vague inkling of the possible international implications if she was drawn into war again.

So by the end of 1937 the *Mein Kampf* strategy was going seriously astray. The probability was that if Germany attempted to expand in Europe Britain and France, with support from the United States, would offer resistance. All Germany could show for her endeavours to date was an understanding of dubious value with Italy. But all was not lost. There was still a chance that Germany might realize her ambitions. For Britain, in Hitler's opinion, would not oppose German expansion by force, at least not in the near future – an opinion which Ribbentrop, incidentally, did not share. And if Britain did not move, neither would France. Resting his policy on this risky assumption Hitler, far from moderating his demands to take account of mounting opposition abroad, deliberately accelerated the pace of German policy. On 5 November 1937 he alerted his advisers to his intention of securing Germany's flank by seizing Austria and Czechoslovakia in the near future if favourable opportunities arose. Conceivably, too, Hitler's conviction that time was running out for Germany militarily and diplomatically was confirmed by his concern that he might not have much longer to live. What one might term the militarization of German policy had begun. Germany started to pursue a policy which ignored diplomatic and political restraints, minimized international opposition to another German bid for hegemony and relied primarily on the maximization of armaments to achieve Germany's political ambitions.

Turning from Europe to Asia, the point was made earlier that in the summer of 1936 the influence of the military was markedly on the increase in both Germany and Japan. The renewal of the war with China in the summer of 1937 and the mounting threat to Czechoslovakia in the summer of 1938 were the first signs of the overt militarization of German and Japanese foreign policy. The only difference was that whereas the attack Hitler planned to launch on

Czechoslovakia was clear proof of his intention to dominate eastern Europe by force, the war in China was an essentially defensive measure to maintain Japan's threatened foothold on the Asian mainland; whether Japan would move later to a positive policy of aggression against Russia or perhaps southwards to dominate the Pacific were issues still unresolved in 1937–8. What is clear, however, is that Germany and Japan were not acting in collusion with each other. So far they had had relatively little contact with each other though no doubt each drew comfort from the lack of punitive measures against the other when they left the League of Nations in 1933. Nevertheless, interesting parallels exist between the course of development in the two countries.

As the effects of the world economic crisis spread throughout the globe and the façade of democracy began to crumble in Germany and Japan, the military establishment in both countries agitated for increased expenditure on armaments. Even before Hitler came to power General Kurt von Schleicher's cabinet approved a plan in November 1932 for the expansion of the army from 10 to 21 divisions. Hitler endorsed the plan and accelerated its implementation. In the same year the Takahashi ministry authorized substantial increases in the armed forces. In the early stages of rearmament orthodox financiers still exerted considerable influence: Schacht in Germany and Takahashi Korekiyo in Japan. Both men were well aware that while the existence of unused capacity in their economies had made rearmament relatively painless in the initial stages, with the attainment of full employment cheap money policies would have to be abandoned and taxation increased, otherwise inflationary pressures would build up in the economy.

When that point was reached, however, dominant factions in both countries were able to prevent any slackening off in the pace of rearmament. In Germany a new alliance between party leadership, army command and IG Farben – all with a vested interest in the speedy creation of an offensive army – swept aside gloomy prognostications from the ministry of economics and from export-oriented industry about the dangers of accelerated rearmament. Hitler bluntly refused to repay the Mefo bills – which had helped finance rearmament and which represented a built-in inflationary element – and Schacht, whose star had been waning since 1936, finally resigned as minister of economics in 1937. Takahashi, who had also fought to keep military expenditure within reasonable bounds, had a more dramatic end, falling victim to an assassin's dagger during the military rebellion in February 1936. The result was the same: an acceleration in the pace of rearmament regardless of the economic consequences. In the summer of 1936 Hitler sided with the dominant faction insisting on absolute priority for armaments while Takahashi's successor, Eiichi Baba, accepted without question the inflated budget estimates of army and navy.

Rapid rearmament led to economic difficulties in both countries. In Germany the rapid recovery of the economy and the mounting pressure of rearmament after 1934–5 sucked in additional food and raw material imports which soon strained the balance of payments. In the spring and summer of 1936, when Russian and Rumanian suppliers of oil demanded hard currency for their products, Germany faced a sharp financial crisis. To cope with these problems the Nazis introduced a Four Year Plan which aimed at making

Germany self-sufficient in key raw materials essential for their aggressive policies. But economic difficulties persisted and intensified on the eve of war as will be seen later.

Japan experienced fewer economic problems in the initial stages of rearmament because a ruthless deflationary policy between 1927 and 1931 had drastically pruned the economy; industry had been re-equipped and productivity increased at the expense of a docile and under-employed labour force totally dependent on the paternalistic Zaibatsu. Reflation and steadily increasing expenditure on armaments did not lead to inflation or to a balance of payments crisis because Japan paid for increased imports through a successful export drive subsidized by the government and assisted by a devalued yen. But by the end of 1936 ominous signs of financial strain showed themselves. Exports began to flag as resources were switched to the production of armaments; the trade gap widened; and Japan's gold reserves started to fall sharply though through control of foreign exchange the government prevented a fall in the value of the yen. Inflationary pressures started to build up at home; prices rose though this was offset to some extent by higher wage rates and agricultural prices; and by the end of 1938 the internal debt stood at 15,000 million yen, for two-thirds of government expenditure was being financed by borrowing and 80 per cent of all expenditure went on armaments.

Finally, heavy industry in both Germany and Japan was ready to support the expansionist policies of their respective governments. In Germany, as indicated above, a consensus emerged in the winter of 1935–6 between powerful sections of heavy industry led by I.G. Farben, army command and the party leadership in favour of accelerated military expansion. There was some variation initially in Japan. The Zaibatsu, tied for the most part to international markets, were not enthusiastic about the military action in Manchuria. Nor were the radical-minded young officers making the running in the Kwantung Army well-disposed to the old-established industries; they deliberately excluded the Zaibatsu from the strictly regimented economy they were attempting to establish in Manchuria in the early 1930s and relied on smaller firms to help them carry out their plans.

By the end of 1937 when it was becoming clear that the Japanese were trapped in a long war in China, a new economic phase commenced characterized by a shift to heavy industry and by vast increases in arms expenditure. To maximize production the Control Group realized that the full co-operation of the Zaibatsu was essential. Already in March 1937 the government was making plans for the mobilization of the economy for war by 1941. In the next two years industries such as coal and iron and steel were placed under state control; others, such as shipbuilding and engineering, were bribed with lavish subsidies and tax concessions; the government assumed powers to regulate prices and profits and to direct labour; in October 1937 a Cabinet Planning Board dominated by the military was set up to monitor these developments; and in 1938 a reluctant Diet passed the National Mobilization Act which gave the state virtually unlimited powers over the whole economy. A deep sense of patriotism which had infused Japanese industry from its earliest beginnings and a desire to limit government interference as much as possible were as important as the profit motive in bringing the Zaibatsu into line. Whereas in

Germany the Nazi leadership quickly brought radical anti-capitalist elements to heel in the summer of 1934 and entered into a working partnership with industry guaranteeing it a degree of management autonomy and huge profits in return for its co-operation, first, in getting the economy moving again and, later, in producing vast quantities of armaments, in Japan this type of understanding with industry was retarded by internal struggles in the army. Not until 1936–7 when the Control Group got the upper hand over the anti-capitalist radicals was co-operation for mutual advantage possible, though admittedly state control was much more extensive and effective than in Nazi Germany.

During the period of mounting crisis which commenced in the Far East with the outbreak of the Sino-Japanese War in July 1937 and in Europe with the deepening crisis over Czechoslovakia in the summer of 1938 the global implications of German and Japanese expansionism began to assume importance. Three developments call for comment: the growing animosity between Japan and the United States; the deterioration of relations between Germany and the United States; and attempts by Germany to strengthen her ties with Japan.

Turning to the first of these developments. The outbreak of war in the Far East threw into sharp relief the basic dilemma of American policy. Ever since it became apparent in the mid 1930s that Japan would no longer tolerate subordinate status in the Pacific concern had been growing in Washington. In December 1934, under pressure from radical-minded officers in the middle echelon of naval command, men bitterly resentful of Japan's 'humiliation' after the First World War and convinced of the inevitability of war with the United States, the Japanese government gave notice of its intention to terminate the 1922 Washington Treaty; in November 1936 the Anti-Comintern Pact was signed; and in December, when her request for parity of status was rejected, Japan withdrew from the London Naval Conference making a new naval race with the United States a distinct possibility.

Renewed hostilities in China naturally increased American fears about Japanese ambitions. But American policy failed conspicuously at this moment of crisis to establish a proper balance between aspirations, resources and political realities. The emotional commitment of the American public to China – shared by the policy-makers – inhibited them from taking full account of certain political realities: that America's political commitment in the Far East would decline after the Philippines achieved independence in 1946; that America's economic stake in Japan was greater than in China and growing throughout the 1930s; and – most important of all – that the United States lacked the military potential at that time to oppose Japan by force for the sake of China. No policy reappraisal took place. Instead Roosevelt and Hull continued to rely on the high moral principles enshrined in the Non-Recognition Doctrine to see them through and pinned their hope to China's ability to resist Japanese encroachments without American assistance, the old mixture of moral intransigence and military disengagement which had failed during the Manchurian Crisis.

Within days of the outbreak of hostilities Hull had roundly condemned the Japanese but went on to make it clear that the United States did not intend to intervene in Asian affairs and expressed his earnest hope that Japan would seek an early settlement of the conflict. Japan and the United States were good neighbours, he insisted, and must stay that way. It is conceivable that Hull may even have hoped that a moral appeal might arouse the Japanese masses against war, isolate the army and discourage aggressive moves in Europe as an added bonus mark. The president acted in the same schizophrenic fashion; he eagerly supported the initiative of the League of Nations in inviting the signatories of the Washington Treaty to meet in Brussels in November. On the other hand, he reassured the great American public that the conference would under no circumstances seek to coerce the belligerents; its aim was simply to encourage China and Japan to make peace. In fact, Japan did not come to Brussels. And as America was not prepared to undertake coercive measures against Japan, and Britain would not unless forced into it, the conference quickly foundered. Through their failure to agree on concerted action the last chance of working out a settlement between China and Japan was lost.

Clearly there had been no new departure in American policy on 5 October 1937 when Roosevelt declared in a speech in Chicago that 'the epidemic of world lawlessness' was spreading and that 'when an epidemic of physical disease starts to spread the community approves and joins in a quarantine of the patients in order to protect the health of the community against the spread of the disease'.[4]

It is true that since the mid summer he had been thinking of an Anglo-American blockade of Japan to stop her in her tracks if she committed fresh acts of aggression in the future. This operation, he thought, could be carried out successfully without leading to a formal state of war. An added attraction was that, in his capacity as commander-in-chief, he could authorize this kind of warfare whereas a formal declaration of war would require the assent of Congress which clearly would not be forthcoming. But when the cautious references in the Quarantine Speech to co-operation among peace-loving nations to halt aggression met with widespread approval outside the hard-core isolationist press, Roosevelt was taken aback. The next day he floundered, back-tracked, categorically denied that he was contemplating physical sanctions, and took refuge behind the nebulous concept of 'neutral co-operation'. As he explained later to Norman Davis, his chief adviser on foreign affairs, all he had in mind was a group of neutral nations seeking to influence the aggressor but without resorting to the use of force.[5] Thus it is difficult to maintain that the speech was proof that Roosevelt was a staunch internationalist determined to take firm action against aggression. Though the temperature of the water was inviting, he refused to leap in.

This time the Far Eastern problem did not go away as it had so obligingly done in 1933. On the contrary. Signs that Japan, Germany and Italy were acting in concert were a new and ominous complication at the close of 1937; in

[4]S. Rosenman, ed. *The Public Papers and Private Addresses of Franklin D. Roosevelt* (New York, 1938–50) VI, p. 410.

[5]Roosevelt had turned down the draft prepared by the State Department and substituted the quarantine passage for one declaring America's readiness to fight for certain principles: see D. Borg, 'Notes on Roosevelt's Quarantine Speech', in *Political Science Quarterly* LXXII, pp. 413–17.

September Mussolini visited Berlin where the two European dictators ostentatiously reaffirmed their belief in the Rome–Berlin Axis; and in November Italy joined the Anti-Comintern Pact, turning it into an agreement *à trois*. With hindsight it is clear that the three 'have-not' powers had relatively little in common and were not able to co-ordinate their foreign policies to any marked degree; indeed, ideological declarations were a substitute for agreement on practical co-operation at an international level. Still, in international politics appearances are frequently more important than reality. The Anti-Comintern Pact is a case in point. Official circles in Washington immediately concluded that a secret offensive alliance committed the three powers to expansionist policies aimed at world conquest. Consequently when one of the Axis powers resorted to the use of force, the Americans never evaluated such actions in their immediate local context but assumed automatically that this must be a deliberate premeditated act in a carefully constructed global conspiracy which called, therefore, for a riposte with global implications for American policy. Furthermore, at a time of recession in the United States the prospect of co-ordinated action by the three autarky-minded powers, each with designs on neighbouring territories from which they would squeeze out American trade, represented a serious threat to the international trading position of the United States.

The pervasive myth of Anti-Comintern solidarity helped persuade Roosevelt that a show of strength was necessary to deter imminent aggression. In January 1938 he announced the commencement of negotiations for a trade treaty with Britain whilst simultaneously suspending negotiations for one with Italy; and he took to Congress a new naval programme providing for a 20 per cent increase on treaty levels. Nevertheless, whilst fears about Axis intentions were uppermost in his mind, considerations of domestic policy were also involved. An Anglo-American trade treaty would, it was hoped, increase American trade with the important markets of the British Empire and so appease the farming lobby. And in the case of naval expansion, to maintain full employment in the shipyards during a sharp recession, new orders for 69 new vessels would fill the void left by the completion of the ships built under the Vinson–Trammell Act.

The darkening international scene helped Roosevelt secure substantial majorities in the House of Representatives and in the Senate for the new programme. In mid December 1937 Japanese aircraft sank an American naval vessel, the USS *Panay*, in Chinese waters. Naval command was deeply shocked and demanded the fleet be got ready for immediate action. Determined to avoid a direct confrontation, Roosevelt resisted these demands. But the crisis encouraged him to revive the idea of an Anglo-American naval blockade to deal with future incidents, and to consider a freeze of Japanese assets in the United States. However, the Japanese government, anxious to avoid war, got him off this hook by tendering the necessary apology and the *Panay* incident blew over. What Roosevelt finally decided to do had, in the long run, quite important consequences for American policy. In the first place, the president instructed Admiral William D. Leahy, chief of naval operations, to begin work on strategic planning for a two-ocean war on the assumption that Britain and the United States would co-operate with each other. Secondly, in response to British suggestions, he sent Captain Royal E. Ingersoll, director of the war plans division in the navy, to London to confer with his British counterpart.

Ingersoll arrived in London with instructions to discuss general strategy and explore the possibility of joint action with the British fleet against Japan. Although no binding agreements emerged, and the reluctance of both governments to launch a blockade of Japan in the near future killed that proposal, nevertheless, much general information about the respective fleets was freely exchanged. In effect, the first tentative step had been taken on the long road to the combined strategy of Britain and the United States during the Second World War.

During the 18 months between the sinking of the *Panay* and the outbreak of the European war in September 1939 American–Japanese relations continued to deteriorate as the China incident dragged on. When the Japanese allowed the Marco Polo Bridge affair to escalate into war in the summer of 1937 what they had in mind in all probability was a short sharp campaign to put Chiang Kai-shek in his place. Having inflicted defeats on the Chinese, Japan was quite willing to accept a German offer of mediation. On 5 November relatively moderate peace terms were handed to Chiang Kai-shek who procrastinated in the vain hope that the Brussels Conference would come out strongly in support of China. The conference, however, proved a fiasco. After further military victories including the conquest of Shangai and the fall in December of Nanking, the Nationalist capital, Chiang Kai-shek was ready for peace. It was too late. As indicated earlier, nationalist elements in the Japanese cabinet, in a fit of mindless euphoria, stiffened the terms on offer, much to the dismay of the army general staff, most of whom feared involvement in a long-drawn-out war when they would have preferred to prepare for the coming conflict with Russia.[6] Chiang Kai-shek rejected the new terms, set up a new capital, Chungking, far in the interior of China and continued the war. To make matters worse the Konoe cabinet, carried along on a wave of xenophobic nationalism, declared in Janaury 1938 that it would never negotiate with Chiang Kai-shek but would prosecute the war against him to the bitter end.

By the autumn of 1938 it finally dawned on Japan's leaders that they could not force Chiang Kai-shek to his knees in the near future. Konoe quickly repented of his hasty declaration and the general staff renewed its efforts to end the fighting, this time supported by the war ministry. In November 1938 army representatives negotiated secretly with an influential Kuomintang supporter, Wang Ching-wei, who believing China needed peace above all else, was prepared to part company with Chiang Kai-shek and accept peace terms leaving Japanese forces in parts of north China and Inner Mongolia on condition they withdrew from the rest of China within two years. This agreement came to nothing because Chiang Kai-shek suppressed the peace party in his own camp, and because when it came to the crunch neither the soldiers nor the civilian politicians in Tokyo could bring themselves to withdraw any Japanese forces from occupied territory. Already by the end of 1938 there were ominous

[6]On 5 November Japan was ready to settle for *de facto* recognition of the Japanese presence in Manchukuo and of the autonomy of Inner Mongolia. China was to cease 'anti-Japanese' activities and form a common front with Japan against communism. By the end of December Japan was demanding recognition of her right to establish 'special regimes' wherever she wanted in China, close economic co-operation and payment of an indemnity.

signs that under the corrosive influence of war Japanese ambitions were growing. On 3 November 1938 the Konoe government declared publicly that the objective of Japanese policy was the establishment of a 'New Order' in east Asia. To guarantee the stability of the region, Japan, China and Manchukuo must work together as 'good neighbours'; they would seek to secure international justice, co-operate economically and culturally, and take active steps to combat communism in the area. This new political concept was to some extent rooted in Pan-Asianism, an ideology growing in Japan since the turn of the century. Pan-Asiatics rejected individualism, liberalism, nationalism, Marxism and imperialism as wholly negative manifestations of western penetration of Asia and called for a return to the traditional virtues of harmony, mutual respect, selflessness and co-operation by all for the greater good of Asia with Japan, supposedly the repository of these virtues, as the centre-piece of the new scenario.

Behind the idealistic verbiage of the New Order lay harsh economic realities. Japan's trading position was deteriorating sharply in the late 1930s. Exports were declining partly because of the switch from light to heavy industry and also because of rising tariff barriers and trade boycotts. And as the armaments industries sucked in increasing volumes of raw materials, Japan's trade gap widened and her gold reserves dwindled rapidly. The only alternative to economic collapse and the abandonment of an expansionist policy was autarky.

In the so-called yen bloc – Japan, Manchukuo, north China, Korea and Formosa – inter-regional trade was expanding fast; between 1936 and 1938 Japanese exports to the United States declined from 22 to 15.8 per cent while exports of manufactured goods to Manchukuo and north China increased from 25 to 40 per cent and their exports of food and raw materials to Japan rose from 14 to 22 per cent. Japan invested heavily in Manchukuo and north China developing sources of raw materials, laying the foundations of heavy industry – especially steel and chemicals – and building up markets for Japanese cotton goods. The experiment was only partially sucessful. A country as dependent on the outside world as Japan was for oil, rubber and steel alloys could never become self-sufficient. Even in respect of coal and iron ore from Manchukuo and north China time was needed for investment to pay off while the ruinous war in China, accounting for half Japan's military expenditure, militated against success. Meanwhile Japan remained dangerously dependent on the goodwill of the United States for essential machine tools, oil and scrap metal.

As Japan's new imperialism took concrete shape, concern deepened in Washington. By the summer of 1938 the myth of global conspiracy had taken deep root in official circles. Japanese military action in China and German expansionism in Europe were not treated as unconnected episodes – which to a large extent they were – but as part of a co-ordinated plan inimical in its totality to American interests. To this new and threatening situation the military planners were now turning their attention. Hitherto the navy, which exerted decisive influence on military strategy until 1939, had thought exclusively in terms of war with Japan. Under Plan Orange the army was expected to remain on the defensive holding on to the Philippines as long as possible while the navy took offensive action; the intention was to destroy the Japanese fleet in one decisive naval engagement after which it was confidently expected that a blockade of Japan would force her into submission. But in the winter of 1938–9 the Joint Army–Navy Planning Board reached the momentous conclusion that the only war the United States was likely to face in the near future would be against the combined forces of Germany, Italy and Japan. By April 1939 five so-called Rainbow Plans had been drawn up. However, differences between army and navy precluded a final choice. The navy was still reluctant to abandon its traditional commitment to offensive action in the Pacific for the prospect of war with Japan had been its *raison d'être* from the very beginning. Much as the Japanese navy advocated southern expansion to justify increased expenditure on their arm of the service, so the American fleet kept alive the concept of the inevitability of conflict with Japan to justify its existence. But the army – now at last beginning to exert some influence on policy-making – was already moving to the view that the United States should stay on the defensive in the Pacific and win the battle against Germany in the Atlantic and in Europe; three of the five Rainbow Plans were based on this assumption.

Nor were civilian policy-makers in complete agreement about the direction to take. As the crisis of American policy deepened in 1938–9 the merits and demerits of alternative tactics for dealing with Japan were energetically debated in the State Department. Roosevelt, lumbering hesitantly towards positive action, was exposed to pressure from opposing camps – the 'hawks' and the 'doves' – in the corridors of power. He reacted in characteristic fashion siding first with one and then the other camp, vacillating in his attitude to the Axis powers between resolute action and conciliatory gestures.

Secretary of State Hull, on the other hand, was much less of a pragmatist by instinct. He yielded to none in his forthright condemnation of every Japanese move in the power game and in his insistence that the Japanese adhere rigidly to Christian principles in their dealings with other powers. Yet his naïve idealism, which ill-fitted him to deal with people of a vastly different cultural tradition, was tempered by a high degree of political caution and a desire to avoid conflict, which ordinarily put him on the side of the 'doves' over both Japan and Germany.

The 'hawks' were led by powerful and influential figures such as Henry L. Stimson, appointed secretary for the army in 1940; Frank Knox, appointed navy secretary also in 1940; Henry Morgenthau Jr, secretary of state for the Treasury; and Stanley K. Hornbeck, the chief of the division of Far Eastern Affairs in the State Department from 1928 to 1937 and from 1937 to 1941 chief adviser on the Far East to the secretary of state. Deeply convinced that the Axis powers were plotting to disturb the peace, the 'hawks' insisted that a tough policy towards Japan was the only way to stop her dead in her tracks; a trade embargo would effectively cripple her so heavily dependent was she on imported raw materials; then her leaders, like sensible Anglo-Saxons, would see reason, abandon the war in China and leave the United States in command of the situation without a drop of American blood being spilt.[7] Events were to

---

[7]As Stimson remarked: 'To get on with Japan one had to treat her rough, unlike other countries',: D. Borg and S. Okamoto, eds., *Pearl Harbor as History. Japanese–American Relations 1931–1941* (New York, 1973), p. 85; see Stanley K. Hornbeck, 'The Japanese speak and understand the language of force', *FRUS* 1934 IIII, p. 193.

prove that when Japan was forced into this situation and faced with the painful choice between capitulation and national suicide she chose the latter. Furthermore the 'hawks' refused to distinguish between civilian governments and the military faction in Japan, mantaining that all shared the same expansionist objectives. Whatever may be said about ultimate objectives, this was certainly not true of methods: the 'hawks' underestimated the possibility that tactical changes on the Japanese side might open up genuine opportunities for mutually advantageous negotiations.

The 'doves' were represented by men such as Joseph C. Grew, ambassador in Tokyo; Francis Sayre, assistant secretary of state; Maxwell Hamilton, Hornbeck's assistant chief in the State Department from 1930 to 1937 when he became chief of the division; and Joseph W. Ballantine, assistant chief under Maxwell from 1937. They cautioned the president against a hard-line policy not, it must be emphasized, out of any sympathy for Japan – they were as convinced as the 'hawks' that the Axis powers were conspiring against world peace – but simply because they reckoned that a tough policy would drive civilian politicians with moderate views into the arms of the military extremists thereby increasing the likelihood of further aggression and encouraging other Axis powers to follow suit. In differentiating between the factions in Japan the 'doves' showed rather more insight into the complexities of Japanese politics than the 'hawks'. However, it should be said here that the terms 'moderate' and 'extremist' are somewhat misleading when applied to Japan and are only used in this text for want of more accurate nomenclature to describe an ever-changing and highly personalized balance of forces in a system wracked by institutional and factional rivalry and characterized by the peculiarly Japanese phenomenon of *ringisei*, i.e. the practice whereby proposals were initiated at the bottom of the bureaucratic pyramid and percolated upwards to be accepted as policy by senior officials, a situation which enabled middle-echelon officers in the army and navy to exert a degree of influence over policy unknown in western-style governments.

Under the influence of the 'hawks' the American attitude to Japan hardened perceptibly in the summer of 1939. Already in June 1938, incensed by bombing raids on Chinese cities, Roosevelt had imposed a moral embargo on the export of aircraft to Japan and supplied Chiang Kai-shek with his first credit of $25 million. Japan did not greatly care for the embargo but her requirements were not for aircraft but for oil and scrap metal and neither of these was affected. On 28 December 1938 the United States protested sharply against Konoe's 'New Order' concept, denouncing its autarkical basis as a violation of the principle of the Open Door to which the Americans were so deeply committed. By the summer of 1939 popular pressure for effective action against Japan was mounting. Opinion polls revealed heavy support for an arms and trade embargo on Japan. In Congress a number of motions were tabled to restrict trade with Japan.[8]

[8]A perceptive observer commented on the frenetic state of public opinion that the United States 'which bolts like a frightened rabbit from even remote contact with Europe, will enthusiastically take a step which might well be a material day's march on the road to a Far Eastern war': Beatrice Berle Bishop and Travis Beal Jacobs, eds., *Navigating the Rapids 1917–1971. From the Papers of Adolf A. Berle* (New York, 1973), pp. 231–2.

Hull feared that an outright arms and trade embargo would lead to war and that eventuality both secretary of state and president were resolved to avoid at a time when events in Europe were clearly moving to a crisis. In the end Hull persuaded Roosevelt to announce on 26 July that the 1911 commercial treaty – which accounted for 40 per cent of Japan's total foreign trade – would lapse in 1940. This would provide a six-month delay in which Hull hoped passions might subside and Japan might see reason. When the treaty eventually expired in January 1940 without the Japanese coming to heel, Hull announced that trade with Japan would now continue on a day-to-day basis in the vain hope that this would keep the Japanese guessing about America's ultimate intentions and incline them to caution.

The reality was that America's middle-of-the-road policy combining moral condemnation with the avoidance of steps likely to lead to war had precisely the opposite effect on Japan. Apart from young radical officers itching for war, Japanese government circles and the army and navy commands did not desire war with the United States and remained supremely confident that their forward policy would not lead to armed confrontation with her. Verbal abuse they expected, having grown accustomed to high-sounding declarations with no sting in the tail. Provided Japan did not directly threaten American security interests in the Philippines and refrained from threatening her economic interests in the Far East, the policy-makers in Tokyo supposed that they could realize their ambitions in east Asia and still remain on tolerable terms with the United States. When unfortunate incidents such as the USS *Panay* occurred, bland apologies were immediately forthcoming in accordance with this general strategy. What the Japanese obstinately shut their eyes to was the irrational element in American policy: the growing emotional commitment to China which proved to be the rock on which Japanese ambitions foundered.

The deterioration in American–German relations was the second major development in 1938–9. Over Germany there were also sharp differences of opinion with Roosevelt in the middle of the argument siding sometimes with the hardliners and sometimes with the appeasers.

Prominent among the hardliners were George Messersmith, assistant secretary of state from 1937; William E. Dodd, ambassador in Berlin from 1934 to 1937; William D. Leahy, director of naval operations; Harold L. Ickes, secretary of the Department of the Interior; and Henry Morgenthau who was also a 'hawk' over Japan. These advisers were profoundly pessimistic about the probable outcome of Nazi foreign policy. They feared that economic pressures generated by massive rearmament and intensified by autarkical policies disruptive of international trade coupled with the political ambitions of Nazi extremists would drive Germany to war if nothing were done to prevent it. The danger was acute because moderate elements had been ousted by Ribbentrop, Goebbels, Hess and Rosenberg, all extremists committed to the seizure of *Lebensraum* as the ultimate answer to Germany's mounting difficulties. The proper course of action was not to conciliate the Nazis but, on the contrary, to refuse to make any concessions and encourage Britain and France to abandon their ill-conceived political appeasement and stand up to Nazi aggression. If the Nazis were confronted with a determined anti-fascist front led by the western democracies then, so the hardliners hoped, the extremists might still be replaced by a more sensible regime backed by the army and ready to come to terms with the democracies.

The appeasers disagreed with this diagnosis. Under-secretary of State Sumner Welles; Assistant Secretary of State Adolf A. Berle; Jay Pierrepoint Moffat, head of the European division in the State Department; William Bullitt, American ambassador in Paris; and Joseph Kennedy, American ambassador in London, all believed that the way to avoid war was not to create an anti-fascist front likely to goad Germany into war but to appease her economically. About the British connection the American appeasers were deeply sceptical. Instead of aligning herself with the British imperialists the United States ought to stand aloof from all European entanglements and take independent action to preserve the peace. As they believed that moderate elements in the German army, civil service and industrial world had not been routed by the extremists but were still in charge – an erroneous assumption by this time – it seemed to make sense to try to steer them away from the temptation of war; this could be done, so the appeasers believed, by helping Germany gain access to sources of raw materials and generally by reintegrating her into international markets. This diagnosis clearly overestimated the significance of Germany's economic problems and ignored the strategic, diplomatic and ideological determinants of Nazi policy.

At first Roosevelt sided with the hardliners. That was the real significance of the Anglo-American trade treaty of November 1938. The treaty did, of course, confer substantial benefits on United States agriculture in an important market; in 1937 41 per cent of American exports went to the British Empire and 36 per cent of her imports came from that region. An agreement with an industrial nation was urgently needed by the administration because the farm lobby was deeply critical of a trade policy which had so far benefitted manufacturers not farmers. But political considerations were uppermost in Hull's mind. Tough trading policies were intended to put pressure on the Germans – with whom he refused to negotiate a trade agreement – and would he hoped lead them to abandon their autarkical policies and come to terms with the United States.[9] For example, Germany was deliberately excluded from the most-favoured-nation clauses which extended concessions made to British goods in American markets to other nations, a step which greatly increased the difficulties German exporters faced in those markets. Germany did not on that account alter her commercial policies. But the existence of the treaty served as a reminder in

[9]As Hull remarked 'if a great trading nation like Britain and another great trading country like the United States became inert and undertook further self-containment alone, such countries as Japan, Germany and Italy with their armies and navies would in two or three years dominate every spare foot of trade territory other than that under the immediate control of Great Britain and the United States. That would leave our two countries in an amazingly disadvantageous situation'. But if free trade principles were more widely adopted then 'nearly forty nations would be marching across the Western World proclaiming a broad, concrete basic program to restore international order and promote and preserve peace and the economic well-being of people everywhere. The tremendous economic and moral influence of all those nations would be exerted upon any country not disposed to join with them'. C. Hull, *The Memoirs of Cordell Hull* (New York, 1948) I, p. 522; pp. 524–5.

Berlin that the United States was a potential opponent prepared to underwrite British opposition to Nazi ambitions.

At other times Roosevelt inclined towards the appeasers. In January 1938 he supported a plan resurrected by Welles and Berle for an international conference to discuss arms limitations, tariff reductions and equal access for all to sources of raw materials. Possibly he felt that, having increased defence expenditure and just authorized negotiations for an Anglo-American trade treaty, he had gone far enough in demonstrating American readiness to stand up to the dictators. Welles's woolly and naïvely optimistic plan was likely to win popular support in America, a factor which could not be overlooked with mid-term elections due in the autumn. Furthermore, should an international conference succeed against all the odds it could ease America's current economic difficulties by reintegrating an old customer, Germany, into the international trading network. And success in Europe might even loosen the ties between Berlin and Tokyo and force the Japanese to make a reasonable peace with China. The plan – which never had the slightest chance of success – did not even get off the ground. This was partly because the British Prime Minister, Neville Chamberlain, poured cold water on it; already peeved by the refusal of the United States to work with Britain at the outset of the Sino-Japanese War, he feared that an ill-prepared conference with broad issues like disarmament on the agenda would probably alienate the dictators and prejudice his own plans for appeasing Germany and Italy by patient negotiation on specific issues; he wanted the president to hold fire to see what progress Britain could make on her own. President and secretary of state were disturbed by Chamberlain's iconoclasm, especially by his readiness to recognize the Italian conquest of Abyssinia. And although Chamberlain was subsequently persuaded by Foreign Secretary Anthony Eden to dispatch another message to Roosevelt in which positive support for a conference was promised, the damage had been done. Ever after, Washington remained mistrustful of Chamberlain fearing that he was uninterested in a general settlement and would gladly surrender central and south-eastern Europe to the Germans in return for political guarantees and a bilateral agreement protecting British economic interests in that region at the expense of the multilateral trading pattern so dear to the American heart.[10] But it is also likely that Britain's cool response came as a relief to Roosevelt who, as in October 1937, was without any clear plan for peace.

American policy towards Germany up to the time of the Munich Crisis was 'ambiguous at best and on the side of misguided appeasement at worst'.[11] Privately Roosevelt was on the side of the hardliners in fulminating against Chamberlain's continued appeasement of Hitler despite the annexation of Austria in March 1938. But in public he refused to take a really firm stand against the dictators. When some pressure built up in Congress in 1938 for the repeal of the embargo on arms to Spain so that the Spanish Republic could buy arms on a

---

[10]This was a complete misunderstanding of the appeasement policy; see S. Newman, *March 1939. The British Guarantee to Poland. A Study in the Continuity of British Foreign Policy* (Oxford, 1976).

[11]Offner, *American Appeasement*, p. 246.

cash-and-carry basis Roosevelt and Hull refused to budge.[12] No doubt they had no wish to tangle with a Congress majority already rebellious over Roosevelt's fight with the Supreme Court. Nor did the president wish to alienate the powerful Catholic vote by allowing the 'Red Republic' to buy arms. But in this, as in other actions, one detects a desire to keep his options open. He had pressed for the embargo imposed by Congress in 1937 primarily to support the Anglo-French non-intervention policy. To agree to repeal the embargo would undermine their policy. That he wished to avoid. For if, despite the odds against it, Chamberlain's appeasement policy succeeded, the United States, having kept her secret anxieties to herself, could clamber unashamedly onto the bandwaggon which would then start to roll, and exert influence to secure a broader European settlement more in keeping with American economic and political objectives.

As the Czech crisis reached a critical point in September 1938 Roosevelt, thoroughly perplexed by the prospect of war, oscillated violently between hard-liners and appeasers in the State Department. On 1 September he announced the creation of an Atlantic squadron equipped with seven of the latest cruisers. On 10 September two of them docked in British ports. On 9 September, however, correcting a misreported speech in which Ambassador Bullitt, speaking extemporaneously, had pledged America to stand by France, Roosevelt categorically denied that the United States had the slightest intention of creating an anti-German front. A week later he was lamenting in private that Chamberlain was for peace at any price and prophesied that Hitler would destroy the Czechs while Britain and France washed 'the blood from their Judas Iscariot hands'.[13] Talking to the British ambassador in mid September, he suggested a world conference to reorganize frontiers on rational lines. If, however, Britain and France went to war, he urged them to wage a defensive campaign and restrict themselves to the blockade of Germany. American opinion might well approve of the blockade in which case he could help them, but not with munitions – these he believed (wrongly) could be imported quite legally via Canada.

When British mediation attempts broke down at the Godesberg Conference, Roosevelt was finally forced into the open. Though he resisted Welles's suggestion that he offer to mediate – as did Hull – he did appeal on 26 and 27 September to the interested parties to negotiate, especially as Germany and Czechoslovakia were agreed in principle on the cession of the Sudetenland. But he was careful to explain to Hitler that the United States would not attend a conference as she had no political interests in Europe; nor would she undertake political commitments there. When the Munich Conference resolved the crisis Roosevelt did not fail to congratulate Chamberlain and even told him that

[12]The legal embargo was imposed because a New Jersey scrap dealer defied the administration's plea for a moral embargo on all arms to Spain. The dealer planned to export $3 million worth of aircraft parts and engines to the Spanish government. Roosevelt, though sympathetic to the Republican cause, condemned the plan as 'unpatriotic' and asked Congress to pass legislation forbidding it.

[13]Harold L. Ickes, *The Secret Diary of Harold L. Ickes II. The Inside Struggle 1936–1939* (New York, 1956), p. 468.

'today there is the greatest opportunity in recent times to establish a new order based on justice and right'.[14]

Hitler's unco-operative attitude after Munich and, above all else, the horrors of *Reichskristallnacht*, when Hitler loosed the Brownshirts on the Jews of Germany, destroyed American hopes that the leopard might change its spots. This event coincided with Ribbentrop's attempts to strengthen the Anti-Comintern Pact, with evidence of a German trade offensive in Latin America and with German political machinations in Brazil. All this re-kindled in Washington fears of a world conspiracy directed by the Rome–Berlin–Tokyo Axis. The ranks of the appeasers thinned with the defection of Welles and Bullitt. By the end of 1938 Roosevelt was firmly committed to the hardline policy of employing the economic power of the United States to contain Nazi aggression.

The object of the new policy, it must be emphasized, was not to carry the United States into war but to avoid that catastrophe by assuring Britain and France of American economic support on condition they resisted the Axis powers. Eventually, it was supposed, the democracies would be able to negotiate from a position of strength; either Hitler would be forced to negotiate with the West or, more likely, he would be overthrown by his own people as Germany's economic difficulties deepened. As Roosevelt remarked in his address to Congress in January 1939, though no nation was safe from aggression, nevertheless America had decided 'rightly' not to intervene militarily to prevent acts of aggression. With characteristic ambiguity reminiscent of the Quarantine Speech, he went on: 'Words may be futile but war is not the only means of commanding a decent respect for the opinion of mankind. There are many methods short of war but stronger and more effective than mere words of bringing home to aggressor governments the aggregate sentiments of our own people'.[15] That sentence reflected accurately the stage he had reached in his pilgrimage away from isolationism. He now knew that the United States could no longer ignore the threat facing the democracies but must act positively to help them. But he was just as firmly resolved as ever to keep them out of war, of which he had a deep and abiding horror.

Rearmament, not economic appeasement, was central to the new American strategy. Already in October 1938 he was planning to ask Congress for an additional $500 million to build up a huge American airforce which he thought would be a more effective deterrent than a land army.[16] As part of his campaign to show that the United States was behind the democracies, he overruled army objections and permitted France to purchase aircraft in the United States.[17]

[14]Quoted in C.A. MacDonald, *The United States, Britain and Appeasement 1936–1939* (London, 1981), p. 105; cf. Welles's views in *DDF* second series II XI, pp. 753–4: de St Quentin to Georges Bonnet 1 October 1938.

[15]Rosenman, *Public Papers* VIII, p. 3.

[16]It was also likely to prove a much less sensitive political issue. In fact Roosevelt's initial demands for a 10,000-strong airforce and the capacity to produce 20,000 planes a year were abandoned under pressure from the military authorities, which insisted on a balanced build-up of armaments.

[17]The military were reluctant to share their secrets with foreigners, and in the end production difficulties substantially reduced the number of aircraft delivered to the French to a mere 200.

And in April, to persuade the British to concentrate their navy in the Mediterranean and hold the Italians in check, he ordered the American fleet, on manoeuvres in the Atlantic, back into the Pacific. By so doing he assumed a moral obligation to protect British as well as American interests in that area.

Diplomatically he did all he could to encourage Britain and France to stand firm. He refused to recognize the German conquest of Rump Czechoslovakia in March 1939, and imposed countervailing duties on German exports to the United States. That the Germans, despite mounting exasperation, did not retaliate by breaking off diplomatic relations with the United States underlines once more the importance they attached to the purchase of raw materials from America. When negotiations between Britain, France and Russia faltered in the summer of 1939 Roosevelt urged the Russians to conclude an agreement before Hitler picked them all off one by one.

Where he failed was in the attempt to revise the Neutrality Act. Convinced that the repeal of the embargo on the sale of arms to all belligerents would do more than any other measure to persuade Germany that America was in earnest, he encouraged attempts to effect the necessary changes. However, whether because his political stock in Congress had fallen to a low level after the mid-term elections, or because he feared the isolationist backlash on this sensitive issue, or because he felt safer following rather than leading public opinion, or more likely because of a combination of all three, he preferred to leave the initiative to others, a fatal error as it turned out. For without a clear lead from the White House or State Department, the Senate quickly deadlocked on a bill which proposed to repeal the embargo and place all trade with belligerents on a cash-and-carry basis – a proposal which obviously favoured Britain and France who had command of the seas and the financial resources to secure supplies from America. Not until May did Roosevelt intervene openly and urge the leaders of the House of Representatives to support a similar bill on the grounds that this was the only way of preventing war in Europe or, if it occurred, of preventing a victory of the fascist powers. Even then he refused to take a public stand on the issue. In June the House by a majority of two votes retained the embargo on arms and ammunition but not on 'implements of war'. Roosevelt now switched his attentions back to the Senate and attempted to persuade the Senate Foreign Relations Committee to reconsider the bill it had been sitting on since March. That stratagem failed when the committee decided by 12 votes to 11 to postpone action on neutrality legislation until January 1940. The last scene was enacted at the White House on 18 July when Roosevelt failed to persuade a group of influential senators that war in Europe was likely. When they made it plain that the Senate would not change its mind, Roosevelt finally abandoned his efforts but not before declaring to a press conference that the failure of Congress had fatally weakened the influence of the United States in the event of a crisis in Europe. That was a gross if pardonable exaggeration; it is extremely unlikely that the repeal of the arms embargo would have had the slightest effect on the German decision to attack Poland.[18]

[18]The sorry outcome that the arms embargo remained in force but the cash-and-carry clause lapsed so that American merchantmen could now trade freely with belligerents.

The Italian decision to join the Anti-Comintern Pact in November 1937 had helped to confirm the belief in Washington that Rome, Berlin and Tokyo were hatching a plot to dominate the world by force. Reports in the summer of 1938 that Germany was seeking a formal alliance with Japan – the third significant development in the years 1938–9 – increased these fears still further. Nothing came of the attempt for in reality wide differences of opinion kept the two powers apart.

When Hitler finally came off the fence early in 1938 and opted for Japan, he seems to have encouraged Ribbentrop to work for an alliance with her. Ribbentrop had been convinced of the need for closer relations with her since the autumn of 1937. But not until his appointment as foreign minister was the way clear. Even then Germany had to liquidate the Chinese commitments so that in practice Ribbentrop was not ready for serious negotiations until the summer of 1938.

With Hitler's approval Ribbentrop tried to persuade Japan to agree to a comprehensive three-power pact committing the signatories to mutual assistance in all eventualities. This does not mean that war with Russia was uppermost in German minds. On the contrary; what they wanted was an agreement directed against Britain whom they now feared would prove a serious obstacle to the realization of their ambitions in Europe. With Japan as an ally they calculated that the threat of Japanese pressure hanging over British possessions in the Far East would be enough to force London to temper its anti-German policy. But Japan was determined at all costs not to prejudice her relations with Britain and the United States because by the summer of 1938 not only did she face the prospect of a long drawn-out war in China but confrontation with Soviet Russia was now a serious possibility.

Tension between Russia and Japan had been building up since 1934, along the border between Manchukuo and Inner Mongolia. Japan, firmly entrenched in the former region, was making a bid to ingratiate herself with Inner and Outer Mongolia by promising Mongolians in Hsingan province (in Manchukuo) a degree of autonomy in the expectation of eventually taking over both Mongolias. In 1935 Japanese and Russian forces clashed on the borders of Manchukuo and Outer Mongolia. In March 1936 Stalin publicly declared that Soviet Russia would defend Outer Mongolia which had been under Russian control since the 1920s. The next month he signed a formal pact with this tributary state. Russian suspicion of Japan deepened with the signature of the Anti-Comintern Pact in November. Then in 1937 came the fearful episode of the great purges which decimated the higher echelons of the Russian army. Heartened by this unexpected sign of weakness, Japan pursued a more belligerent line. When in May 1937 Soviet troops occupied two islets in the Amur river claimed by Manchukuo Tokyo demanded the instant withdrawal of the Russians. A sharp clash occurred between Russian and Japanese troops. Russia, in a conciliatory mood, withdrew her forces and one islet was handed over to Manchukuo.

The outbreak of the Sino-Japanese War set the alarm bells ringing in Moscow where it was assumed – as in Washington – that Japan was out to dominate all China. Accordingly help was sent to Chiang Kai-shek via Sinkiang (effectively under Russian control by 1934). Against this background the Changkufeng incident occurred in July 1938. When a dispute broke out over an obscure hillock on the borders of Manchukuo, Korea and Russia the Soviets resisted Japanese advances and very heavy fighting broke out. Even though the cease-fire in August left both sides in a status quo position, Japanese army command was deeply impressed by the superiority of the Russian Far Eastern Army both in equipment and tactics. War with Russia was still regarded as inevitable one day but the military would not risk it now until all preparations were completed, i.e. not before 1942. The other lesson of Changkufeng for Japan was that the only agreement with Germany worth having was one directed against Russia which might conceivably scare her into abandoning aid to Chiang Kai-shek.

There were other reasons why an anti-British agreement aroused no enthusiasm in Tokyo. Senior naval officers were convinced that the fleet was not ready for war with the Anglo-Saxon powers. And in any case a country heavily dependent on the United States for raw materials dare not risk confrontation with that power. Furthermore, court, government and naval circles remained supremely confident, as always, that Japan was destined in the fullness of time to become the dominant power in the Far East at the expense of the Anglo-Saxons and that this could be accomplished without war.

The deadlock between Germany and Japan persisted when Ribbentrop renewed the negotiations for a three-power pact in October 1938. At first Ribbentrop made no headway in Rome either, for Italy felt she had as much to lose as Japan by falling in behind the Germans. Then in January 1939 Mussolini decided to throw in his lot with the Germans, largely because he thought a German alliance would strengthen his hand against France in the campaign to extract from her Nice, Savoy, Corsica and Tunis. But the forces opposed to an anti-British alliance still remained in the ascendancy in Tokyo. In March Ribbentrop finally abandoned hopes of securing Japan as an ally and concentrated on Italy instead. Negotiations with her led in May 1939 to the signature of the Pact of Steel committing the two powers to mutual defence in the event of war.

Finally, we turn back to Europe to the events preceding the outbreak of war in 1939. Between the summer of 1936 and the spring of 1938 a combination of factors – political, military and economic – came together to put Germany on the road to war. As the pace of German policy quickened between the Czech crisis and the attack on Poland, these factors continued to sustain the impetus of German expansionism.

In recent years the role of economic pressures in precipitating the outbreak of war has been hotly debated. Marxists, not unnaturally, have been in the forefront of the argument in emphasizing a factor too often undervalued by the older generation of liberal historians. For Marxists of the orthodox school the machinations of monopoly capitalism on their own are a sufficient explanation of what happened in 1914 and again in 1939. Fascism is seen by them not as a time-bound and place-bound phenomenon rooted in the historical conditions of particular countries but as a universal manifestation of capitalism at a certain stage of development. In the words of the Comintern definition of 1935, which still enjoys the seal of official approval in communist countries, fascism is 'the open terroristic dictatorship of the most reactionary most chauvinistic and most imperialist elements of finance capitalism'.[19] This definition reduces Hitler to the status of a puppet manipulated by a sinister coterie of industrialists who put him in power to further their own ends: the destruction of the trade union movement, the intensification of the exploitation of the working class and the preparation of Germany for wars of aggression to secure new markets and sources of raw materials.

The crudity of this interpretation of the relationship between fascism and capitalism, which tends to substitute the machinations of industrialists for those of politicians in bringing Hitler to power, has not prevented historians in the German Democratic Republic, who subscribe to it officially, from making valuable contributions to the debate about the role of industry in the Third Reich. For example, they have demonstrated how active German banking corporations were in advancing their interests abroad in 1938–9. At the time of the *Anschluss* the Deutsche Bank obtained a dominant influence over the Österreichische Creditanstalt-Bankverein A.G. while the Dresdner Bank took over the Mercurbank A.G. Months before Hitler seized Rump Czechoslovakia in March 1939 these banks were planning to do the same to their Czech competitors; immediately after the march into Prague the Deutsche Bank gained control of the Böhmische Escompte Bank and the Dresdner Bank took over the Böhmische Union Bank while I.G. Farben, the giant industrial combine already playing a key role in the execution of the Four Year Plan, seized the Aussiger Verein and the Dynamit-Nobel A.G. to become the leading chemical concern in south-eastern Europe.

This does not, however, prove that these or other monopoly capitalist concerns determined the course of German foreign policy but only that they co-operated with the regime in its aggressive designs. And despite the Comintern definition, economic imperialism does not necessarily lead to war as the attitude of American business in 1939 amply demonstrates. What gave economic imperialism its thrusting and ruthless character in Germany and made it the handmaid of the Nazis was a lethal convergence between the economic ambitions of the giant concerns and the territorial ambitions of the Nazi regime.

A more sophisticated explanation is offered by younger Marxist historians who have revived the so-called Bonapartist theory according to which quasi-authoritarian regimes such as Napoleon III's as well as Hitler's totalitarian state gradually detach themselves from the capitalist order that spawned them and impose their will on it. Timothy Mason argues that while heavy industry played a possibly decisive role in helping Hitler to power and remained in loose alliance with the Nazis for some years, after 1936 the Nazis were the dominant political force in Germany. Industry was forced to do the bidding of the Nazis and exerted negligible influence on German foreign policy.[20]

[19]W. Pieck, G. Dimitroff, P. Togliatti, *Die Offensive des Faschismus und die Aufgaben der Kommunisten im Kampf für die Volksfront gegen Krieg und Faschismus. Referate auf dem VII Kongress der Kommunistischen Internationale 1935* (Berlin, 1957), p. 87.

[20]T.W. Mason, 'The Primacy of Politics – Politics and Economics in National Socialist Germany', in S.J. Wolff, ed., *The Nature of Fascism* (London, 1968).

Economic factors were still important in determining the timing of the outbreak of war. Central to Mason's thesis is the deterioration of the economy referred to earlier. Put quite simply, the economy could not accommodate escalating rearmament and the lavish building programme Hitler embarked on after 1937 while also maintaining a contracting but still significant consumer goods sector to provide the goods and services a fully employed work force expects. Inflationary pressures showed themselves in the shape of shortages of skilled labour and raw materials, lengthening of delivery dates, a shortage of capital, decline of the agricultural sector and the upward movement of some wages and prices. Faced with this the Nazis did not damp down consumer demand drastically and ensure absolute priority for rearmament because, Mason argues, they feared that if they pressed the working class too hard it would explode in revolt as in 1918-19. Yet as the Nazis persisted in rearming at breakneck speed, inflationary pressures increased still further, retarding their own efforts to rearm faster and trapping them in a vicious spiral leading to a general crisis of the economy and of the system of government. To escape from it the Nazis plunged into war. In fairness to Mason, it should be pointed out that he does not claim that the economic dimension need necessarily have been the decisive one.[21]

The evidence leaves little doubt that the German economy was seriously overheated in 1938-9 and was moving towards a crisis. Whether it had arrived there in 1939 seems doubtful. More important, the Nazi leaders do not appear to have thought they were in the grip of a make-or-break economic crisis as the Japanese leadership undoubtedly was in 1941. Through Goering Hitler was kept informed of the mounting economic difficulties though whether he read key documents placed before him is uncertain. But disinclined though he was on principle to intervene in the economic sector, his acute political sense led him on occasions to oppose increases in bread prices and the introduction of rationing. Fleeting references to economic problems appear in some of his major speeches. In January 1939 he declared bluntly to the Reichstag that 'In the final instance the economy of the Reich today is bound up with its external security. It is better to see that while there is still time than wait till it is too late'.[22] And addressing the commanding generals on 22 August, on the eve of the onslaught on Poland, he remarked that 'we have nothing to lose only to gain. As a result of restrictions our economic situation is such that we can only hold out for a few years. Goering can confirm that. There is nothing else for it, we have to act'.[23] But it is difficult to believe that these remarks were more than arguments *ad hominem* to justify a course of action decided upon for other reasons. This is not to deny that the deteriorating economic situation did introduce a note of urgency into Hitler's calculations. But on present evidence one cannot conclude that it was of primary importance in the decision to attack Poland.

[21]See T.W. Mason, 'Innere Krise und Angriffskrieg 1938-9', in F. Forstmeier and H.E. Volkmann, eds., *Wirtschaft und Rüstung am Vorabend des Zweiten Weltkrieges* (Düsseldorf, 1975); also his *Arbeiterklasse und Volksgemeinschaft. Dokumente und Materialien zur deutschen Arbeiterpolitik 1936-1939* (Opladen, 1975).

[22]M. Domarus, ed., *Hitlers Reden und Proklamationen 1932-1945* (Würzburg, 1962-3) I, p. 1054.

[23]*DGFP* D VII, no. 192.

It is much easier to demonstrate that strategic considerations were in the forefront of Hitler's mind in 1938–9. British, French and Russian rearmament was well under way by this time, an inevitable riposte to Hitler's militarization of German policy. British rearmament greatly perturbed him so that when Britain announced substantial increases in the wake of the Munich Conference he immediately ordered a five-fold increase in the airforce, acceleration of naval rearmament and increased production of heavy guns and tanks for the army – a programme which could not, incidentally, be achieved by an over-burdened economy. At this time Hitler still seems to have been thinking of war with the western powers in four to five years time (i.e. 1942–3). But by the spring of 1939 Poland's refusal to become an obedient satellite and his decision to strike at her despite the British and French guarantees to that country exposed Germany to the prospect of war with them in the near future. While he clearly hoped that he would not have to fight in the west and east simultaneously and on balance believed almost to the very last that he could avoid it, nevertheless he seems to have persuaded himself that Germany was ready for war even with the western powers in 1939. On 22 August he told the commanding generals that 'all these favourable circumstances [i.e. for war in 1939] would no longer prevail in two or three years time'.[24] And to Mussolini in March 1940 he declared that 'the conditions of the struggle would in two years time at best not have been more favourable for Germany'.[25] It is true that addressing some of his generals in May 1939 he said that Germany must be prepared for a war lasting 10 to 15 years but he spent much of his time at that meeting minimizing the effectiveness of British rearmament; far from resigning himself to a long campaign against Britain, he insisted that if she intervened over Poland the aim must be to deal her 'at the start a smashing blow or the smashing blow'.[26]

Up to a point Hitler's calculations were rational enough. The German armed forces with a total mobilized strength of 103 divisions, 26 more than in 1938, were capable of defeating Poland even though not yet fully equipped and – in the opinion of their commanders – not ready for war. Through her economic control of south-eastern Europe Germany possessed adequate supplies of raw materials, particularly oil and grain from Rumania, for a 'lightning' war against a small neighbour. And the *Luftwaffe* enjoyed a position of superiority over all potential opponents, an advantage which, as the British military attaché observed, would begin to decline after mid June 1939 as the balance of air-power moved against her. If Germany seized bases in Belgium and Holland, as Hitler suggested at the May 1939 conference, German air power could then be exploited to cripple Britain's lines of communication. Thus war in 1939 was not a completely irresponsible act granted Germany's determination to dominate Europe.

The irresponsible elements enters the picture in that if Britain and France went to war in earnest – which Hitler doubted – and if a lightning strike at them did not succeed then Germany would face a long war before she was

[24]*Ibid.*
[25]M. Muggeridge, ed., *Ciano's Diplomatic Papers* (London, 1948), p. 361.
[26]*DGFP* D VI, no. 433.

properly equipped to wage such a struggle; and if the United States aided the democracies Germany would be committed to a war she was almost certain to lose in the end. In other words, the degree of risk Hitler was running in 1939 was infinitely greater than the risk he had run over Czechoslovakia. Precisely for this reason the Non-Aggression Pact Germany negotiated with Soviet Russia in the summer of 1939 was of crucial importance because it removed whatever lingering doubts he had and encouraged him to believe that Britain and France would not dare to intervene; but even if they did, he could face the prospect of a longer war with a reasonable chance of winning in the end. So the general diplomatic situation, to which we now turn, contributed significantly to the German decision to risk a general war in 1939.

The attack on Poland was not intended to be the prelude to an immediate attack on Soviet Russia to secure *Lebensraum* for Germany. The evidence suggests that its purpose was to safeguard Germany's flank for the showdown with the western powers, particularly with Britain, now making the running in the Anglo-French camp. For as a result of their active intervention to prevent war over Czechoslovakia Hitler had concluded that Britain and France would not, after all, allow Germany to dominate Europe as he had hitherto hoped they would, and that war with them was, therefore, unavoidable. Already in the summer of 1938 naval command started to plan for war with Britain. In January 1939 Hitler approved and gave absolute priority to the so-called Z Plan for the creation by 1944 of a large fleet containing six battleships. The *Luftwaffe*, too, in the winter of 1938–9 worked out a detailed strategy for aerial warfare against the British Isles. In March 1939 the Nazi press began an orchestrated campaign against the western powers, the representatives of 'world Jewry' and 'world bolshevism' seeking to 'encircle' Germany and deny her legitimate claims to *Lebensraum* in the east.

Initially Hitler hoped to woo Poland. In October 1938 negotiations between Germany and Poland commenced for the return of the Free City of Danzig to Germany, extra-territorial rights for Germany across the Corridor (the strip of territory separating Germany from East Prussia) and the adherence of Poland to the Anti-Comintern Pact; in return Germany would extend the 1934 Non-Aggression Pact with Poland for 25 years. When Poland hesitated Hitler dangled before her foreign minister, Colonel Josef Beck, the prospect of territorial gains in the Ukraine, bait which Beck feared to take because of probable Russian reactions. When it became clear to Hitler in March that agreement with Poland was unlikely, he decided on military action in the near future. The British guarantee to Poland on 31 March simply confirmed him in his decision. On 3 April he ordered Army High Command to work out Plan White with 1 September as the deadline for the attack on Poland. Shortly afterwards he denounced the Non-Aggression Pact with Poland and the Anglo-German Naval Convention of 1935. From then on he gave no further thought to negotiation with Poland being firmly resolved not to be trapped into agreement as he had been in September 1938 but this time to smash his enemy by military force.

A major complication arose in the spring of 1939 when Britain and France hesitantly approached the Soviet Union and opened negotiations for an agreement to contain German aggression which dragged on to a fruitless conclusion in August. Had a three-power pact emerged from the discussions Germany would run the risk of being trapped in a two-front war if she persisted in her resolve to attack Poland. Of course, a habitual *va banque* player like Hitler, a man who had succeeded in 1938–9 precisely because he had been willing to run (calculated) risks, might not have backed down even in the face of an Anglo-Franco-Russian front. On the other hand, there is some evidence that he might have been deterred by a three-power agreement. In which case he had two alternatives: either to call off the attack and re-adjust German policy to take account of a drastically changed strategic situation or else prevent the negotiations reaching a successful conclusion by approaching the Russians with a better offer.

Another factor making an agreement with Russia attractive for Germany was Ribbentrop's failure to turn the Pact of Steel into a Tripartite Pact. On 12 August Japan terminated the negotiations with Germany. It was now clear that Japan would remain neutral in the event of war. This had, incidentally, other important consequences. It meant that Britain was relieved of anxiety in respect of her Far Eastern possessions should she be called upon to honour her obligations to Poland. Indeed, Britain had already arrived at a *modus vivendi* with Japan late in July in the Craigie–Arita declaration in which she recognized Japan's special position in China.

Economic factors appear to have played no more than a secondary role in bringing Russia and Germany together. It is true that both powers were interested in maintaining a limited volume of trade. Germany wished to purchase oil, manganese ore and wood from Russia. But in March 1938 and in February 1939 negotiations had broken down because Germany was not able to find room in her economy to supply Russia with the capital goods she demanded in return. No further progress was made until Vyacheslav M. Molotov, the new Soviet foreign minister, made it clear that Stalin wanted a political agreement with Germany first. Once Germany agreed to this in principle, the trade discussions were resumed in June and formed a useful cover for the political negotiations. But the trade treaty signed on 19 August was important for Germany. The prospect of increased trade over the next two years – partially financed by German credits – offered Germany the possibility, in theory at least, of becoming independent of overseas raw materials in the event of a long war though that would still depend on Germany's ability to supply Russia with machine tools.

It is unnecessary to examine the negotiations between Germany and Russia in the summer of 1939. Suffice to say that the discussions were speeded up once Hitler decided in mid August that he would attack Poland by the end of the month. On 14 August Hitler resolved to send Ribbentrop to Moscow to clinch the deal. When Russia seemed unwilling to receive the German foreign minister before 26 or 27 August, Hitler intervened with a personal message to Stalin on 20 August requesting him to receive Ribbentrop by 23 August at the latest. The next day Stalin agreed. On 22 August Ribbentrop left for Moscow and in the early hours of 24 August the Russo-German Non-Aggression Pact was signed.

Under the terms of the agreement both parties pledged themselves to refrain from aggressive action against each other either singly or in combination with others. If one partner was the object of military action by a third power the other would remain neutral. The partners promised to consult with each other about questions relating to their common interests. Neither partner would join any grouping of powers directed against the other. In the event of any contentious issue arising between them the partners agreed to settle this peaceably. Finally, the treaty was of 10 years' duration; it was to come into force at once and be ratified as soon as possible. Significantly the pact omitted the clause Russia habitually included in non-aggression pacts; that a party to the treaty would only be neutral if the other party was the victim of an unprovoked attack. That it was to come into force at once was another unusual feature; for Germany this was a necessity with only a week to go before the attack on Poland, whilst Russia was anxious to tie her new friend's hands at once lest Hitler try to use the threat of signature to strike a bargain with the western powers.

Appended to the pact was a notorious secret protocol in which Russia and Germany defined their respective spheres of influence in eastern Europe. In the event of territorial changes in the Baltic region (Finland, Estonia, Latvia and Lithuania) Lithuania would be in the German sphere of influence. In the event of territorial changes affecting the area ruled by Poland, the boundary separating the German from the Russian sphere of influence would be formed by the line of the rivers Narew, Vistula and San. Whether an independent Polish state should continue in being or not would be decided later by Russia and Germany. Finally, Russia emphasized her interest in Bessarabia and Germany declared that she was not interested in that area.

Whether Hitler would have gone ahead with his attack in the absence of an agreement with Russia we cannot be sure. What is certain is that he was greatly relieved by Ribbentrop's success. On 22 August, informing his commanding generals that the signature of the pact was imminent, he commented: 'I have knocked this weapon – Russian assistance – out of the hands of the western powers. It is now possible to strike a blow at the heart of Poland. The way for a military solution is free by any human reckoning.'[27] On 23 August he ordered the attack to begin on 26 August. And when he received news of the signature he banged the desk going red in the face as he shouted: 'I've got it; I've got it'.[28]

The pact also opened up an alluring last-minute prospect of fighting a localized war in the east should Britain and France now decide to abandon their Polish obligations. That Hitler preferred this to general war is clear from the efforts he made on 25 August to detach Britain from Poland. Warning the British ambassador, Sir Nevile Henderson, that the Russian pact struck out of Britain's hand the traditional weapon of blockade, he proposed an Anglo-German alliance once the Polish problem had been settled. Of course, the attack was to go ahead as planned – one hour after talking to Henderson he had given the necessary orders – but in a fit of euphoria brought on by the Russo-German Pact he seems genuinely to have believed his offer would deter Britain from intervening militarily. In the case of France he tried to place the onus for intervention fairly and squarely on her shoulders by informing the French ambassador that Germany had no wish for war with France.

The stratagem did not work. Two nasty surprises were in store for Hitler on

[27]*IMT* XLI Document Raeder-27.
[28]A. Speer, *Inside the Third Reich* (London, 1970), p. 176.

the late afternoon of 25 August. In response to Hitler's request on 24–5 August that Italy fulfil her obligations under the Pact of Steel, Mussolini replied that Italy was not ready yet for what he was certain would be a general war. Secondly, news arrived in Berlin of the signature of the Anglo-Polish alliance, clear proof that the Russo-German Pact had not intimidated Britain. Hitler cancelled the order for attack but only because he still hoped that Britain might reply favourably to his alliance offer. Quickly disappointed in this, on 30 August he confirmed 1 September as the new date for the attack. To shift responsibility for the war onto Polish shoulders Hitler made play with the British statement that Poland was ready for direct negotiations with Germany, and demanded that Warsaw send a plenipotentiary to Berlin by 30 August. In fact, the Poles refused to fall into that trap. When Sir Nevile Henderson met Ribbentrop at midnight on 30–1 August with a request for a delay to allow German–Polish talks to begin, the foreign minister, acting on Hitler's orders, read out the allegedly generous terms Germany would have offered but refused to give the ambassador a copy and declared that the terms were in any event no longer on offer. There could have been no clearer proof that Hitler intended to go ahead with the attack and accepted the near certainty of war with the western powers as well. In the early hours of 1 September German troops crossed the Polish frontier and Europe was again at war.

What were the motives of the Soviet Union in agreeing to the pact with Germany? As long as the Russian archives remain closed to scholars any analysis of·Stalin's motives in preferring the Germans to the British and French in 1939 can only be speculative. Whether Soviet Russia was ever in earnest in seeking an agreement with Britain and France is doubtful.[29] But even if she had been, she could hardly have been blamed for suspecting that the western powers were only half-hearted about the Russian connection. The more they defended the rights of small nations and refused to abandon the Baltic states to the Russians, the more it looked to the latter as if the west lacked all under-standing of Russia's security problem in having to defend long vulnerable frontiers against a line of aggressors who had plundered Russia from the seventeenth century onwards. And what sense did it make to fight for Poland or Rumania? Both states had good reason to fear Russia for both had seized territory from her when the young bolshevik state was fighting for its very existence. Under the Treaty of Riga in 1921 Poland acquired territory in the east inhabited by White Russians and Ukrainians while in the south Rumania had taken Bessarabia. To fight to preserve these frontiers would simply not be in the Russian interest. In addition, if war broke out the hard fact was that Russia would have to bear the weight of the German offensive while France remained on the defensive behind the Maginot Line and Britain relied on naval blockade to squeeze the life out of Germany without spilling British blood.

So it may well have seemed to Russia that she had more to gain by coming to terms with the Germans. That was the only way of avoiding war. And to stay out of the fighting as long as humanly possible was an imperative for a state just emerging from the most momentous economic and social revolution in modern

[29]G.L. Weinberg, *The Foreign Policy of Hitler's Germany. Starting World War II 1937–1939* (Chicago, 1980), p. 556.

times. Russia deperately needed peace to consolidate the breakneck progress made in the 1930s. Furthermore, Russia's strategic situation forced her to pursue a cautious policy. Hitler was not the only or the most immediate threat to peace. In the Far East Russian forces were engaged in heavy fighting with the Japanese in mid May at Chalcun-Gol on the border between Manchuria and Outer Mongolia. Though Russia had held her own during the Nomonhan incident, she could not afford to be dragged into war in Europe, and for no apparent gains, while Japan attacked again in the Far East. A pact with Germany was preferable to a possible pact between Germany and Japan leaving Russia to face Germany in Europe and Japan in the Far East.

Soviet policy seems to add up to a calculating piece of *realpolitik*. But it would be a profound error to ignore the ideological framework of Marxism–Leninism on which it rested. This is not to deny that Russia used all the skills of the old diplomacy to defend herself, playing one power off against another with considerable success; nor does it mean that she was incapable of pursuing a nakedly imperialist policy reminiscent of the old Tsarist regime – events between May 1940 and May 1941 tell their own story. But Soviet *realpolitik*, unlike that of Peter the Great or Catherine the Great, was not simply and solely a relentless pursuit of national or imperialist interest. Marxist–Leninists believed that history was moving inexorably by a dialectical process to a grand finale: the destruction of their imperialist opponents and the victory of socialism on a world scale, but a victory which according to Lenin would be preceded by a series of bloody conflicts among the imperialist powers. That moment seemed to be approaching in the 1930s as the rivalries in the imperialist camp deepened and war between the have-not powers – Germany, Italy and Japan – and the established powers – Britain, France and the United States – seemed increasingly likely. As conflict lay in the logic of history, it was not the duty of the Soviet Union to prevent its occurence but to ensure that when it did break out it would last long enough to smash the imperialist system to pieces and open the way for socialism to be carried into Europe on the bayonets of the Red Army. As early as 1925 Stalin outlined Soviet strategy very clearly when he declared to the Party Congress that 'our banner is and remains the banner of peace. If a war begins however we will not be able to stand idly by – we will have to intervene in order to tip the scales and exert a decisive influence'.[30]

There was an additional complication. War must break out in the right place, i.e. between the imperialist powers and must not involve the Soviet Union in the initial stages. For as the crisis of capitalism deepened, it was always within the bounds of possibility that the imperialist powers might temporarily bury their differences and turn against the common enemy: the Soviet Union, as they had done during the Civil War. Stalin and Molotov may well have harboured a suspicion that Britain and France were only going through the motions of negotiating with Russia in order to impress Hitler and pressurize him into being 'reasonable' about Poland. If another Munich could be arranged, might it not be followed by an anti-Soviet crusade during which the 'have-powers' stood back and watched the 'have-nots' attack the Soviet

---

[30] J.W. Stalin, *Werke*, (Berlin, 1952) Bd. 7, p. 11.

Union? The fact that there is no convincing evidence that Britain and France were pursuing such a Machiavellian policy in 1939 is beside the point; it is not objective reality that counts in international affairs but the perception policy-makers have of reality. Russia dare not stand 'idly by' and let events take this course. The only way to ensure that war broke out without dragging in the Soviet Union was to encourage Hitler to attack Poland. That is precisely what the Non-Aggression Pact guaranteed as Stalin was well aware. Speaking to Sir Stafford Cripps in July 1940, Stalin revealed the truth when he remarked that whereas Russia and Germany wanted to change 'the old equilibrium' Britain and France did not; 'this common desire to get rid of the old equilibrium had created the basis for the rapprochement with Germany'.[31]

Starting the war was one thing; keeping it going another. For Stalin and Molotov, like most of their generation, thought in terms of the First World War. They assumed that the balance of military power still favoured the French and that Germany would be defeated fairly quickly. To prevent this happening before the imperialist system had been fatally weakened, Stalin was prepared to offer more than a negative neutrality. So that Germany would not collapse, he was prepared to supply her with vital raw materials and food. Even if the amounts involved did not come up to German expectations, they still represented a significant contribution to the German war effort. And despite the deterioration in Russo-German relations in 1941, Russia continued to make deliveries right up to the eve of the German onslaught.

[31]Quoted in G.L. Weinberg, *World in the Balance. Behind the Scenes of World War II* (Hannover, 1981), p. 7; note the instruction from Moscow to the Russian ambassador in Tokyo 1 July 1940: 'the conclusion of our agreement with Germany was dictated by the need for a war in Europe'. Quoted in James W. Morley, ed., *The Fateful Choice: Japan's Road to the Pacific War* (New York, 1980), pp. 311–12.

3

War and Peace:
September 1939–March 1940

The attack on Poland commenced in the early hours of 1 September. Eighteen days later effective resistance to the Germans had ceased. On 1 October the last Polish opposition was overcome, and on 2 October Hitler took the salute at a parade of German soldiers through the battered streets of Warsaw. This impressive victory represented a resounding triumph for the superior technology and tactics of the *Wehrmacht* though it was facilitated greatly by Poland's military weakness and by the defensive strategy pursued by the western powers.

Roughly the same number of soldiers faced each other in September 1939 on the eastern front: 1.5 million Germans and 1.3 million Poles. Each had 37 infantry divisions. But the Germans had at their disposal six armoured divisions, four motorized divisions and four light divisions compared with one Polish armoured brigade and eleven cavalry divisions. In the air Germany had over 2,000 aircraft to Poland's 750. It was this unique combination of armoured power and airpower, producing a flexibility of firepower and movement quite new in the science of warfare, that was the key to the German victory.

Quite early in the 1930s German army command realized that in the tank they had a weapon for winning wars quickly and avoiding a repetition of the terrible war of attrition between 1914 and 1918. In 1935 three armoured divisions were formed; two were added in 1938 and one more in 1939. Each division consisted of 250–300 tanks supported by motorized light infantry. In battle the attack was spearheaded by heavy tanks whose task was to breach the enemy lines. They were followed by medium tanks which widened the gap and guarded the flanks whilst the light infantry passed through and mopped up remaining resistance. Liaising closely with the armoured divisions Goering's *Luftwaffe*, the core of which was a formidable force of 1,400 light twin-engined bombers, attacked enemy positions, supply lines, railway centres and centres of population, thoroughly demoralizing the enemy, destroying his airforce on the ground and generally breaking his resistance. This was the essence of the lightning warfare for which Germany gained a formidable reputation between 1939 and 1941.

The Poles, on the other hand, not only suffered from a woeful deficiency in both tanks and aircraft. Their command organization did not bear comparison with the German and their military tactics proved their undoing. Certainly Poland's military leaders faced a forbidding task. They were defending very long frontiers and terrain ideally suited to the kind of mobile warfare the Germans were planning. The Polish mistake was not the delay in the completion of mobilization – for which British and French pressure was responsible, in an attempt to avoid provoking Hitler – for it is certain that a few more poorly equipped infantry divisions would have had no appreciable effect on the outcome. But the deployment of two-thirds of their forces west of the river Vistula undoubtedly robbed them of their room for manoeuvre. This was largely Hobson's choice. Poland's vital industrial areas and her coal and iron resources, which she could not do without, lay west of the Vistula; and the Poles, committed to an offensive not a defensive strategy, were determined to hold on to every inch of Polish territory possibly for up to three months – so unrealistic was their estimate of the Germans – until the western powers launched an offensive and forced the Germans to reinforce the western frontier. However, once the fast-moving Panzer divisions had overrun their positions the slow-moving Polish infantry west of the Vistula had little hope of withdrawing across the river to defend Warsaw.

German strategy was still modelled along the lines laid down before the First World War by Count Helmuth von Moltke and Count Alfred von Schlieffen, i.e. the aim was to outmanoeuvre the enemy in a war of movement, surround him and annihilate him. By implication the war would be short, sharp and decisive. A speedy victory was essential over Poland for another reason. There was widespread concern in army command that the French would seize this golden opportunity to launch an offensive in the west. All that stood in their way was the *Westwall*, 600 kilometres of fortifications only partially completed running from Basle to Geilkirchen and defended by 32 reserve divisions of poor quality. Even though it would take the French three weeks to mobilize all 91 divisions – by which time German army command hoped to have won decisively in Poland – after the tenth day of mobilization France would have 50 divisions ready to launch an attack, which could gravely interfere with operations in the east.

Five armies were deployed around Poland's northern and western frontiers on 1 September 1939. In the north General Günther-Hans von Kluge's Fourth Army advanced across the Polish Corridor, cut off one-third of the Polish army on the Tucheler Heide, made contact with General Georg von Küchler's Third Army in East Prussia and then swung southwards. Küchler's army meanwhile advanced into north-eastern Poland and headed for Warsaw and Brest Litovsk. However, the major offensive was launched across Poland's western frontier by General Gerd von Rundstedt's Army Group South: the Eighth Army commanded by General Johannes Blaskowitz thrust towards the industrial centre of Lódź; General Sigmund List's Fourteenth Army thrust towards Cracow and Lwów while General Walther Reichenau's Tenth Army, to which two armoured and four motorized divisions were allotted, had the major task of thrusting towards Warsaw. Already on 1 September the *Luftwaffe* had made a major contribution to the success of the entire campaign when it struck a devastating surprise blow at Poland's airfields putting them out of action and ensuring air superiority for the Germans.

The invasion of Poland went more or less according to plan. Within a few days Lódź, Cracow and Lwów had fallen. The Polish army was now completely disorganized. Hundreds of thousands of Polish soldiers were encircled and quickly forced to surrender. And by 8 September Reichenau's forward reconnaissance units, which covered a remarkable 140 miles in seven days, were on the outskirts of Warsaw. So even before Russian troops moved into their allotted sphere of influence in eastern Poland the armed forces of Poland were in a hopeless plight. On 18 September the Polish government and high command fled to Rumania. The last significant action commenced on 25 September with a grand assault on Warsaw. Three days later the Polish commander surrendered, and on 29 September the Polish defence force marched out of the ruined city. During the campaign 70,000 Poles and 11,000 Germans had fallen in action. And 700,000 Polish soldiers were in German captivity and 300,000 in Russian. Devastating though the defeat was for Poland, it was only the beginning of the martyrdom of that unhappy country.

We turn now to the Russian occupation of eastern Poland. On 3 September Ribbentrop urged Russia to take immediate action pointing out that Poland's total collapse could only be a few weeks away. Possibly he hoped that if Russia seized her share of the booty this would prove that she did intend to implement the Non-Aggression Pact and might deter Britain and France from launching an offensive in the west; or they might even declare war on Soviet Russia thereby extinguishing any possibility of a reconciliation between west and east at the expense of Germany. Stalin was too wily a bird to fall into the German trap. Molotov replied blandly to Ribbentrop on 5 September that the time was not ripe for Russian action.

There were weighty reasons for caution. Heavy fighting between the Russian Far Eastern Army and Japanese troops on the frontiers of Manchuria made intervention in Poland inadvisable. Stalin also had a delicate public relations exercise on his hands. As Molotov informed the German ambassador, Friedrich Werner von Schulenberg, on 10 September action must be postponed until the Kremlin had persuaded the Soviet people that, because of the disintegration of the Polish state, all agreements between Russia and Poland were null and void, and that Russia must intervene to protect herself against 'hazards and surprises'. It was necessary for the Red Army to come to the assistance of the Ukrainian and White Russian minorities in eastern Poland, maltreated by the Polish government in the past and now threatened by the advancing Germans. Not an explanation flattering to their new German friends but one forced on the Russian leadership by the domestic situation. The Soviet people was clearly bewildered by the pact with Germany. On 14 September a propaganda campaign was under way to reassure Soviet citizens that Russia was not going to war and that the pact with Germany was a guarantee of peace, but that a local 'police action' was essential to protect their 'kith and kin'. On 15 September a major obstacle was removed with the signature of a Russo-Japanese agreement terminating the fighting in Manchuria. The way was open for intervention in Poland. Mobilization of the invading force was now complete and on 17 September Red Army units moved into the area delineated as the Russian sphere of influence. They met with little resistance. In a broadcast on Moscow radio Molotov spoke of Russia's 'sacred duty to extend a helping hand to brother Ukrainians and brother White Russians who live in Poland'.[1] On 18 September a joint Russo-German statement was issued which declared that their troops were simply restoring order in Poland and assisting the Polish people to reconstruct their national existence.

On 20 September Molotov proposed to Berlin a joint settlement of the frontiers of Poland. On 27 September Ribbentrop flew to Moscow and in an atmosphere of remarkable cordiality the two foreign ministers quickly resolved the points at issue. In the Frontiers and Friendship Treaty signed on 28 September and in supplementary protocols Germany and Russia declared that in view of the collapse of the Polish state they had assumed an obligation to restore law and order in the area. To this end they had finally delineated the frontier between their respective spheres of influence. As one of the secret protocols revealed, Lithuania had been moved from the German to the Russian sphere while certain territory west of the river Bug in the vicinity of Lublin and Warsaw had been handed back to Germany.

The effect of these territorial changes was twofold. By withdrawing from the line of the rivers San, Vistula and Pisa to the line of the rivers Pisa, Bug and San (70 miles east of Warsaw) Russia ensured that she had as few Poles as possible under her control. This enabled her to maintain that she had virtually no part in the subjugation of Poland as such but had merely re-occupied territory east of the Curzon Line which the western powers had themselves proposed as Poland's frontier in 1919 but which a chauvinistic government had refused to accept.[2] Secondly, in return for surrendering part of her share of Poland, Stalin persuaded Hitler to agree to transfer Lithuania to the Russian sphere of influence. Once this was agreed the Soviet Union would, as Stalin informed the Germans, 'immediately take up the problem of the Baltic countries in accordance with the protocol of 23 August', a clear indication that in the very near future these states would be pressurized by Russia into agreeing to her demands.[3]

While Hitler would have been quite prepared for propaganda reasons to allow a nominally independent Polish state to continue in being, Stalin, having no wish to surrender any territory already occupied for this purpose, argued that such a creation would only be a cause of friction between them. What he may well have feared was an alliance between Rump Poland and Germany directed against Russia. On this point also Hitler yielded to Russian pressure and agreed in another secret protocol signed on 28 September not to tolerate Polish agitation for an independent state in the occupied territories. No more was heard of Congress Poland after that.

Once any hope of the western powers making an immediate peace with Hitler disappeared with Chamberlain's brusque rejection of the German offer on 6 October, the Germans went to work in earnest on the ruthless exploitation of the 15 million Poles and 2 million Jews they now controlled. West Prussia/Danzig and Poznan (Wartheland) were annexed by Germany. The remainder of Poland was turned into a *Generalgouvernement* under the jurist *Gauleiter* Hans

---

[1]Joan Degras, *Soviet Documents on Foreign Policy* (Oxford, 1953) III, p. 375.
[2]Only in the south did the demarcation line coincide with the Curzon Line. In the north for strategic reasons Stalin insisted on a line running 140km. further west than Curzon.
[3]*DGFP* VIII, no. 131.

Frank residing in his splendid castle at Cracow. Hitler, determined to give vent to his destructive racism, set out to transform the Poles into hewers of wood and carriers of water for the Germans. From the annexed territories thousands of Poles and Jews were brutally expelled mostly to the *Generalgouvernement*, and their farms and homes handed over to Baltic Germans as part of a systematic attempt to colonize the area and so advance the racial frontiers of the German Reich to the east. When the German armies advanced into Poland four *Einsatzgruppen*, or murder squads, followed in their wake with express orders from Hitler to 'liquidate' the Polish ruling class and deprive the Poles of political and spiritual leadership. Thousands of government officials, priests and intellectuals were summarily shot. With the appointment of Heinrich Himmler as 'Reich commissioner for the strengthening of Germanism' the Poles were subjected to a reign of SS terror. Finally, the industrial resources and labour force in the *Generalgouvernement* were ruthlessly exploited in the interests of the Reich.

Meanwhile in their zone of occupation, which still included five million Curzon Line Poles as well as 4.5 million Ukrainians, 1 million White Russians and 1 million Jews, the Russians at once prepared the way for its annexation to the Soviet Union. In October free elections along Soviet lines with one candidate in each constituency were held. These led to the formation of West Ukrainian and White Russian assemblies which at once requested incorporation in the USSR.

The two republics were quickly subjected to sovietization. Thousands of Russian administrators, judges and secret policemen moved into the area. Large estates, banks and factories were nationalized. In many cases plant was dismantled and taken to Russia as were stock piles of raw materials. The highest priority, however, was given to the systematic removal of Poland's national leaders. Landowners, officials, political leaders, clergy and professional soldiers were rounded up by the secret police. Some were summarily shot, the remainder ended up in labour camps in the far north of Russia. In the course of the next two years the families of those arrested were deported as well as the Jewish population of artisans and small traders, in all about 10 per cent of the whole population of the two republics.

Finally, in a statement signed on 28 September Germany and Russia declared that it was in the true interests of all peoples that the war be ended. They promised to act jointly and with other friendly powers to bring about this desirable end. However, should they fail, it would be clear that Britain and France were solely responsible for the continuation of the war. In that event, the declaration continued ominously, Germany and Russia would consult about the necessary measures to adopt.

Neither power was in earnest. Hitler did not expect the declaration to weaken the resolve of the west to fight on, nor did he want it to. From Stalin's point of view there was everything to be said for the continuation of hostilities to keep the imperialist powers divided, undermine the system in the long run and allow Russia time to build up her defences. Stalin's attitude bore some resemblance to that of the leader of the other great non-belligerent: Franklin Roosevelt. Both had universalist ambitions for their countries. Roosevelt hoped that with American help Britain and France would win in the end and that the United States would then be able to dictate peace terms based on the principles of democracy and free trade. Stalin, on the other hand, was indifferent to the rival merits of the belligerents and interested only in the revolutionary potential of a long drawn-out struggle likely to end in the triumph of a world-wide socialist system. Neither the American nor the Russian peace objectives – mutually exclusive though they were – could be achieved in the short-term.

Only the communist parties throughout the world found themselves working for an immediate peace. To maintain the newly forged friendship with the Nazis, Stalin ordered them, through the Comintern, to abandon their unrelenting war on fascism. Instead they had to abandon the ideological habits of a lifetime, denounce the western powers for prolonging a blatantly imperialist war and call on the masses everywhere to demand peace based on justice at once. How Hitler was to be persuaded to agree to this desirable proposition was left shrouded in mystery. The story of the energetic but misguided efforts of the communists which met with a singular lack of success in the democratic countries – the only ones where they were allowed to conduct their defeatist propaganda – is a sad one reflecting little credit on international communism.

On the evening of the day Britain and France declared war on Germany Roosevelt, in a broadcast to the American people, announced that the United States would be strictly neutral in the conflict although he added that he did not expect Americans to be 'neutral in thought' – as Woodrow Wilson had expected them to be in 1914. The president's overriding objective was quite simply 'to keep war from our firesides by keeping war from coming to the Americas'. He went on: 'As long as it remains within my power to prevent, there will be no blackout of peace in the United States'.[4] On 5 September, in accordance with the provisions of the Neutrality Act, he placed an embargo on the sale of arms, ammunition and implements of war to all belligerents.

Simultaneously he turned to the task of securing the repeal of this embargo. Encouraged by favourable soundings of public opinion, he avoided his earlier error and came out openly for revision. On 21 September a special Congress met to debate the issue. This time he succeeded thanks to more careful preparation – Republicans were consulted as well as Democrats – and to his own brilliant advocacy of the case for repeal.

In fact the Fourth Neutrality Act passed by Congress on 4 November represented a partial reversion only to the practices of traditional neutrality which he personally favoured. The arms embargo was repealed by convincing majorities but in response to isolationist pressure several provisions of the 1937 Act were retained. American vessels were forbidden to carry goods or passengers to belligerent ports; American citizens were forbidden to travel on belligerent ships; American vessels were not to be armed; the president was empowered to define combat zones which American ships, aircraft and citizens were forbidden

[4]S. Rosenman, ed., *The Public Papers and Private Addresses of Franklin D. Roosevelt* (New York, 1938–50) VIII, pp. 463–4.

to enter; only short-term loans could be offered to belligerents; and all purchases from the United States were to be paid in cash and carried in belligerent
ships, i.e. the cash-and-carry clause which lapsed in May 1939 was reintro-
duced and extended to all purchases. The new act was indeed the 'very epitome
of American isolationism, embracing every conceivable device to protect the
country from the dangers to which it had been exposed in 1914–1917'.[5]
Nevertheless, it achieved Roosevelt's principal objective: the act made it possible for Britain and France to purchase war material from the United States,
always provided they had the money and the ships.

Precisely because of this Roosevelt has been accused of misleading the American people for throughout the debate he maintained in season and out of
season that the aim of the new legislation was to keep America out of war, not to
aid the democracies.[6] Of course had the former been the main objective then, as
isolationist critics pointed out, a more effective course of action would have
been the retention of the arms embargo and the re-enactment of the cash-and-
carry clause to cover all other goods. For, as one of their spokesmen in the
House of Representatives remarked prophetically: 'First, we furnish munitions, second, we furnish money; and finally we furnish men'.[7] While
Roosevelt made no secret of his belief in the moral rectitude of the cause of the
democracies and his detestation of fascism, he deliberately concealed from the
American people his awareness of the vital strategic stake the United States had
in the survival of the democracies; privately he wrote to a political colleague: 'if
. . . Germany and Russia win the war or force a peace favourable to them, the
situation of your civilization and mine is indeed in peril. Our world trade
would be at the mercy of the combine, and our increasingly better relations
with our twenty neighbours to the south would end – unless we were willing to
go to war on their behalf against a German–Russian dominated Europe'.[8] To
have confessed this in public would have jeopardized the repeal of the arms
embargo. Political expediency dictated that he gloss over the material advantages to the democracies, presenting this as an accidental by-product of a policy
designed solely to keep the United States out of war. That does not, of course,
mean that he was not as firmly resolved as his opponents to avoid American
entry into the war.

What role did economic advantage play in the repeal of the embargo? Introducing the amendment on 2 October 1939 Senator Key Pittman observed that
a further decline in American exports, the consequence in his view of the
retention of the embargo, would bankrupt large sections of the economy. But
his main argument was not economic but political: by tightening up existing

[5]W.L. Langer and S. Everett Gleason, *The Challenge to Isolation 1937–1940* (New York, 1952),
p. 232.

[6]His attitude coincided with and was influenced by the public opinion polls which showed that
while 80 per cent favoured the democracies and 50–60 per cent favoured aid to them, 70 per cent of
the latter category wanted the United States to stay out of the war.

[7]*Congressional Record* November 1 1939, p. 1,167.

[8]E. Roosevelt, ed,. *The Roosevelt Letters 1928–1945* (London, 1952) III, p. 293; cf. Hull's blunt
comment that 'if Britain and France won the war we could remain at peace whereas if Germany
won there was every likelihood that we should soon have to fight': C. Hull, *The Memoirs of Cordell
Hull* (New York, 1948) I, p. 684.

legislation to prevent American ships carrying supplies to belligerents the danger of American involvement in war could be avoided even at some cost to American trade. This ploy, designed to disarm the opposition, was copied by supporters of repeal so that in Congress political and legalistic arguments dominated the debate with only occasional references to economic consider-ations. All the same, the latter may well have been an important factor in explaining the easy passage of the legislation. By the spring of 1939, although farming interests opposed revision, the business community was over-whelmingly for it. And business interests lobbied effectively to amend the bill. For example, the West Coast Export Group, supported by the Maritime Asso-ciation of New York, protested that cash-and-carry in its original form would cripple American trade with the Far East, putting ships out of service and men out of work. In the end the clause was restricted to the North Atlantic so that American merchantmen were able to continue their trade with British posses-sions in the Far East. It is significant, too, that the greatest support for repeal came from the north-east and south of the United States where economic ties with Europe were strong.

Repeal of the arms embargo did not, in fact, bring immediate relief to the American economy because Britain and France were slow to increase their purchases from the United States, basically for two reasons. As Britain believed the war would probably last three years, proceed at a leisurely pace and end in the collapse of Germany through economic strain, she was confident she could build up her armaments without having recourse to the Americans. Secondly, as the Johnson Act of 1934 prohibited loans from the American money market to all countries who had defaulted on their war debts in the 1930s, financial problems would clearly arise if the western powers became heavily dependent on the United States. Instead they husbanded their gold and dollar reserves switching imports from non-essentials such as tobacco and fruit to raw materials, food stuffs, machine tools and aircraft. Nor at bottom did they wish to switch to a war economy disruptive of their own trading position if there was any chance of the Hitler regime collapsing in the near future. It was Hitler's victory in the west in the summer of 1940 that dramatically trans-formed the situation making Britain dependent overnight on the United States for survival. When that happened Roosevelt increased defence expenditure substantially in the interests of national security. Then, and then only, did the American aircraft and munitions industries move into top gear and unemployment fell dramatically at last.

If the United States was 'to keep the war from coming to the Americas', it was essential to work very closely with the countries of Latin America, a vulnerable area on the American defence perimeter where the Axis Powers were building up their trade and intriguing against the Americans. Fortunately the Latin American countries, only too well aware that the war would in all probability disrupt their European trade, were anxious to co-operate with their mighty neighbour. In September representatives of 21 countries met in Panama to discuss inter-continental defence and economic arrangements to offset the anticipated loss of trade.

Three decisions were reached. First, the American republics declared their neutrality in the European conflict. Second, in the so-called Declaration of

Panama it was agreed to establish a safety zone around the western hemisphere south of Canada and extending from 300 to 1,000 miles out to sea depending on the geographical indentations of the coastline. In this zone belligerents were warned not to undertake naval action. The zone was of questionable legality. As the British were not prepared to respect the zone unless the United States could guarantee that the Germans would not be allowed to use it, Roosevelt was obliged to order the navy to provide 80 destroyers for patrol duties. But it was not his intention nor that of the American republics to fight to uphold the sanctity of the zone. They relied on the goodwill of the belligerents to respect it. This they did only when it suited their convenience. That was made abundantly clear when three British destroyers pursued and attacked the German pocket battleship *Graf Spee* off the Uruguayan coast. On the other hand, a week after the security zone was announced Roosevelt's unneutral attitude became apparent when he gave permission to American patrols to inform British patrols of the presence of foreign submarines in these waters, a step clearly intended to give them a chance to move in and destroy the enemy.

The third decision of the Panama Conference was the establishment of an Inter-American Financial and Economic Advisory Committee to study and make recommendations about the effect of trade dislocation and to plan closer financial ties and a more balanced economic relationship between the Latin American countries and the United States. Progress was at first extremely slow for this was no easy problem. United States markets could not absorb competing surpluses of food and raw materials from countries such as Uruguay, Argentina and Chile with whom North America did relatively little trade. This situation became extremely urgent in the summer of 1940; unless positive action was taken at once the Latin American states would inevitably be forced to accept whatever terms a victorious Germany deigned to offer them. That this would imply an unwelcome degree of political and economic subjection to Berlin was certain. The State Department's riposte in the form of an imaginative proposal in June 1940 for the establishment of an organization to market and control the production of food and raw materials throughout the western hemisphere had Roosevelt's enthusiastic support. But it was too radical a departure for American farmers fearful of overproduction. In Latin America the plan aroused old fears of Dollar Imperialism. So in the end Roosevelt dropped the scheme. Orthodox methods prevailed; in July 1940 Congress approved an increase of $500 million in the capital and loan power of the Import–Export Bank.

On the eve of the European war Japanese foreign policy was in ruins. The Japanese government, confident that it would get its way with Germany and that she would not dare violate the secret protocol to the Anti-Comintern Pact in which she had promised not to conclude any political agreement with Russia, resolutely disregarded repeated warnings from diplomatic representatives that this was precisely what the Germans had in mind. So the news of the Russo-German Pact came as a great shock and enraged public opinion in Japan. German explanations were brushed aside by Foreign Minister Arita Hachirō who broke off formal negotiations with Germany on 25 August. Three days later the pro-German government of Baron Hiranuma Kiichirō fell. After unsuccessful attempts by Hirota and Konoe to form new administrations a caretaker regime headed by a political nonentity, General Abe Nobuyuki, took over on 30 August with instructions from the emperor to pursue a conciliatory policy towards Britain and the United States.

This was a logical step for Japan to take. Badly let down by Germany, on the verge of war with Russia and on bad terms with Britain, France and the United States, a realignment of policy was urgently necessary. An improvement in relations with the democracies seemed the obvious course to follow. There was already speculation in Washington that Japan would be forced in this direction although, typically, the administration expected Tokyo to make all the concessions. Britain, on the other hand, as the Craigie–Arita declaration demonstrated in July 1939, was ready to come to terms with Japan in order to free her hands as the European crisis deepened. The appeasement of Japan continued after the outbreak of war and Britain gave way in the winter of 1939–40 to demands for the withdrawal of most British garrisons and heavy naval vessels from China. This raises an interesting but unanswerable question: had it not been for the running sore of the China episode, might not Japan have obtained enough by blackmail to persuade her to remain neutral?

In mid September Japan's position improved somewhat when the crisis with Russia subsided. It commenced in May 1939 when Outer Mongolian soldiers clashed with the Japanese garrison at Nomonhan, a lonely area on the north-western frontier of Manchukuo. Early in July hostilities flared up again when the Kwantung Army, a law unto itself, decided to teach the Russians a lesson and attacked in strength against the advice of both war ministry and army general staff, neither of which saw much sense in committing scarce resources in this remote area. The Japanese suffered a sharp defeat at Nomonhan. Undeterred, they launched a new offensive late in July when they were again repulsed. On 20 August the Russians launched a heavy counter-attack with five infantry divisions and five tank brigades. The Japanese, heavily outnumbered, lost 18,000 men and were obliged to withdraw from Nomonhan. The Kwantung Army, incredibly, was preparing a new offensive when the general staff at last intervened; the offensive was suspended and the Kwantung commander replaced. By this time the Japanese and Russians wanted to draw a line under the Nomonhan incident. On 16 September Russia and Japan announced a cease-fire and it was agreed that a boundary commission delineate the frontier later.

The immediate benefit for Russia was that she could move into Poland. For Japan the easing of tension enabled her to concentrate on ending the war in China. The Abe government turned to this task with renewed vigour for a new and alluring prospect was unfolding; if Japan could free her hands of China she would be able to exploit the favourable situation likely to develop in the Far East as the European powers, locked in internecine warfare, gradually relaxed their grip on their colonial possessions. Hope flared in Tokyo that under cover of the European war Japan could become the dominant power in the Pacific. Whether this could be achieved by peaceful means and in agreement with the United States, as moderates advocated, or by force, as the extremists predicted, was as yet unclear.

Towards China Japan relied on a mixture of stick and carrot. Military operations were intensified; an offensive was launched into Kwangsi province to cut Chiang Kai-shek's strategic links with Indo-China; in November Canton fell and the Nationalists were left with the Burma Road and the Hanoi–Kunming railway as their only outlets to the sea. At the same time Japan re-affirmed her objective of creating a New Order in East Asia but, in the hope of wooing the Chinese, emphasized the importance of mutual co-operation and assistance between Japan, China and Manchukuo in the economic, political and cultural fields. Finally, in an attempt to facilitate peace negotiations, Japan declared her intention of setting up a new central government headed by a former Chiang Kai-shek supporter, Wang Ching-wei. But in practice the China policy of the Abe government proved to be a major obstacle preventing it making any progress towards the second objective: an improvement of relations with the democracies, especially with the United States. This became apparent at the close of 1939 during the conversations between Ambassador Grew and Foreign Minister Nomura Kichisaburō.

The Japanese, upset by the decision to terminate the 1911 trade treaty, were anxious for a dialogue with the Americans. When the treaty ran out in January 1940 Tokyo feared that the United States might then impose a trade embargo with the most serious consequences for Japan; without scrap metal and petroleum from America Japan simply could not continue military operations in China. Even the pro-Axis faction in the military advocated conversations with the Americans although, as usual, they deluded themselves in thinking that no substantial concessions would be required of the Japanese.

No progress whatever was made by Grew and Nomura. The more Japan tried to assure the United States that the New Order in east Asia would not violate the Open Door Policy or infringe the established rights of the white powers, the more Washington feared that Japan's real objective was precisely that, and that a closed economy would be created in China and Manchukuo under Japanese political control. The present Japanese monopoly of the carrying trade on the Yangtze river was particularly obnoxious to the Americans. But Nomura's offer to open the lower reaches of the Yangtze to foreign trade – a fairly minor concession – in return for a new trade agreement with the United States stood no chance of acceptance. And the more Japan maintained that present interference with American property and trade was a purely temporary phenomenon due to the exigencies of the military situation, the more Washington was convinced that it was only a foretaste of what was still to come. There was never any hope of a *modus vivendi*; nothing short of a complete change of heart in Tokyo would have satisfied Washington.

Japan's assurances that the Wang Ching-wei government, set up in Nanking in March 1940, was completely independent were contemptuously rejected in Washington where Hull denounced it as a Japanese tool designed to establish Japan's exclusive rights in China. The revelation in January 1940 of the peace terms Wang Ching-wei was (allegedly) prepared to accept confirmed the American suspicions; China was to recognize Manchukuo and join the Anti-Comintern Pact; although Japan promised to withdraw her troops from central and south China within two years, troops would stay in Inner Mongolia and north China; the latter would become a semi-autonomous region, while throughout China Japan was to have special privileges to exploit mineral resources, manage Chinese communications and develop industrial concerns. Terms such as these spotlighted the real problem; the Japanese military, though anxious to end the fighting, could not bring themselves to make major concessions to the Nationalists, especially as control of Inner Mongolia and north China was considered essential strategically in the likely event of war with Russia. So Chiang Kai-shek's determination to continue the struggle was strengthened and all hope of an early peace faded.

But although the conversations, temporarily revived in June, ended in failure, Roosevelt and Hull still refrained from imposing sanctions on trade with Japan. There was the usual clash between 'hawks' and 'doves' on the issue. Stimson, Morgenthau and Hornbeck argued strenuously that only economic sanctions could bring the Japanese to heel and force them to negotiate with Chiang Kai-shek on a reasonable basis. The opinion polls showed that 75 per cent of the American people supported this view.

Grew, however, though pessimistic about Japan's long-term intentions, urged that every effort be made to conciliate the moderates in the Abe cabinet including the offer of a new trade treaty. The 'doves' had powerful allies in Britain and France who were anxious to avoid precipitate action in the Far East. Their fear was that, tempted by the European war, Japan might seize their colonial possessions. Economic sanctions would only resolve any doubts the Japanese might have and force them into forward action. As neither power could resist Japanese aggression, appeasement seemed the only viable alternative. This course the 'doves' recommended to Hull throughout the autumn of 1939 urging in particular that the United States act as mediator and work for a speedy settlement of the war in China, even one highly favourable to Japan.

Roosevelt's own instinct was to support the 'hawks' over economic sanctions. But he eventually temporized agreeing with Hull that they should not be imposed forthwith. At the same time he instructed Hull to make it clear to Japan that in return for this he expected her to act in conformity with those immutable principles from which the Americans refused to deviate on China. So the old middle course between coercion and appeasement continued to determine the American attitude to Japan. And the Japanese continued to delude themselves that they had little to fear from America.

The point was made in the last chapter that the Second World War is generally assumed to have broken out in 1939 because in September Britain and France declared war on Germany and continued the struggle until she surrendered unconditionally in May 1945. The fact that all the British self-governing Dominions joined in (with the exception of Eire) and that the British and French colonial territories were automatically committed to war gave a quasi-global character to what was essentially a European war about Poland.

Arguably the European war only became a world war when the super powers, as it became customary to call the United States and Soviet Russia in the 1940s, became directly involved in the fighting. For they alone possessed the economic potential and the manpower to fight the war to a finish. A not dissimilar situation existed during the First World War. Tsarist Russia had been involved in the war from the very beginning but although her seemingly inexhaustible manpower proved a serious drain on Germany and Austria–Hungary, she was quite unable to defeat the Central Powers on her own. So by 1916 the war had stalemated. This deadlock was broken by the intervention of the United States, then the only power capable of bringing the war to a decisive conclusion.

But was it inevitable that the United States and the Soviet Union were drawn into a second European conflict turning it into a truly global struggle? Are we confronted here with the inexorable working of some historical law by which minor wars involving some great powers always escalate until they include all the great powers? These are not pointless questions. Much can be learnt about .the nature of historical phenomena through the consideration of alternative scenarios. As Lord Dacre remarked in a defence of Counter-Factual History in his valedictory lecture at Oxford: 'History is not merely what happened, it is what happened in the context of what might have happened. Therefore we must incorporate as a necessary element the alternatives, the might-have-beens. . . . It is only if we live for a moment as the men of the time lived, in its still fluid context . . . [that we can truly recreate the past]'.[9] It is well worth asking ourselves whether there was any possibility that the belligerents might have patched up their quarrel in the winter of 1939–40. Because if the war in Europe had ended that winter, the United States would have been driven in on herself, unable to help the cause of democracy but compelled to watch helplessly from the sidelines while Germany established her dominance over Europe with all that this implied for the future. And if, as most historians believe, Hitler always intended to attack Russia one day the date of that attack might well have been advanced and the outcome of that titanic struggle might then have been very different.

Certainly there was no desire in Britain and France to escalate the war. Both powers pursued a defensive strategy on military and economic grounds. For Britain with only six regular infantry divisions (four in France by the end of September) there was no question of any other strategy. In the case of France with 88 divisions and 1,700 tanks when fully mobilized (which took three weeks from 23 August) an offensive strategy might seem to have been a distinct possibility. Indeed, much criticism was levelled at her for failing to attack in the west when the bulk of the German army was deeply committed in Poland and 32 divisions, only 11 being regular divisions of high quality, guarded the western fortifications. Gamelin had actually promised the Poles in somewhat ambiguous language to attack 'in strength' in the west as soon as the German offensive in Poland gathered momentum. In fact, a minor sortie was all he ever intended and all that France was capable of. For French High Command had stubbornly refused to take cognizance of German experimentation with armour in the late 1930s and persisted in relegating tanks to an infantry-support role so that the army was woefully undermechanized; there were only two mechanized divisions in the whole French army in 1939. Nor was the airforce, which consisted of 700 fighters and 625 bombers, capable of giving massive support to an attacking army. Consequently there could be no question of emulating German tactics and striking quickly through Belgium (even if the latter had

[9]'History and Imagination', in *The Times Literary Supplement* 25 July 1980.

allowed the French through their country, which is extremely doubtful), crossing the Rhine and seizing the Ruhr. On the other hand, the French did not intend to repeat the costly tactics of 1914–18: massive bombardment of enemy positions followed by infantry attacks. The dilemma of how then to help Poland was soon resolved; by 16 September Polish resistance had already crumbled. The order for limited offensive actions was promptly countermanded. And French reconnaissance troops already on German soil were withdrawn as German reinforcements arrived from the east. Gamelin was greatly relieved at this turn of events. Despite his promise to the Polish war minister, he had never believed that France could launch a serious offensive before 1941 and then only with British support and American equipment. Instead the French gave up all thought of offensive action and stayed in the formidable Maginot Line defences throughout the winter of 1939–40. It was symptomatic of the desire of the political and military leadership both in Paris and London not to provoke the Germans that an RAF plan for dealing Germany what might have been a crippling blow by bombing her industrial heart, the Ruhr, was not activated. Daladier and Gamelin readily agreed with Chamberlain and Halifax that it would bring upon the democracies the opprobrium of being the first to bomb civilians and so offend neutral opinion as well as leading to reprisals likely to damage the allied war effort at a critical stage in rearmament.[10]

Of course, Gamelin did not expect the war to go away. He anticipated a German attack through Belgium in the spring of 1940. But he remained surprisingly confident that a well-prepared and by then fully-mobilized army would move into Belgium and contain the Germans and that the internal situation in Germany would then explode.[11] The defensive strategy of 1939–40 had another advantage: it avoided a repetition of the savage carnage of the First World War, the consequence of incessant frontal attacks on the enemy to capture a few square feet of territory, and an experience which had bitten deep into the French soul. And in a country so divided politically, uneasily aware that her greatness lay behind her and that the Germans were probably more than a match for her, it made sound political sense to ensure that the war caused the minimum inconvenience to the maximum number of Frenchmen for as long as humanly possible.

Economic arguments pointed in the same direction. It was widely believed in British government circles that Germany's Achilles' heel was her economic condition. A country which had – so it was erroneously supposed – been mobilizing her total resources for war for some years must soon feel tremendous strain. Therefore, provided Britain could survive whatever initial offensive Hitler launched against her, it seemed certain that the slow strangulation of economic blockade would force him to his knees in two to three years at most. In this way Britain would avoid the bloody war of attrition of 1914–18.[12] Mean-

---

[10]The chief of the imperial general staff commented in his diary on the war cabinet discussion of the feasibility of bombing the Ruhr: 'I noticed how relieved the cabinet was at not being asked to make a decision': R. Macleod, ed., *The Ironside Diaries 1937–1940* (London, 1962), 23 October 1939, p. 143.

[11]*Op. cit.*, 30 December 1939, pp. 173–4.

[12]Chamberlain thought Germany would collapse inside 18 months and that she would not even launch an offensive in the west in 1940.

while Britain would mobilize her immense overseas resources in order to deliver the *coup de grâce* to a much weakened Germany. Already in September 1939 the cabinet decided to build up an army of 55 divisions within two years for this purpose. The mood of complacency about the outcome of the war was encouraged by the plain fact of German isolation. Italy's declaration of neutrality removed any threat for the time being to Britain's vital lines of communication through the Mediterranean and Suez Canal to the Indian Empire. Also the fact that the long-anticipated aerial bombardment of Britain did not take place in the early days of the war confirmed Chamberlain – and Churchill – in the belief that Hitler had 'missed the bus' and passed up a golden opportunity to strike at the democracies at a time of maximum weakness.

Behind the military, economic and political arguments for a defensive strategy lay at bottom a hope that the war might still go away. That Britain and France had done their level best to avoid war in 1938–9 is a matter of record. They had finally declared war partly – in Britain's case – in response to the pressure of public opinion but mostly because they were driven to the reluctant conclusion that Hitler had personal ambitions to dominate Europe and perhaps rule the world which had to be resisted. During the critical 48 hours between the German attack on Poland on 1 September and the declarations of war Chamberlain and Daladier did not waver in their resolve; they torpedoed Mussolini's desperate attempts to preserve the peace by insisting on an immediate withdrawal from Poland as a *sine qua non* for any discussion with Hitler. Similarly at the end of the Polish campaign when Hitler offered peace terms on 6 October, Chamberlain and Daladier refused them point blank.

Nevertheless, throughout the early months of the war Britain maintained many unofficial contacts with Germany, in particular with the Swedish businessman Birger Dahlerus who had attempted to mediate between Britain and Germany in the summer of 1939 and supposedly had the ear of both Hitler and Goering. For what the British government really wanted was to restore the status quo of 31 August 1939. The government sensed, as Foreign Secretary Sir Edward Grey had done in August 1914 when he made his celebrated remark about the lights going out all over Europe, that an all-out war against Hitler would be destructive of the entire social, political and economic order Britain was seeking to uphold. Apart from the threat to Britain's imperial possessions and the near certainty of her decline as a world power, pressure for social change at home quite unacceptable to the National Government would be the inevitable consequence of total war.[13] The economy would be completely disrupted, the modernization of British industry seriously retarded and the precarious balance of payments destroyed by the loss of overseas markets which Britain might never recover after the war. The financial burdens of war were already a matter of serious concern to the Treasury which estimated that the creation of 55 divisions by 1941 and the commitment to produce 2,500 bombers a month would use up Britain's reserves by the end of 1940 and force her to

---

[13] Ambassador Joseph Kennedy reported on 31 October that while everybody hated Hitler, they did not 'want to be finished economically, financially and politically and socially, which they are beginning to suspect will be their fate if the war goes on very long': Langer and Gleason, *Isolation*, p. 259.

realize her overseas assets, further endangering the balance of payments. Similarly ruling circles in France felt little enthusiasm for the prolongation of the war. As a contemporary remarked bitterly: 'for the initiated war was not "a leap into the unknown" but a sort of gigantic charade acted out by mutual consent from which nothing serious could emerge if we played our part right'.[14]

The British government kept the secret lines to Berlin open, not it should be emphasized because it reposed any confidence in Hitler, a thoroughly discredited figure in Britain, but because it was hoped that Hitler might be replaced in a palace revolution by Goering, a man widely regarded in official circles as the representative of conservative forces in industry, civil service and army with whom a reasonable peace might yet be arranged and the economic and social cost of total war mobilization avoided. It was, to say the least, convenient while such hopes were alive, that Britain kept a low military profile.

Too much should not be made of these possibilities. By December 1939 Chamberlain had ended the contacts with Dahlerus having come to the reluctant conclusion that he was only Hitler's mouthpiece gaining time for the Führer, who was quite uninterested in making any concessions. When Chamberlain and Sir Samuel Hoare made comments to Sumner Welles during the latter's visit to London in the spring of 1940 which suggested that they had not completely closed their minds to an agreed settlement, these were echoes from a distant past. All hopes of peace with Nazi Germany, if they had ever been more than wishful thinking, had died by the end of 1939.

For a proper understanding of the peace manoeuvres in the winter of 1939-40 it is necessary to diverge from the main thread of the story to explain the American attitude during the early months of the war. It was to be expected that the greatest neutral on earth would be called upon by prominent individuals inside and outside the United States to intervene and prevent the escalation of the war. When the king of Belgium and the Finnish foreign minister appealed to Roosevelt to mediate and forestall the expected German offensive in the west, senior State Department officials early in October discussed the feasibility of intervention. They concluded that the United States should not seek to mediate in the near future for the good reason that Germany was too strong and they had no wish to humiliate the democracies by forcing them to refuse mediation. Roosevelt thoroughly approved of this line for his hope – though not his expectation in the near future – was that with American material aid Britain and France would shift the balance of military advantage away from Berlin.

Whilst Roosevelt was as determined as ever not to allow the United States to be drawn into war, he did not want to be left out of the rather nebulous peace talk surfacing intermittently in the winter of 1939-40. Not that Roosevelt was at all interested in a patched-up peace based on the recognition of the German conquest of Poland. But he did want the United States to play a leading role in the reconstruction of the world after an Axis defeat – one more reason, incidentally, why Chamberlain was anxious to avoid an escalation of the war certain to make Britain economically dependent on the United States. As early as December 1939 Roosevelt was talking privately of the four freedoms: freedom

[14]André Beaufre, *1940. The Fall of France* (London, 1964), p. 154.

of speech, freedom of religion, freedom from fear and freedom of trade and access to raw materials as a possible basis for a world settlement.

There was in the president's make-up a strong Messianic strain; as an old disciple of Wilson he saw himself succeeding where the master failed, restoring to the United States the economic and political primacy she enjoyed in 1919. At the same time he was too astute a politician not to lose sight of the presidential election in November 1940. If he wanted an unprecedented third term as president – and he had not yet decided whether to stand – then would there not be a double bonus awaiting the candidate who could walk the political tightrope and, whilst avoiding war or any suspicion of foreign entanglements, could stand out as the man who had promoted the cause of peace in the highest American traditions? In so far as pressure groups such as the multinational corporations, concerned about trading links with Europe, and Catholics, convinced that as escalation of the war could only benefit communism, nursed hopes of an early peace which the isolationist press played upon, it did nothing but good to involve their representatives in peace soundings which proved that there was no hope of an immediate peace.

With these objectives firmly in mind he did his best to improve America's image as the apostle of peace. In December he appointed a special envoy to the Holy See, an American Catholic Myron C. Taylor; this step he first contemplated in 1936 but now activated it in the hope of harnessing the moral force of the papacy to future peace initiatives. At the end of the month he authorized the setting up of a special State Department committee, chaired by Sumner Welles, whose remit was to discuss not a patched-up peace in Europe but post-war planning and the creation of a new world order based on respect for international law, large-scale disarmament, a revivified League of Nations and a sound trading system.

At the beginning of 1940 when the Committee for the Problems of Foreign Relations produced an outline plan for a world economic settlement, Roosevelt threw his weight behind it. An organization of neutral states would be created to work together in economic matters and begin discussions on the establishment of a stable world system once the war had ended. Hull initiated these discussions in February 1940 with 46 neutral countries but the rather nebulous scheme – reminiscent of Welles's scheme two years previously for a great international conference – failed to make much headway; the absence of the belligerents limited its practical value; and the German campaigns in the spring killed it off completely.

Roosevelt took other initiatives at the beginning of 1940 as part of his 'peace offensive'. In January he authorized another unofficial visit to Germany by James D. Mooney, a General Motors executive with German contacts, whose attempts in October 1939 to interest the president in Goering's 'peace plans' had proved singularly unavailing. This time he had to go to Berlin to ascertain whether the Nazis were interested in agreed solutions to current problems; if they were, Roosevelt would be willing to try and reconcile the differences between the belligerents – not that he thought there was any chance of this happening.

The second initiative was the mission of Sumner Welles to Rome, Berlin, Paris and London to ascertain the views of the four governments on the establishment of a just and lasting peace. The president's motives are controversial. No doubt he did want to hold off a German attack in the west as long as possible to enable Britain and France to build up their military strength. But it seems unlikely that he had weakened in his aversion to a compromise peace for on the same day as the Welles visit to Europe was announced Hull made public the plans for a post-war settlement. What Welles's mission showed very clearly was that no basis existed for a patched-up peace.

In Rome Mussolini and Ciano assured Welles that peace would only be possible if Germany retained her gains in the east and regained her colonies, terms which probably coincided with Welles's own views. But in Paris and London the signs were unpropitious. Certainly Daladier said he would accept *Grossdeutschland* as a political reality; he would let Austria, the Sudetenland and west Poland determine their own future; and even indicated a willingness to have dealings with the present Nazi leadership but only on condition that France was secured against future German aggression which he had no doubt was still uppermost in Hitler's mind. In London it was the same story. Angered by what they regarded as American interference likely to give Hitler a false impression about British intentions thereby diminishing Chamberlain's hopes for a genuine negotiated peace, government members went out of their way to emphasize Britain's determination to fight on and even dismember Germany when they won. Only if a miracle occurred, would Chamberlain be willing to make peace with Hitler; only in that improbable eventuality would he (Chamberlain) not be intransigent about the frontiers of Czechoslovakia and Poland or jib at the *Anschluss* with Austria. Germany could even have access to her former colonies but she must first of all withdraw from Poland and Czechoslovakia unconditionally, guarantee these and other small nations their independence, and commence to disarm. Chamberlain, like Daladier, did not believe there was the slightest chance of Hitler offering acceptable guarantees against future aggression. Despite this, when rumours of a compromise peace started to circulate Roosevelt immediately denied that the United States was willing to discuss detailed peace plans. When Welles attempted to persuade the president to agree that Mussolini mediate between London and Berlin Roosevelt turned the suggestion down, and obliged Welles to state publicly that no peace plans had been submitted by either side.

To turn now to Germany. It is most unlikely that Hitler ever wavered in his determination to turn on the western powers once Poland had been defeated. At first there were some hints that he was prepared to be flexible in his handling of Poland; in September Hitler spoke of settling for the annexation of the Corridor and Upper Silesia but very probably he was hoping to drive a wedge between Britain and France and encourage opposition to those western politicians who insisted on a German withdrawal from Poland as a prerequisite to negotiation. Even before his peace offer on 6 October Hitler knew that Britain was sure to reject it and immediately after the speech he informed the commander-in-chief of the army, General Walther von Brauchitsch, and the chief of the army general staff, General Franz Halder, of his intention to attack in the west. As the first unfavourable press reactions to his offer were arriving in Berlin, Hitler was busily composing a memorandum in which he emphasized the need for a swift offensive in the west. Though there may have been momentary anger in Berlin when Chamberlain rejected the peace offer on 12 October, it is hard to believe that Hitler seriously expected any other response.

While Hitler permitted the contact with the British to continue through Dahlerus he had no high hopes of a settlement; but anxious to keep his options open as long as possible he could not completely discount a change of heart in London. By the early spring any desire he may have had for peace had vanished. Detailed work was proceeding on a revised Plan Yellow. When Sumner Welles toured the European capitals Hitler only received him because, as he explained to Mussolini, a successful peace offensive would have interfered with his military plans. But to Welles on 2 March he did not mince his words: 'I can see no hope for the establishment of any lasting peace until the will of England and France to destroy Germany can be itself destroyed. . . . there is no way by which the will to destroy Germany can be itself destroyed except through a German victory. I believe that German might is such as to ensure the triumph of Germany but if not we will all go down together'.[15]

One must, therefore, conclude that there was no hope of a negotiated peace in the winter of 1939–40. Does this mean that in the last resort the European war continued because of the intransigence of one man: Adolf Hitler? Whatever side one favours in the long-running battle between 'functionalists' and 'intentionalists' about the degree to which Hitler was his own master, in wartime the power of any ruling group or single individual is immensely enhanced. As peoples cluster around their respective castle walls and propaganda machines swing into action with renewed vigour, internecine feuding diminishes in intensity and military values with their heavy emphasis on loyalty and obedience determine the relationship between ruler and ruled. In dictatorships and democracies alike rulers are able to make decisions confident in the knowledge that their peoples will follow them more or less without question. Still, it would be an error to suppose that when Hitler ordered his commanders-in-chief on 27 September to prepare an offensive in the west before Christmas this can be explained simply in terms of an irrepressible itch for further violence. Uppermost in Hitler's mind was the conviction that time was not on Germany's side. If she stayed on the defensive in the west this would allow Britain and France to complete their rearmament with assistance from the United States, and Germany's temporary military advantage would be lost. Once the democracies had repaired their deficiencies particularly in respect of anti-tank and anti-aircraft defences a repetition of the Polish campaign would not be possible. Furthermore Hitler was worried about the vulnerability of the Ruhr. Though he rightly discounted the possibility of a French onslaught on the *Westwall*, he thought France might pressurize Belgium into allowing French troops to move up to the Belgian–German frontier, from which vantage point heavy artillery could bombard the Ruhr.

Because of the pact with Russia Germany could contemplate an offensive in the west without fear of being trapped in a two-front war. Hitler, however, preferred to use a negative argument to overcome opposition from his military advisers; in a memorandum of 9 October addressed to Armed Forces High Command and to his commanders-in-chief he observed that: 'By no treaty or

[15]*FRUS* 1940 I, p. 49.

pact can a lasting neutrality of Soviet Russia be ensured with certainty. . . . The greatest safeguard against any Russian attack lies in a striking display of German superiority, viz: in a prompt demonstration of German strength'.[16] That did not signify anxiety about Russian intentions. Hitler was perfectly satisfied with Russian behaviour to date; nor was there any reason to suppose Russia was in any state to attack Germany. The reference to Russia was simply an argument *ad hominem* to persuade his military advisers that they must strike quickly in the west.

Similarly he tried to capitalize on fear of possible American intervention in the war remarking in the same memorandum that: 'The attempts of certain circles of the USA to lead the American continent in a direction hostile to Germany, is definitely unsuccessful at the moment, but could still in the future lead to the desired result. Here, too, time is to be considered as working against Germany'.[17]

On the same day Hitler issued provisional orders to his commanders-in-chief: an attack was to be launched as quickly as possible through Luxemburg, Belgium and Holland. The objective was to defeat as much of the French army as possible and to conquer as much territory as possible in the Low Countries and northern France to provide a base for the prosecution of the war against Britain by sea and air, and to act as a protective cover for the Ruhr. As in Poland, co-operation between armoured and mechanized units and airforce would guarantee a quick victory. On this basis army general staff drew up Plan Yellow.

How did the generals receive the news of Hitler's decision to attack in the west? Military leaders such as Brauchitsch, Ritter von Leeb, commander of Army Group C, and von Rundstedt, commander of Army Group A, were filled with foreboding. They expected a hard and protracted campaign against the old enemy France. A frontal onslaught would surely result in heavy casualties and end in a stalemate. The violation of the neutrality of small states would offend other neutrals while the Dominions would rally to the support of Britain, an enemy with a reputation for fighting to a finish. And Germany's position, suffering as she was from a shortage of officer reserves, would steadily deteriorate. Far better to remain on the defensive, from which the enemy would be unable to dislodge her. If an offensive could not be avoided in the west, then at the very least the army needed time to re-equip after the losses sustained in Poland – an argument which, when put to Hitler, he dismissed impatiently as a sign of cowardice.

Attempts to persuade Hitler that he should defer the offensive merely enraged him and aroused in him a deep and abiding suspicion of the generals. When Brauchitsch took his courage in his hands and read him a memorandum summarizing the case against an offensive and containing an allegation that the infantry had not performed with sufficient *élan* in Poland, Hitler flew into a

---

[16]*Nazi Conspiracy and Aggression* (Washington, 1946) VII L-52, p. 802; cf. Hitler's comment to commanding generals on 23 November: 'Russia is at present not dangerous. It is weakened by many developments. . . . It is a fact that at the present time the Russian army is of little account. For the next year or two the present situation will remain'. J. Noakes and G. Pridham, *Documents on Nazism 1919–1945* (London, 1974), p. 573.

[17]*Nazi Conspiracy* VII, pp. 803–4.

rage, accused the army of disloyalty and lack of faith in his genius and swore to stamp out the 'spirit of Zossen'.[18] An hour later he confirmed 12 November as the date for attack. Summoning 200 high-ranking officers to the chancellery on 23 November he boasted of his superior political wisdom over the years, chided the army by implication for its pusillanimity and repeated the arguments first used on 27 September: time was not on Germany's side so that Germany must exploit her (temporary) freedom from a two-front war by attacking at once.

The reservations of the generals failed to deter Hitler. Nor did the small band of active conspirators around Admiral Wilhelm Canaris, head of the *Abwehr*, and Colonel Hans Oster, chief of *Abwehr* staff and head of its central division, make any headway in their attempts to persuade colleagues such as Brauchitsch and Halder to join in a plot to overthrow Hitler. What human agencies could not accomplish, adverse weather reports did. In November and December Hitler postponed and re-instated the attack several times as weather conditions continued to be unfavourable. A further complication occurred in the New Year. On 10 January the details of Plan Yellow fell into enemy hands. An airforce major on a flight from Münster to Bonn was carrying with him the entire operational plan. In bad conditions he lost his way over the Rhine and flew into Belgium where he made a forced landing; part of the plan fell into Belgian hands and the details were quickly handed over to the British and French. Only then did Hitler finally decide to drop this version of Plan Yellow.

By the beginning of 1940 Hitler was already having doubts about the plan which had been the object of much criticism since it was drawn up in October. One of the most energetic critics, General Erich von Manstein, chief of staff of Army Group A, had formulated his doubts in a series of memoranda to army command. He was convinced that the current plan was a recipe for disaster certain to lead to a stalemate on the line of the river Somme. It was also unsatisfactory in that, unlike the Schlieffen Plan of 1914, it did not aim at the total annihilation of the French Army but only at the seizure of territory in the Low Countries. Manstein believed that a knock-out blow was possible and on this assumption devised a new strategy. Introducing an element of surprise absent from the current plan, he proposed to launch the major offensive not north but south of Liége and through the Ardennes, a wooded region of ravines, winding roads and few bridges which the British and French general staffs considered unsuitable tank country. Encouraged by General Heinz Guderian, who assured Manstein that these were not insuperable obstacles, the latter developed his concept further. The prize for success in this salient was a glittering one; once the river Meuse was crossed the road to Paris and the Channel coast would be open and the bulk of the Anglo-French forces – which it was thought would move into the Low Countries once the attack commenced – could be cut off from the main French army.

In the winter of 1939–40 military opinion swung slowly but surely in Manstein's favour. Not least of the factors explaining this change was Hitler himself. As early as 25 October, already uneasy about the obstacles facing an invading army in the north, he had talked vaguely of shifting the centre of gravity of the operation to a point south of Lüttich and then swinging north to

[18]Army headquarters were situated at Zossen just outside Berlin.

entrap the Anglo-French forces. But uncertain of his ground he did not press the point home. Indeed Brauchitsch and Halder, irritated by Manstein's dogged persistence, arranged a posting for him to an obscure command in Stettin. But on 7 February at a war games exercise held to test Plan Yellow Manstein had the satisfaction of seeing his opponent Halder edging towards his (Manstein's) own strategy. Ten days later Manstein was able through the good offices of Hitler's adjutant to the *Wehrmacht*, General Rudolf Schmundt, to arrange a meeting with the Führer. This was a great success. Hitler was immediately impressed with Manstein's exposition and with new-found confidence resolved at last to order that the centre of gravity of the operation be shifted to the southern flank. In fact, when he met army leaders on 18 February there was no trial of strength; their war games had convinced them Manstein was right. Within the next few days the general staff worked out the details of a revised plan of attack known, because of its basic premise, as the 'Sickle Cut'. Thus, by a fortunate convergence of a number of historical accidents: autumnal weather, Hitler's penchant for amateur strategy, Manstein's persistence, Schmundt's intervention and the failure of the western powers to attack, a strategic plan was evolved which four mouths later led Germany to a victory over France more complete than that of 1870–1.

4

The Campaign in the West and its Global Repercussions

Although this chapter is dominated by the campaign in the west in the summer of 1940 and by the consequences of the German victory for Russia, the United States and Japan, nevertheless in the spring of 1940 it was Scandinavia which witnessed the first serious passage of arms between the belligerent powers when Germany occupied Denmark and Norway.

Economic and strategic considerations were closely interlocked for both belligerents in Scandinavia. Britain was relying heavily on the weapon of blockade to bring Hitler down as painlessly as possible. But the blockade was only partially effective. To keep the Italians out of the war and generally to conciliate neutral opinion, Britain did not stop all imports into these countries, leaving a loophole which the Germans exploited to their own advantage. A further complication was the Russo-German Pact; if Germany obtained substantial supplies from this unexpected source, then the blockade would take much longer to bite. It was therefore very much in the interests of Britain and France to neutralize these advantages by taking direct action against enemy sources of supply. Of particular importance to the German war effort was oil from Rumania and Russia and high-grade iron-ore from Sweden.

Little progress was made in respect of oil. To stop Rumanian oil being shipped up the Danube, British agents concocted a cloak-and-dagger scheme for sending ships loaded with dynamite up the river; at the right spot these would be blown up and river traffic disrupted. Wisely the cabinet decided not to proceed with the scheme. In the case of Russian oil an even more fantastic plan was evolved. The French won the grudging assent of the British to the bombing of Russian oil refineries at Batum, Baku and Grozny. Apart from the arrant stupidity of action certain to alienate Russia if it did not lead to war with her, practical difficulties made it a non-starter. The obvious airfields in Turkey and Iraq were not likely to be placed at the disposal of the French. To carry out the crazy plan new bases would have to be built in Syria; furthermore, France lacked suitable aircraft and would have had to modify transport aircraft for the mission; and permission to fly over Turkish territory would not have been granted by Ankara in any case. Not surprisingly Operation Caucasus was quietly interred in the end.

Britain had shown little interest in bombing Russian oil refineries. Swedish ore was a different proposition. As Germany was importing over 50 per cent of her iron-ore from Sweden in 1939 and had reserves for nine months only, the Swedish connection was of vital importance for the continuation of the German war effort. Unlike the French, the British had the means of striking at this source of supply if they chose to do so. During the summer months the ore was shipped across the German-controlled Baltic and was largely beyond allied interference. But in the winter when the Gulf of Bothnia was frozen the iron ore was transported by rail to Narvik, then taken along the Norwegian coast by freighters which sheltered behind a line of islands just inside Norwegian territorial waters until they reached the Skagerrak.

From the earliest days of the war Churchill, now first lord of the admiralty, was convinced that serious damage could be done to the German war economy by reducing this trade. Impatient as always to get to grips with the enemy, in September 1939 he proposed the laying of minefields in Norwegian waters across the three-mile limit to force the ore ships out into the Atlantic. On foreign office advice the war cabinet rejected this drastic proposal fearing that neutral opinion would be offended. Nor had he any more luck with a proposal in November for a barrage of mines across the North Sea. What changed the situation was the Russian attack on Finland on 19 November. Opinion in the western democracies sided instinctively with a small people fighting gallantly against an aggressor. This opened up the possibility of exploiting popular support for Finland to advance strategic objectives: if British forces were sent to help the Finns via Scandinavia then *en route* might they not occupy Narvik and put the Swedish ore fields out of action?

The project was no more feasible than Operation Caucasus. The British made it dependent on prior agreement with the Norwegian and Swedish governments, both of which promptly and predictably refused to allow troops through their territory for fear of German or Russian retaliation. The Supreme War Council still continued to discuss ways and means of sending 100,000 men to Finland until the capitulation of the Finns on 12 March put an end to this talk. Once again Britain and France did not see eye to eye on strategy. French Prime Minister Edouard Daladier, concerned to shore up his crumbling government by some spectacular feat of arms, preferably far away from the French frontier and falling mostly on the British, pressed for action at all costs regardless of Norwegian susceptibilities and even at the risk of conflict with Russia, an eventuality which the British, increasingly sceptical of the whole operation, were determined to avoid. Once the Finns surrendered two of the three British divisions earmarked for the operation were promptly sent to France.

The capitulation of the Finns brought the British government up against the moral dilemma it had been avoiding for six months: if it was serious in its wish to stop Swedish ore reaching Germany then it would have to act without the agreement of the Norwegians. For Daladier this had never been a problem; in March he proposed the seizure of strong points along the Norwegian coast and welcomed the extension of the war this would lead to in the event of German countermeasures. Chamberlain and Halifax were utterly opposed to this proposal as they were to Churchill's renewed pleas for the mining of Norwegian waters; they had still not reached the point where they were prepared to disregard neutral rights for what, it must be admitted in fairness to them, they considered a doubtful advantage. Another cogent reason for caution was the 800,000 tons of ore Britain had imported from Narvik in the six months following the outbreak of war, making this as important a trade for Britain as for Germany.

The fall of Daladier's government on 20 March brought the British government no relief from pressure for action. Paul Reynaud, his successor, presented London with a comprehensive plan left by his predecessor proposing the seizure of strong points on the Norwegian coast, submarine warfare in the Black Sea and air attacks on Russian oil refineries. In the war cabinet Chamberlain opposed the French plan but seems to have succumbed to the growing feeling that action somewhere was almost a moral imperative. In the end a package deal was agreed upon; Britain would lay mines outside Narvik on 5 April and – thanks to pressure from Churchill – send the hastily recalled expeditionary force to Norway if the Germans intervened; in return the French would drop mines in the Rhine and other German rivers. However, the French got cold feet, fearing German retaliation against munition and aircraft factories, and postponed their part of the bargain despite British entreaties. In the end Britain went ahead on her own and started to lay mines on 8 April. Three valuable days had been lost in Anglo-French wrangling. For on 9 April German forces attacked Norway and Denmark in accordance with a plan drawn up some weeks previously.

Why did Germany attack Scandinavia? Initially Hitler had no thought of such action. The Scandinavian people ranked high in the Nazi racial calendar. They were looked upon in Berlin as friendly neighbours who would one day be united with the Germans in a Nordic *Schicksalsgemeinschaft*. Meanwhile their continued neutrality was highly satisfactory enabling the Germans to import the iron-ore they needed.

External events forced Hitler to abandon this optimistic position. The British declaration of war immediately alarmed the German naval authorities who realized that Britain with her superior naval power could do immense damage to Germany in the North Atlantic. In October 1939 Admiral Erich Raeder, commander-in-chief of the navy, was already pressing Hitler to acquire strong points on the Norwegian coast – which he thought could be obtained through joint Russo-German pressure – partly to provide new bases from which to intensify the war at sea and partly to forestall British attempts to bottle the German fleet up in the Baltic. At first Hitler did not respond positively; expansion of the navy was hardly possible when the army was being re-equipped for the attack in the west; in any case he believed Britain would capitulate once France was defeated; meanwhile she would scarcely risk the moral opprobrium of violating Scandinavian neutrality.

The Russian attack on Finland greatly increased the likelihood of British counter-measures. Early in December Raeder returned to the attack insisting that for economic and strategic reasons Germany could not afford to let Britain invade Norway. This time he found a new ally in Vidkun Quisling, the leader of the small Norwegian fascist party eager to collaborate with the Germans. Introduced to Hitler by Raeder, Quisling maintained that British action in Norway was imminent. Though still hopeful that the Scandinavians would uphold their traditional neutrality, Hitler was sufficiently impressed by these warnings to order in January 1940 the establishment of a small group in Armed Forces High Command to draw up operational plans for *Weserübung*, the seizure of Norway and Denmark. Then on 16 February the British destroyer *Cossack* entered Norwegian territorial waters, stopped and boarded the *Altmark*, a German supply ship, and freed 300 British prisoners of war held below the hatches. This decisive British action persuaded Hitler that further violations of Norwegian neutrality were being contemplated. He ordered an immediate acceleration of the planning and on 21 February appointed General Nikolaus von Falkenhorst to command the *Weserübung* forces – characteristically the latter was ordered to return the same evening with a hastily drafted plan of campaign which Hitler approved at once. On 1 March Hitler issued the directive for *Weserübung*. Two days later he decided that it must precede Plan Yellow by a few days. On 2 April Hitler announced that the attack would be launched on 9 April.

The forces Germany committed to the campaign were quite small: no more than 10,000 troops were involved supported by two battle cruisers, one pocket battleship, seven cruisers and 14 destroyers. But the speed and efficiency with which the operation was carried out was such that the Germans outwitted far superior British and French forces. Before dawn on 9 April German forces invaded Denmark and within four hours all resistance had ceased. In Norway, although the government refused to submit tamely, all seven ports and vital airfields were fairly easily captured within 24 hours.

For the next two months Anglo-French forces tried in vain to dislodge the Germans from their strongholds. From the start the campaign was marred by disaster. Although the British fleet had received reports of strong German forces moving northwards through the Skagerrak, the admiralty, instead of attacking the troop transports, preferred to chase after German battle cruisers; the result was that the Germans landed and seized all their objectives with a minimum of interference from the British. Nor did the navy retrieve the situation later by blockading the Skagerrak and cutting off supplies to the Germans in Norway, their argument being that a blockade would expose them to aerial bombardment. In addition, the Anglo-French forces were unprepared for opposed landings and unused to the severe winter conditions. And the unchallenged air supremacy enjoyed by the Germans proved a decisive weapon: operating from captured airfields and in greater numbers than their opponents could muster, the *Luftwaffe* pounded the Anglo-French forces relentlessly. An appalling lack of co-ordination between army and navy and an absence of any clear plan aggravated matters. Churchill wanted to concentrate on the capture of Narvik but the war cabinet opted for an attack on the port of Trondheim in central Norway. At first the plan was to land at Namsos and Aandalsnes, small fishing villages north and south of Trondheim, and attack the port directly. This was abandoned in favour of a wider encircling movement but bad weather conditions and *Luftwaffe* activity forced the British to evacuate their forces. Finally, an attempt was made to re-take Narvik. After much delay, due in part to disputes between army and naval command, the port eventually fell on 28 May. By then disaster had struck the Anglo-French forces in western Europe and on 8 June the forces were hastily withdrawn. This sorry tale of mismanagement had one happy result: it provoked a revolt in the House of Commons which drove Chamberlain from office and brought Churchill to power on 10 May.

The Germans had won a famous victory. The iron-ore supply route was safe; the threat to the Baltic approaches removed; and the German navy had the port facilities and the *Luftwaffe* the air bases for an intensification of the war against

Britain. Only in one respect were the Germans seriously disadvantaged and this was not immediately apparent. On paper both sides had sustained considerable losses at sea; the Anglo-French forces lost one aircraft carrier, two light cruisers and nine destroyers compared with German losses of one heavy cruiser, two light cruisers and 10 destroyers. But the damage done to the German fleet was disproportionately much greater so that when Hitler had, reluctantly, to contemplate an amphibious operation against Britain in the summer of 1940 he discovered that the German navy could not now guarantee safe passage across the Channel for the invasion troops.

In the early hours of the day Churchill kissed hands and accepted the seals of office as the king's first minister, the Germans launched their long-awaited offensive in the west with simultaneous attacks on Holland, Belgium, Luxemburg and France. For the operation they had concentrated 141 divisions in the west leaving only 10 in the east thanks to the security afforded them by the Russo-German Pact. In the modified Plan Yellow the centre of gravity of the operation had been shifted. In the north facing Holland and Belgium were 26 infantry divisions and three armoured divisions in General Fedor von Bock's Army Group B. In the south facing the Maginot Line General von Leeb's Army Group C consisted of 17 divisions. But in the centre, where the main thrust was to come, General von Rundstedt had under his command 34 infantry, seven armoured and three motorized divisions.

On paper the opposing forces on the western front were fairly evenly balanced. France had 104 divisions facing the Germans and Britain now had 10 divisions in France which together with 22 Belgian and eight Dutch divisions made a total of 144 divisions facing 141 German divisions. In respect of armoured vehicles the balance slightly favoured the Anglo-French forces with 3,300 compared with 2,500 German. In fact, the balance was much less favourable than it looked. First, in terms of equipment. The Anglo-French forces were deficient in anti-tank and anti-aircraft defences; and although France had used the six months since the outbreak of war to create three armoured divisions these in no way equalled the 10 battle-hardened armoured divisions on the German side. Nor had the French learnt the lessons of the Polish campaign; the new divisions were in practice employed in an infantry-support role. In the air the Germans were distinctly superior. They had 4,000 aircraft including 1,220 fighters and 1,560 bombers compared with 1,400 French aircraft; and Britain had stationed only 450 of her 1,500 aircraft in France. As in Poland close liaison between the German airforce and the armoured divisions was to prove a winning combination.

Second, the Anglo-French forces laboured under the grave disadvantage faced by any defender awaiting an enemy attack. It was assumed (wrongly) that the Ardennes were impregnable and (rightly) that the Maginot Line would not be attacked so that the major German offensive was expected through Belgium. In that event the French and British planned to send their most mobile forces into Belgium to support the Belgian army and hold a line running from Namur to Antwerp. Although substantial forces remained behind the Maginot Line, the crucial hinge of the allied operation was the Sedan sector where a line of badly constructed fortifications was held by the French Second Army consisting of five infantry divisions, some cavalry, three artillery regiments and only three tank batallions spread out over a 50-mile front. Twenty-five divisions were held in reserve to stem a major advance but as it took four days to transport them, the Germans had broken through at Sedan before effective resistance could be offered.

The campaign opened with dramatic successes for the Germans in Holland and Belgium. In the first airborne operation of the war German paratroopers landed near Rotterdam in the early hours of 10 May and seized vital bridges across the Nieuwe and the Maas rivers. These were held until the Ninth armoured division had raced 100 miles across eastern Holland to join them on 13 May. A secondary attack on the Hague was not, however, successful. When the Dutch commander refused to surrender Rotterdam on 14 May the city centre was destroyed in a savage aerial bombardment, an action which deeply impressed the Dutch. As the Seventh French Army failed to link up with the Dutch, being easily beaten back by the Germans, the Dutch surrendered on 15 May.

The campaign in Belgium started equally dramatically. The Belgians were relying on a line of fortifications along the Albert canal and the Maas river to delay the German advance. But in the early hours of 10 May in a brilliantly executed coup German paratroopers seized two of the three bridges across the canal and put out of action Eben Emaël, a modern fortification dominating the countryside. By 11 May two armoured divisions were over the bridges and fanning out over the plain, forcing the Belgians to fall back to the Namur–Antwerp line where the Anglo-French forces had arrived as planned.

Meanwhile von Rundstedt's Army Group had moved through Luxemburg and crossed the French frontier. On 12 May forward units were on the banks of the Meuse. On 13 May, under cover of devastating air attacks on the French positions, armoured infantry units crossed the river and established a bridgehead on the other side. By the evening of 14 May all Rundstedt's armour was over the river much to the surprise of the French. Now at last it dawned on them that they fallen into a trap; their most mobile units, which had advanced into Belgium with all speed, found their rear suddenly exposed to attack.

It should be remembered, however, that the crossing of the Meuse was a touch-and-go operation. Those German soldiers who believed in the armoured division as a campaign-winning weapon had a hard time struggling against the exponents of the traditional view of the tank as an infantry-support weapon. And had the traditionalists won and forced the armour to wait for the infantry, the French might well have succeeded in regrouping their forces and offering stiffer resistance to further German advances. The struggle started on 15 May when General Ewald von Kleist, who was in overall command of the armour, ordered the advance to halt until the infantry had consolidated the bridgehead. It was Guderian, the tank enthusiast now commanding three armoured divisions, who persuaded his superior to allow his advance to continue. By 16 May Guderian had advanced 50 miles. Once again caution got the upper hand, this time at a higher level still. Although Hitler had been one of the first to recognize the potential of armour, in the battle situation he was on the side of caution. Fearing that a too rapid advance would expose them to flank attacks – a view shared by General Wilhelm Keitel, chief of Armed Forces High Command, and by his deputy Colonel Alfred Jodl – he ordered the advance to halt for two days to allow the infantry to catch up. Guderian protested and in the end was given permission to continue 'strong reconnaissance' which enabled him to maintain the pressure on the enemy and race for the Channel coast. On 20 May he reached Abbeville. Hitler, who had spent his time vehemently denouncing the army for reckless conduct certain to ruin Plan Yellow, was now full of praise for what his generals had achieved. Not without justification a military historian said of this crucial contest of wills: 'Guderian and his tank men pulled the German army along after them and thereby produced the most sweeping victory in modern history'.[1]

The importance which the action of individuals in battle situations can have on the outcome of an entire campaign is illustrated once again by the episode of the Dunkirk evacuation. After cutting the supply lines of the Anglo-French forces in Belgium, Rundstedt's armour swung northwards in a bid to seize the Channel ports. On 21 May two British divisions, supported by one tank brigade, tried to break out of the trap closing on them and join up with the French armies in the south. The attempt failed and now under increasing pressure from Bock's forces which had broken through the Belgian defences and were advancing to the coast, the British Expeditionary Force fell back on Dunkirk. On 24 May Rundstedt's armour had reached the commanding heights along a line of canals 10 miles from Dunkirk when it was suddenly ordered to halt. Why? For a variety of reasons. Feeble though the British counter-attack at Arras was, Hitler and Rundstedt feared that further attacks on the German flank were likely; they also feared heavy losses if tanks were committed in the difficult terrain around Dunkirk; and this would be disastrous when the armour was needed to deal with 65 French divisions still in the field, from whom fierce resistance was anticipated. Possibly Goering's boast that the *Luftwaffe* could finish off the British carried some weight with Hitler. There is certainly no evidence that Hitler wished to spare the British, a legend still revived from time to time, most recently in the forged Hitler 'diaries'. On the contrary; a resounding defeat for the British at Dunkirk would increase the chances of them capitulating. What the Germans did not at first realize was that the British were preparing to evacuate their forces. By the time the order was countermanded on 26 May – Halder having convinced Hitler that the infantry had caught up with the armour – the British had prepared some defences to cover the evacuation between 26 May and 2 June. Goering's proud boast quickly turned to ashes; bad weather impeded the *Luftwaffe*'s operation while British Spitfires took a heavy toll of the bombers when they did come over the beaches at Dunkirk. When the operation was broken off on 4 June 337,000 allied troops had escaped the German trap, a small victory but one which gave great encouragement to the British people in the dark days of June 1940.

The final stage of the campaign began on 5 June when the Germans launched a major offensive along a 400-mile front on the Somme and Aisne rivers which the French, now commanded by General Maxime Weygand, had not had time to defend properly. Not that there was much hope of delaying the

[1]B. H. Liddell Hart, *History of the Second World War* (London, 1970), p. 73.

Germans for long; the French had lost their best troops in Belgium; and the *Luftwaffe*, enjoying complete mastery of the skies, gave their opponents no respite. Within two days the Germans had crossed the Seine and the government left Paris. On 10 June Mussolini at last declared war – a formality Hitler ridiculed in private – though when the Duce launched his offensive 10 days later the French, weakened though they were, easily beat it off. But after 15 June effective resistance ceased. On 16 June the French cabinet decided to sue for an armistice. Reynaud resigned and the new cabinet led by Marshal Philippe Henri Pétain approached the Germans on 17 June. Four days later on 21 June the French delegation signed an armistice in the railway coach in the forest of Compiégne where the Germans had signed their armistice 22 years previously.

Germany had won a dazzling victory completely defeating her old enemy in less than 40 days. Even harsher terms might have been imposed on the French had Hitler not intervened in the negotiations. His handling of the French was governed by two factors. As he told Mussolini and Count Galeazzo Ciano, the Italian foreign secretary, in Munich on 18 June it was convenient and less costly to have a legal French government running the country on behalf of the Germans. For had the government left France and established itself overseas, perhaps in Britain, the chances of restoring peace in the west would have been greatly reduced in Hitler's opinion.

More important, by allowing this government its own area of jurisdiction it might be possible to prevent the French fleet being dispatched to Britain; if that happened, the British fleet would be doubled in size and the British surrender Hitler was hoping for would be much less likely. So in the end Hitler persuaded Mussolini to forego territorial claims on France for the time being. Under the terms of the armistice the Germans occupied three-fifths of France including the north and the whole coastline down to the Spanish frontier, placing them in a position to continue operations against Britain if need be. The remaining two-fifths remained under the control of the authoritarian-minded government of Marshal Pétain at Vichy. The Germans renounced all claim to the French fleet when peace was eventually negotiated with France but the bulk of it was to be put out of commission. Three days after the signature of the armistice the French signed a similar agreement with the Italians. But as the latter were virtually abandoned by Hitler to their own devices, they succeeded only in establishing a 50 km. demilitarized zone on the Franco-Italian frontier and made no significant territorial gains.

The German victory in the west had profound effects upon Russia, the United States and Japan. In the case of Russia it resulted in an acceleration of the policy she embarked upon immediately after the signature of the Russo-German Pact: the extension of Russian influence over neighbouring states, cashing the blank cheque Hitler had willingly signed in return for a free hand with Poland.

Stalin set about this task with characteristic single-mindedness. The day Russian troops entered Poland the campaign against the Baltic states got under way. With no hope of German support these states quickly knuckled under. On

28 September Estonia signed a mutual assistance pact with Soviet Russia, leasing her certain naval bases and airfields and allowing her to station troops in the country. Latvia signed a similar pact on 5 October and Lithuania on 10 October. By mid October with a minimum of unpleasantness Russia effectively controlled the Baltic coast from East Prussia to the Gulf of Finland. This ensured that the southern approaches to Leningrad could never again be used, as they had been during the Civil War, to threaten the city.

The Finns were less obliging largely because they assumed that Russia would hesitate to attack a country as well respected as Finland in the community of democratic nations. On 5 October Molotov bluntly informed them of Russia's demands: she must have a 30-year lease on Hango peninsula in south-west Finland in order to build a naval base and thus control both sides of the Gulf of Finland. Secondly, 2,700 square miles of the Karelian isthmus – on which a major defensive barrier, the famous Mannerheim Line, stood – must be handed over together with five islands in the Gulf of Finland, to remove for ever the danger of an artillery bombardment of Leningrad by hostile powers operating on Finnish soil. In return Russia offered to cede some territory to Finland in the far north. Thirdly, the Finnish–Russian frontier must be demilitarized and all fortifications demolished. The Finns were disinclined to give way even though when they appealed to their traditional friend Germany Hitler made it crystal clear that he was not prepared to help them; indeed he underlined German lack of interest on 6 October when he reversed previous policy and announced that all Germans in the Baltic region would be repatriated. By early November relations between Finland and Russia were deteriorating. Russia, probably quite surprised to find that threats had not brought the Finns to heel, remained determined to have her way. On 26 November after a minor frontier incident led to Russian casualties Molotov demanded the withdrawal of Finnish troops from the Karelian isthmus. Finland refused to comply unless Soviet troops also withdrew, whereupon Molotov broke off relations with Finland. On 30 November Red Army units crossed the Finnish frontier and Soviet aircraft bombed Finnish cities. Technically Russia maintained that she was not at war but merely supporting the new 'People's Government of Finland' formed in Moscow by the Finnish communist Otto Kuusinen; in Russian eyes it had replaced the Helsinki government and had, most obligingly, signed an agreement with Russia conceding all the points at issue. When the Finns appealed to the League of Nations Russia stuck blandly to the story that she was not at war with Finland. When they were expelled from the League in December for this act of aggression the Russians dismissed the League as a weapon of the Anglo-French military bloc whose aim was the extension of the war.

After initial setbacks – which led the outside world to underrate Russian military power – the tide turned in favour of the Russians. A reorganized and reinforced Russian army of 45 divisions well equipped with tanks and artillery broke through the Mannerheim Line in February. Significantly Stalin did not exploit the victory to impose even harsher terms on Finland. He was probably anxious to end the war fearing that Britain and France would come to the aid of the Finns, and that if the war dragged on Russia would miss her opportunity to advance her interests in the Balkans. Germany, also anxious to avoid Anglo-

French intervention, was urging Finland behind the scenes to make peace. And as Norway and Sweden refused to allow foreign troops through their territory, Finland could not avail herself of western offers of aid. Therefore on 12 March she made peace. This represented a considerable victory for Soviet Russia; she abandoned the Kuusinen government unceremoniously but the Finns met her demands in respect of Hango and the Karelian isthmus, a shift in the balance of power which left Russia in complete command of the Gulf of Finland.

However reprehensible the bullying methods Russia employed to attain her objectives, in the light of past history and the growing might of Nazi Germany she had legitimate reasons for concern about the security of her Baltic frontiers, and acted no differently from many great powers over the centuries in seizing a favourable opportunity to strengthen her defences at the expense of weak neighbours.

That Russia must strengthen her defences still further was the lesson Stalin drew from the German victory in the west. The assumption that the imperialist powers would destroy themselves in a war of attrition had been completely exploded. France had fallen and Germany was dominant in Europe, a shift in the balance of power which increased the danger to Soviet Russia from which the Russo-German Pact had temporarily freed her. The approaches to Moscow and Leningrad had been secured already. But the wheat of the Ukraine and the oil of the Caucasus remained vulnerable to attack. To compensate for this strategic weakness Russia had far-reaching plans to establish herself in south-eastern Europe; via Bulgaria she aimed ultimately at controlling the passage through the Straits into the Black Sea, an old Russian ambition going back to the days of Catherine the Great. As a first step Russia started to press her claim to Bessarabia, the province Rumania took from Russia in 1918, through which the Danube flowed into the Black Sea.

Unhappy Rumania found herself squeezed three ways: between the Germans determined to secure control of her oil; the Magyars seeking to recover Transylvania; and the Russians out to recover Bessarabia in accordance with the terms of the Russo-German Pact. On 23 June, the day after the French signed the armistice in the west, Molotov informed the German ambassador that the Bessarabian question must be settled forthwith; at the same time he laid claim to Bukowina. When the Germans resisted this claim, Molotov back-tracked and left the non-Ukrainian south of Bukowina to the Rumanians. On 26 June Russia demanded that all Rumanian forces be withdrawn from Bessarabia and northern Bukowina within 48 hours. The Germans and Italians urged Rumania to comply with the ultimatum which she did at once. Soviet troops promptly moved in and early in August the 3,500,000 million Ukrainians became part of Soviet Russia.

Simultaneously Russia tightened the screws on the helpless Baltic states. At the end of May Molotov accused Lithuania of negligence in not investigating a trivial incident concerning the disappearance of two Soviet soldiers in Lithuania. A few days later he added a fresh charge: Lithuania was violating her pact with Russia by maintaining a military agreement with Estonia and Latvia dating back to 1923. On 14 June Lithuania was ordered to form a new government acceptable to Russia, and approve an increase in the size of the Soviet forces stationed in the country. The next day Lithuania capitulated, the government resigned and Russian tanks rolled into Lithuanian cities. On 16 June similar 24-hour ultimatums were sent to Estonia and Latvia and accepted by them with alacrity. Soviet forces now moved in strength into the three states. New left-wing governments were formed under the supervision of high Russian officials. Although no communists were at first included in these governments – a technique employed extensively by the Russians in eastern Europe after the end of the Second World War – party members were appointed to key posts in the administration, and press and broadcasting came under Russian control.

By the end of June Russia was ready to assimilate these states completely. The parliaments were dissolved and fresh elections held. Only communist candidates were allowed and were returned predictably with overwhelming majorities. The new assemblies announced the nationalization of land, banks and large-scale enterprises. On 21 July they requested admission to the USSR. Early in August all three became constituent republics of Soviet Russia along with Bessarabia and northern Bukowina. As in Poland, the secret police went to work rounding up political opponents. By 1941 over 100,000 had been deported from the Baltic countries and possibly as many as 200,000 from the former Rumanian territories.

While strategic considerations clearly loomed large in Russian calculations in 1939–40, this may not be the whole story. In Molotov's speech to the Supreme Soviet on 1 August there were hints of something else: a reawakening of the old imperialist ambitions slumbering beneath the surface in respect of Bessarabia and the Baltic. 'It should be noted', he remarked with obvious pride, 'that nineteen-twentieths of this population previously formed part of the population of Soviet Russia, but was forcibly torn from her by the western imperialist powers at a time when Russia was militarily weak. . . . The fact that the frontier of the Soviet Union will be shifted to the Baltic coast is of first-rate importance for our country. At the same time we shall have ice-free ports in the Baltic of which we stand so much in need'.[2]

We turn now to the United States. Although the attack on Norway and Denmark aroused sympathy for the latest victims of Nazi aggression, it failed to stir the American people. Roosevelt condemned these new acts of aggression; more than doubled the size of the combat zone round the British Isles by extending it to the north and west of the Norwegian coastline and into the Arctic Ocean 200 miles east of Murmansk; and froze Norwegian and Danish funds in the United States.

However, the subject preoccupying the administration in the spring of 1940 was not Nazi aggression but anxiety about a possible British or Canadian occupation of Iceland and Greenland to prevent enemy moves in that direction. In fact, the United States recognized the inevitability of the occupation of Iceland by British forces on 10 May 1940 in view of its proximity to the British Isles. Greenland was a different proposition being part of the American hemisphere and subject to the Monroe Doctrine. Roosevelt and Hull spent much

[2]Jane Degras, *Soviet Documents on Foreign Policy* (Oxford, 1953) III, pp. 463–4.

time and effort persuading Britain and Canada not to occupy Greenland whilst avoiding any suggestion of an American occupation certain to arouse the fury of the isolationists.

But the attack in the west had a cataclysmic effect on the American people. Hitherto Americans assumed that the conflict in Europe would be long drawn-out, that the democracies would survive and with American aid would tip the balance against Germany. This mood of complacency extended to the War Department as the low level of defence spending in the winter of 1939–40 indicates. In January Roosevelt asked Congress for the modest sum of $2 billion but still too large for that body, which spent months trying to reduce the appropriation. The world of illusion was only shattered in May 1940 by the rapid advance of German armour through France. At last the mass of the American people – even in the isolationist Mid-West – began to appreciate what a German victory would mean: without the French army and the British fleet to protect them the security of their own country would be seriously at risk.

Roosevelt responded promptly to the mood of near panic which gripped the country. On 16 May he proposed a massive build up of America's defences; within two weeks Congress had voted $1,500 million for this purpose. And as the crisis deepened at the end of May, the Navy Board demanded a fleet strong enough to dominate both Pacific and Atlantic. In June Congress voted another $1,000 million and in September a further $4,848 million to provide for a two-ocean navy as well as equipment for an army of 1,200,000 men and 9,000 additional planes for the airforce.

American strategy was radically modified by events in Europe. Of the five Rainbow Plans worked out in the spring of 1939 to deal with the emergence of the Rome–Berlin–Tokyo axis, Rainbow Two had up to now been the navy's favourite. This plan assumed that war with Japan was still the most likely eventuality. But in the event of a Japanese thrust towards the Dutch East Indies America hoped to avoid the costly naval battles envisaged under Plan Orange; instead of fighting across the Pacific from atoll to atoll the navy planned to strangle Japan painlessly by economic blockade. This strategy rested on an important premise: that while the United States concentrated on the Pacific, the British and French fleets would still be guarding the Atlantic as they had done for generations. It was the prospect of these navies passing under Axis control completely upsetting the balance of naval power in the Atlantic that brought about a radical reappraisal of American strategy. Forced to choose between two oceans, the naval authorities had to admit that the new strategic situation in the Atlantic posed the most serious threat to American security. When Roosevelt ordered the fleet to remain at Hawaii (where it had been on manoeuvres in April) as a deterrent to keep Japan at bay, the navy, once so anxious to fight in the Pacific, now clamoured for its return to base at San Diego. But Roosevelt insisted on keeping the fleet at Hawaii; whilst confrontation with Japan was far from his mind, he felt he had to assure the American people that the United States did not intend to abandon its interests in the Far East.

Safely re-elected, Roosevelt gave in to British pressure for joint military conversations in the near future. Before these could take place, however, it was essential to finalize American strategic priorities. Out of the reappraisal discussions in the autumn of 1940 emerged the famous Plan D memorandum. In it Admiral Harold R. Stark, chief of naval operations, came out firmly in support of the proposition that it was in the vital interests of the United States that Britain and her Empire survived. America's top priorities must be the defence of the Atlantic and the defeat of the Axis powers which, it was frankly admitted, would necessitate large-scale invasion of Europe. Although the possibility of a limited war in the Pacific could not be excluded, nevertheless, every effort must be made to avoid hostilities with Japan. Drafted initially by naval planning staff, the plan was endorsed by the army in December 1940. It was typical of the hesitancy with which Roosevelt approached major decisions that he avoided giving formal approval to the new strategy Rainbow Five worked out in the spring of 1941 on the basis of Plan D.

To return to the summer of 1940. As the situation deteriorated in early June, Roosevelt decided to speak out boldly. The news that Italy had attacked France despite America's strenuous efforts to keep her out of the war, reached him as he boarded the train for Charlottesville on 10 June and strengthened his resolve not to mince his words. In the course of the address at the University of Virginia Roosevelt roundly condemned the illusion that the United States could exist as 'a lone island in a world dominated by the philosophy of force'. Victory for 'the gods of force and hate' would endanger democracy in the western world and America's sympathies were, he emphasized, whole-heartedly on the side of those nations fighting these evil forces. There were two overriding priorities now for the United States: firstly, to give to the opponents of force 'the material resources of this nation' and, secondly, to speed up America's own defence preparations.[3]

The Charlottesville speech, though it contained nothing new, is often regarded as a turning-point on the road to armed intervention in the war. It was at least a half-turn. Roosevelt did all he could to keep the fighting going in the west; in June 1940 140 bombers, 900 field guns, 80,000 machine guns and 250,000 rifles were sold to Britain despite State and War Department advice that American defence must have priority. The appointment on 20 June of Stimson as secretary of war and Knox as secretary of the navy was a further sign that Roosevelt had the bit firmly between his teeth. But, of course, there were limits beyond which Roosevelt could not and would not go. When Reynaud appealed on 10 and 14 June for direct military intervention as well as for accelerated arms deliveries Roosevelt predictably refused to commit American troops to an overseas campaign for which the United States was, in any event, totally unprepared.

Then momentarily he seems to have wavered in his enthusiasm for aiding Britain. For a few weeks after the fall of France much less assistance reached her. Several factors conspired together to counsel caution. American military chiefs did not rate the chances of British survival highly; Roosevelt personally put it at no higher than a one-in-three chance. Secondly, he knew that the British cabinet had discussed the possibility of a negotiated peace on

---

[3] S. Rosenman, ed., *The Public Papers and Private Addresses of Franklin D. Roosevelt* (New York, 1938–50) IX, pp. 261, 264.

26 and 27 May.[4] Thirdly, this pessimistic prognosis of Britain's future strengthened the hands of Army Chief of Staff General George Marshall and Admiral Stark in insisting that top priority must be given to American rearmament. Fourthly, isolationism was still a powerful force even in the summer of 1940; on 28 June the Senate Foreign Relations Committee had voted to forbid the sale of weapons unless the chief of staff or chief of naval operations declared them surplus to requirement, a step which tied Roosevelt's hands to some extent. Fifthly, the fact that he would be fighting a tough election campaign in the autumn in a bid for an unprecedented third term as president made him scrutinize his every action with great care; any suggestion that he was throwing good money after bad in aiding a doomed country was certain to rebound to his discredit.

His response to Churchill's request for 40 to 50 over-age destroyers to protect British sea lanes across the Atlantic and patrol the British coastline reveals something of the fluctuation in his attitude between May and September. When the request was made on 16 May Roosevelt was anxious to do all he could to accommodate Churchill but was perplexed by the legality of such a transfer requiring, as he then thought, Congressional approval which he did not want to ask for. However, by the time Churchill repeated his request in mid June with France on the point of collapse Roosevelt was much less willing and resisted strong appeals from Morgenthau, Stimson and Knox.[5]

But when Churchill's third request arrived on 31 July Roosevelt had largely resolved his doubts. Two events restored his faith in Britain. The first was the British attack on the French naval forces at the North African base of Mers-el-Kebir on 3 July. Under the terms of the Franco-German armistice all French vessels had to proceed to French metropolitan ports to be disarmed under German and Italian supervision. Despite Germany's solemn promise not to use them in the course of the war, Britain feared the worst and decided on direct action to prevent them sailing to France. French ships in British ports and at Alexandria were seized without difficulty. When the naval forces at Mers-el-Kebir refused to surrender British vessels opened fire and sank two battleships, two destroyers and an aircraft carrier at a cost of 1,000 French lives. After that Roosevelt no longer doubted the determination of Britain to fight on.[6] The second event strengthening his newly restored faith was Halifax's brusque dismissal of Hitler's peace offer made on 19 July.

On 19 July in his acceptance speech as Democratic candidate for the presidential race Roosevelt completed the turn he had commenced at Charlottesville. To stiffen Britain's resolve in the face of Hitler's latest peace

---

[4]At the end of May a majority of the cabinet including Churchill was ready to consider any terms Germany might offer. However, they agreed that they must not approach the Germans and ask for terms as this would be construed as a sign of weakness. Their hope was that Hitler would realize he could not beat Britain and offer her peace on reasonable terms: D. Reynolds, *The Creation of the Anglo-American Alliance 1937–1941. A Study in Comparative Co-operation* (London, 1981), p. 104.

[5]On 4 June he told Ickes that destroyers would be of little use to Britain but would enrage Hitler: 'We cannot tell the turn the war will take and there is no use endangering ourselves until we can achieve some results for the allies': Harold L. Ickes, *The Secret Diary of Harold L. Ickes* (New York, 1953–4) III, pp. 199–200.

[6]Roosevelt told Lord Lothian on 1 July that American opinion expected Britain to seize the French vessels rather than let them fall into German hands and that he personally would do all he could to help bring this about: Reynolds, *Anglo-American Alliance*, p. 119.

offer he launched a vehement root-and-branch attack on totalitarianism. By the beginning of August he had overcome whatever doubts he had had and was ready to reply positively to Churchill's appeal for destroyers. A number of factors came together to clinch the decision. Hitler's invasion of Britain had still not taken place and the British were holding their own in the Battle of Britain; American opinion was now strongly in favour of the destroyers' transfer thanks to the strenuous efforts of the newly formed Committee to Defend America by Aiding the Allies; the reluctance of his Republican opponent in the presidential race, Wendell Willkie, to exploit the issue; the declaration of Admiral Stark that the destroyers were surplus to requirements because of corresponding gains in respect of the bases that Britain was prepared to lease; the view of the legal experts that the transfer could be authorized by executive action and did not, after all, need Congressional approval; the happy suggestion of the Committee to Defend America that Britain allow the United States to build naval and air bases on certain British Caribbean islands as a quid pro quo; and British acceptance of this as well as the promise that Britain would neither scuttle nor surrender her fleet – an assurance to which Roosevelt attached great importance.

On 3 September Roosevelt announced the deal to Congress. Britain was giving the United States 99-year leases on eight British territories in the western hemisphere on which the United States would construct bases. In return 50 over-age destroyers would be handed over to Britain. Roosevelt's fears that he might overreach himself in an election year proved groundless. The deed was immensely popular partly because it offered Britain help she desperately needed but mainly because the acquisition of bases on exceptionally favourable terms greatly enhanced the security of the United States at a critical moment.[7]

In one respect his caution was justified; after the destroyers deal it was no longer possible to pretend that the United States was a neutral power. Churchill had no doubt that it was 'a decidedly unneutral act' and welcomed the implication that the British Empire and the United States would become 'somewhat mixed up together in some of their affairs for mutual and general advantage', a prospect which naturally afforded him great satisfaction.[8] Predictably the Axis powers denounced the deal as a hostile act although Hitler and Mussolini continued to handle the Americans with kid gloves. Without doubt the acquisition of bases, the assurance about the British fleet and the Ogdensburg Agreement taken together did reassure the United States.[9] All the same, she had abandoned her neutral status and by moving to the uncertain category of non-belligerent was taking a giant step towards eventual involvement in the war, though such was not the intention of people or president.

[7]One hostile senator explained succinctly why the Destroyers Deal could not be successfully opposed: 'If you jump on the destroyer transfer you're jumping on the acquisition of defence bases in the Western Hemisphere. And the voters wouldn't stand for that. Roosevelt outsmarted us all when he tied up the two deals'. Quoted in W. L. Langer and S. Everett Gleason, *The Challenge to Isolation 1937–1940* (New York, 1952) p. 772.

[8]W. S. Churchill, *The Second World War*. II: *Their Finest Hour* (London, 1949), pp. 358, 362.

[9]On 18 August the American president and the Canadian prime minister agreed to joint studies of the defence of the northern hemisphere by air, sea and land. In November they agreed that each would grant the other facilities for the building of ships.

By the summer of 1940 the cabinet headed by Yonai Mitsumasa had fallen between two stools exactly like its predecessor. It had not succeeded in ending the China incident. All attempts to force Chiang Kai-shek to make peace had failed. So pessimistic had Japan's military leaders become that on the very day the puppet Nanking government was set up in March 1940, a conference of senior army and general staff officers concluded that, if no settlement was arrived at by the end of 1940, all Japanese troops would have to be withdrawn from China by 1943 leaving only token forces in north China, Mongolia-Sinkiang and near Shanghai. And as the Wang Ching-wei regime was contemptuously dismissed by the Americans as a Japanese puppet, hopes of improved relations with the United States – Yonai's second objective – were also dashed.

At the same time there was a growing belief in Tokyo, by no means confined to right-wing radicals and army circles, that Japan would be forced to take action in the near future to alleviate the mounting economic pressure being exerted upon her by the United States. The obvious alternative source of supply was the Dutch East Indies with its oil, rubber, tin, bauxite, manganese and nickel. In Washington fears began to mount that Japan intended to seize the area, a matter of economic as well as strategic concern to the Americans who imported 80 per cent of their rubber and tin from the Dutch East Indies. Nevertheless, the United States still adhered to her middle-of-the-road policy pleasing neither to 'hawks' nor 'doves'. President and State Department refused to impose an embargo on Japanese trade fearing that this would most likely stampede the Japanese into attacking the Dutch East Indies. But the Americans still kept dangling the threat of an embargo in front of the Japanese in the vain hope of intimidating them. As an additional deterrent Roosevelt, as noted already, sent the fleet on manoeuvres in April 1940 to Hawaii and despite Japanese annoyance insisted on keeping it there.

The German victory in the west transformed the Far Eastern situation. As France and the Low Countries went down to defeat and Britain fought for her life, the balance of power swung dramatically in favour of Japan. Not surprisingly the Yonai government came under increasing pressure to exploit this new situation and establish Japan as the dominant power in the Pacific at the expense of the defeated white powers.

However, the government had no intention of attacking Britain and the United States, though encouraged by the Germans to do so. Yet it dare not do nothing and in a desperate bid to hold on to power decided to try to take the wind out of its opponents' sails by some bold stroke of policy. In June Foreign Minister Arita demanded that Britain close the Burma Road and withdraw her troops from Shanghai, and that France close the frontier between Indo-China and China. These moves would, it was hoped, cut off supplies from Chiang Kai-shek and force him to seek peace. The western powers turned to the United States for help. Under Churchill appeasement was out of fashion in London. The British government asked the Americans either to impose an embargo on Japanese trade and so force Tokyo's hand, or else, in view of the heavy British commitment in home waters and in the Mediterranean, to send naval forces to Singapore even if it led to war with Japan. These were the preferred hawkish solutions. A less desirable but logical alternative would be an American initiative to restore peace between China and Japan at the cost of substantial concessions to the latter.

The American response was entirely negative and irresponsibly high-minded. America refused to send naval forces to Singapore arguing, rightly, that this did not make strategic sense in view of the overriding priority of the Atlantic theatre of war. Yet she was not prepared to appease Japan, believing this would only encourage further demands. She refused point blank to mediate in the Sino-Japanese War. While not objecting to British mediation, charac-teristically she refused to approve any peace not based on her own immutable principles which, of course, doomed all peace talks to inevitable failure. Washington agreed that Britain had little alternative but to acquiesce in local setbacks but still insisted that she keep her hands unstained morally and care-fully avoid initiatives likely to amount to approval of Japanese aggression. Denied American help, Britain settled for the only practical alternative: in the Anglo-Japanese Agreement of 18 July 1940 she agreed to close the Burma Road for three months and help Japan commence negotiations with Chiang Kai-shek, a decision which aroused great displeasure in Washington.

The capitulation of Britain and France did not save the Yonai government. On 18 July a new Konoe government came to power with General Tōjō Hideki, the former chief of staff of the Kwantung Army, as war minister; Yoshida Zengo as navy minister; and Matsuoka Yōsuke, a strong-minded and belligerent diplomat who led Japan out of the League of Nations in 1933, as foreign minister.

The second Konoe cabinet represented the triumph of the military over the civilians. Its actions mirrored faithfully the mood of extremism now gripping the articulate sections of public opinion. The political parties were to be dis-solved, Konoe announced, because their conflicting philosophies distracted the people from their overriding duty of loyalty to the emperor. The parties obedi-ently dissolved themselves at his behest; so much for what was left of parlia-mentary government. By October they had been replaced by the so-called Union for the Support of the Imperial Throne, a nationalist organization chaired by Konoe and designed to mobilize support for government policy and stamp out 'subversion'. Radical educational reforms were promised to create a new generation totally dedicated to the service of the Japanese empire. So that Japan could 'seize the inevitable trends of these world historical developments' a national defence state would be established with a planned economy at its core to maximize arms production. On 26 July Konoe confirmed that the first steps towards the realization of Japanese objectives would be the creation of a New Order in Greater East Asia founded on close co-operation between Japan, China and Manchukuo. The same day Matsuoka, commenting at a press conference on Japanese objectives coined the phrase 'Greater East Asia Co-Prosperity Sphere', which for him included not only Japan, Manchukuo and China but also French Indo-China, the Dutch East Indies, Malaya, Burma, Borneo, India and Siam.

Another sign of the dominance of the military was the setting up of the Liaison Conference. At the meetings of this unofficial body for which there was no place in the constitution, the three civilian members – prime minister, foreign minister and president of the council – were outnumbered by the military men who included the ministers of war and navy, the chiefs of staff and their assistants – the latter from the influential middle echelons of the services where policy was really made. This device in theory guaranteed the dominance of military thinking over the civilian cabinet; if the civilians still possessed some freedom of manoeuvre this was only because army and navy were not yet finally agreed about the direction in which Japan should move.

It was the Liaison Conference which decided on 27 July on the immediate tactics. First of all, a determined attempt must be made to settle the China incident. To cut Chiang Kai-shek's supply lines Japan would pressurize French Indo-China into handing over bases. In the hope of weakening Nationalist China still further Japan would try to settle her differences with Russia. At the same time Japan would seek closer relations with Germany and Italy to strengthen her international standing. To obtain the raw materials Japan could not do without, diplomatic pressure would be exerted on the Dutch East Indies. However, when the China incident was ended – or even if it was not settled but should very favourable conditions obtain – Japan would use force to 'solve the southern problem'. Efforts would be made to limit any conflict to Britain alone but as the United States might be drawn in, military preparations would have to be made to meet that eventuality also.

These decisions leave no doubt that Konoe and his colleagues intended to break decisively with the temporizing policy of the Yonai government, and seize the golden opportunity presented by the defeat of the French and Dutch. Nevertheless, this was not a decision for war. Konoe still hoped that the Americans could be dissuaded from taking military action while Japan took over the mantle of the white powers in east Asia. The alliance with the Axis powers in September 1940 and the Neutrality Pact with Russia in March 1941 were not preparations for conflict in the Pacific but rather weapons of diplomatic coercion designed to avoid war if at all possible. Furthermore, despite the decisions of 27 July the military policy-makers were still not in complete agreement about the direction in which Japan should expand. The army was anxious to end the China incident as quickly as possible in order to concentrate on protecting the northern frontiers against what it regarded as the main enemy: Russia. For that reason army leaders insisted that the pact with the Axis powers, of which they were the strongest advocates, must have an anti-Russian bias. So, while by no means opposed to an advance southwards – thought essential sooner or later to secure vital raw materials – for the army the 'southern problem' remained of secondary importance.

The strongest advocates of southern expansion were in naval circles, essentially for three reasons. To justify its own existence and to obtain a larger share of scarce resources, which went mostly to the army, the navy had found it expedient over the years to argue the case for the conquest of south-east Asia. Secondly, Dutch oil was of crucial importance for the navy – which switched to it from coal in the 1920s – but of much less significance to a largely unmechanized army. Finally, American naval expansion forced the hand of Japanese naval command; the Third Vinson Plan introduced into Congress in June 1940 envisaged the building of a two-ocean navy which would tip the balance of power decisively against Japan and put paid to any ambitions she might have. Yet, paradoxically, the navy chiefs were frightened of war with the

United States because they were convinced they could not win. Even middle-echelon officers, now gaining the upper hand in the formulation of policy and all distinctly pro-Axis in orientation, were anxious that Japan should not be automatically committed to war by a pact with Germany and Italy. Their influence was strong enough to ensure that before the Tripartite Pact was signed Germany conceded: first, that Japan should be given the former German colonies mandated to Japan after the First World War; and, second, that despite the terms of the pact Japan reserved the right to act independently in an emergency.

Relations between Germany and Japan had reached a nadir in the summer of 1939. But once France and Holland had been defeated, even the Yonai government was forced to approach the Germans, if only to establish whether they intended to take over Indo-China and the Dutch East Indies.

Ribbentrop, eager to construct a vast anti-British bloc including Japan and Russia, was quite prepared to write these colonial territories off. On 22 May he assured Japan that Germany was uninterested in the Dutch East Indies hoping to encourage Japan to seize them, which in its turn would lead to war with Britain and force Japan to come to terms with Germany. However, Hitler was at first utterly opposed to any alliance with the 'harvest helpers' as he contemptuously called them.[10] He abruptly rejected Japanese overtures for a free hand in the South Seas because he was certain of British capitulation in the near future and had no desire to advantage the Japanese at the expense of the British Empire. When it dawned on him in August that the British were not minded to surrender and that they could count on increasing material support from the United State – Churchill made the first public reference to the impending destroyers deal on 20 August – Hitler decided that he could use Japan after all as part of his peripheral strategy.

Towards the end of August he dispatched his plenipotentiary, Heinrich Stahmer, to Tokyo. Hitler's hope even at this late hour was that he could avoid the invasion of Britain, about which he had mounting reservations, and through a Japanese alliance pressurize Britain into surrender and keep the United States out of war. He may also have feared that Japan was seeking to come to terms with the United States, which, if it came off, would completely upset his global strategy. The negotiations led to a formal alliance, the Three Power Pact, signed on 27 September 1940. Under its terms Germany, Italy and Japan agreed to co-operate in establishing New Orders in Europe and Asia respectively. If one of the three powers was attacked 'either openly or in a concealed form' by a power not involved in the European war or in the Sino-Japanese war (i.e. the United States), they would assist one another with all political, economic and military means. Furthermore, Stahmer assured Japan that Germany would help bring the China incident to a close and would do all she could to facilitate a Russo-Japanese agreement – not only did Tokyo hope that this would isolate Chiang Kai-shek but it was thought likely by those favouring southward expansion to have an additional deterrent effect on the United States.

The Tripartite Pact was much less formidable than it looked. As a result of

[10] *Wilhelmstrasseprozess*, p. 7,472.

the navy pressure referred to above Matsuoka secured important modifications of the terms; the words 'undertake to declare war' were dropped from Ribbentrop's original formulation. And in a secret letter to Matsuoka the German ambassador, Eugen Ott, conceded that that there was no automatic military commitment by the signatories; whether an attack had occurred would be decided jointly by them. Ott and Stahmer did not in fact inform the Berlin government of this yawning lacuna in the pact.[11]

To recapitulate: Tokyo was convinced that, with no end to the China incident in sight and faced with mounting economic pressure from the United States, Japan's position was bound to worsen. If she was to exploit the developing situation in south-east Asia her last hope lay in an alliance with the Axis powers for which she intended to pay nothing in return. Completely oblivious to the likely reactions her policy would provoke, Japan supposed that the United States would be impressed by surface appearances and back down in the face of an imposing array of martial nations. Moderates hoped for at least the end of the war in China and improved relations with Soviet Russia. More optimistic policy-makers hoped that America would acquiesce in a new partition of the world leaving Japan in control of east Asia – from which the colonial powers would be completely excluded – and the United States in charge of the western Hemisphere.

The Japanese were quite wrong in their calculations. Unaware of the secret reservations, American opinion regarded the Tripartite Pact as proof positive that Japan had thrown in her lot with the predatory Axis powers and would now no longer hesitate to advance southwards in the near future. As a contemporary remarked: 'Japan's alliance with the Axis has done more than anything else could have done to convince Americans that the war in Europe and the war in Asia are the same war'.[12] Already displeased by the British decision to appease the Japanese over the Burma Road, Washington decided to give the economic screw another twist. On 25 July Roosevelt signed an order forbidding the export of aviation fuel and scrap metal to Japan.

The oil embargo issue led to another sharp clash between 'hawks' and 'doves' struggling as usual to control the person of the president. Early in July he had signed the National Defense Act which empowered him to restrict or prohibit the export of materials deemed vital for the defence of the nation. Roosevelt had at once imposed an embargo on many items hardly any of which seriously affected Japan. On 19 July Morgenthau, with the support of Stimson, Knox and Lord Lothian, the British ambassador, urged the president to impose a total embargo on oil exports to Japan in the hawkish belief that this would force the Japanese to back down. This view was firmly resisted by Sumner Welles temporarily in charge of the State Department in Hull's absence. Meanwhile Stimson informed Roosevelt of heavy Japanese purchases

[11]Ott maintained later that he regarded the concession as a strategem designed to help Matsuoka in his struggle against opposition in Japan but not as an alteration of the substance of the pact. Furthermore, he thought the pact nothing more than a propaganda device to keep the United States out of war: J.W. Morley, *Deterrent Diplomacy. Japan, Germany and the USSR 1935–1940* (Columbia, 1976), p. 189.

[12]Robert Aura Smith, 'The Triple-Axis Pact and American Reactions', in *Annals of the American Academy of Political and Social Science* CCXV (1941), p. 132.

of high-grade aviation fuel likely to create a shortage in America. On 22 July the president agreed to forbid the export of this item. Quite independently Morgenthau drafted a proclamation controlling the export of all petroleum products and sent it to the president for signature. When this proclamation – which Roosevelt signed – was passed over to the State Department Welles made sure that the president approved only the first order prohibiting the sale of high-grade fuel.

At the cabinet meeting on 26 July Morgenthau clashed sharply with Welles in front of the president. The latter, characteristically, 'raised his hands in the air; refused to participate in it and said that those two men must go off in a corner and settle this issue'.[13] Welles won the argument and the order issued on 26 July placed an embargo only on high-grade aviation fuel, lubricants and heavy iron and scrap metal. The embargo did little damage to Japan but it squared the political circle, satisfied Roosevelt's longing for tougher sanctions and went some way towards satisfying the public demand for action against Japan. But the risk of war was minimal as the ban affected only high-octane fuel of the type used by American aircraft; the Japanese simply switched to the purchase of middle-octane fuel which her aircraft could use.[14] Roosevelt was well aware of the true position but like Hull and Welles was firmly of the opinion that a total embargo would trigger off a Japanese invasion of the Dutch East Indies. That was why he resisted all the appeals of the 'hawks' over the next few months to extend the embargo to cover all fuel grades.

The Konoe government was not deterred by such half-measures from turning to the most immediate priority: ending the China incident so that Japan would be free to exploit the situation in east Asia. To achieve this objective Tokyo adopted three approaches.

First of all, Japan tried to tighten her military grip on China. On 1 August Matsuoka demanded that France give Japan bases in Tonkin province, allow Japanese troops the right of passage through Indo-China and enter into closer economic arrangements with Japan. By the end of the month France discovered, as Britain had before her, that the United States would not threaten Japan with military sanctions though perfectly willing to lambast the moral turpitude of the Tokyo government. On 22 September France agreed, in return for recognition of French sovereignty over Indo-China, to allow Japan the use of three airfields in Tonkin province, the right to station troops there and to allow free passage for Japanese troops through Tonkin province to attack the Chinese in Yunnan. A day later Japanese troops entered Tonkin.

Japanese pressure on Indo-China combined with the news of the impending signature of the Tripartite Pact convinced Roosevelt that further action was imperative. An additional reason was pressure from the American steel industry; as it commenced to expand, the price of scrap metal rose; rather than have government control of prices the industry preferred to steady domestic prices through a scrap embargo. On 19 September the president imposed a complete

[13]John Morton Blum, *From the Morgenthau Diaries: Years of Urgency 1938–1941* (Boston, 1965) I, p. 353.

[14]In August 1940 $21 million worth of petroleum products were exported to Japan, which exceeded total purchases from January to July. Similarly, as only the highest grades of scrap metal were embargoed, Japan continued to buy other grades.

embargo on the export of all iron and scrap metal. This was announced to the press on 24 September and took effect from 16 October.

At the cabinet discussion on 19 September 'hawks' and 'doves' clashed yet again. Morgenthau, Stimson and Ickes seized the opportunity to call for a comprehensive embargo including oil.[15] Hull and Welles with strong support from Admiral Stark and Admiral James O. Richardson, commander-in-chief of the United States fleet, argued that an oil embargo would only provoke a Japanese attack which the navy was in no position to contain. They may also have been impressed by the minatory comments of Konoe and Matsuoka that further sanctions could lead to war. And in the background the Dutch East Indies were also urging the Americans to avoid action likely to increase Japanese pressure on them. After the decision had been taken, Roosevelt made encouraging noises to conciliate the 'hawks'; in October he gave Stimson and Ickes the impression that if Japan took military action as a result of the re-opening of the Burma Road, he was contemplating a total trade embargo, and was even thinking of using naval patrols between Hawaii and the Dutch East Indies to intercept Japanese commercial vessels. In the end nothing came of either suggestion.

Konoe's second approach to the China incident was to try to cut off the aid Soviet Russia had been giving Chiang Kai-shek since 1937. Matsuoka put out feelers to Moscow in October for a non-aggression pact. Russia, preoccupied with the problem of deteriorating relations with Germany, and with Matsuoka's visit to Berlin imminent, was not inclined to let Japan off the hook lightly. Russia's terms were the return of south Sakhalin, cession of some of the Kurile islands and an adjustment of the Siberian–Manchurian border, a price unacceptable to Japan. By early December Russia made it clear that she would continue to aid Chiang Kai-shek, so this approach ground to a halt.

The third approach was the diametrically opposed one of trying to come to terms with Chiang Kai-shek. In November 1940 Japan dangled peace terms before him coupled with a warning that in the event of refusal, Tokyo would formally recognize the Nanking government. Ribbentrop intervened to add his weight to this warning. Desperate though Nationalist China's position was with the economy on the point of collapse and shortages of military supplies casting serious doubt on the Nationalists' ability to continue the struggle, Chiang Kai-shek refused terms which would have made China a Japanese satellite. In retaliation Japan formally recognized the Nanking government on 30 November 1940. This had precisely the opposite effect to that intended. Chiang Kai-shek curtly dismissed any thought of recognizing a puppet regime with no authority to speak for anyone in China. More serious for Japan was the increasing American commitment to Chiang Kai-shek. Since October negotiations for a large loan to the Nationalists had been proceeding without making much progress. At the end of November Roosevelt suddenly intervened and

---

[15]In a letter to Roosevelt on 17 October 1940 Ickes put the hawkish position succinctly: 'We didn't keep Japan out of Indo-China by continuing to ship scrap iron, nor will we keep Japan out of the Dutch East Indies by selling it our oil. When Japan thinks that it can safely move against the Dutch East Indies and is ready to do so, it will go in, regardless. It will make it all the more difficult for it to go in if it is short on oil and gasolene'. Quoted in W.L. Langer and S. Everett Gleason, *The Undeclared War 1940-1941* (New York, 1953), p. 35.

announced that Washington was considering a loan of $100 million, though it proved difficult in practice to supply China with arms and munitions. A further sign of American displeasure was Roosevelt's extension of the export licensing system; between December 1940 and February 1941 many more restrictions were placed on exports, including 'machine tools, refining machinery and certain chemicals and several metal products. In their totality these restrictions seriously affected the Japanese economy; by the spring of 1941 her industry was suffering from shortages of supplies, stockpiles were exhausted and the production of key items was being impeded.

By the end of 1940 the Konoe government's policy had run into'a cul-de-sac. The advantages confidently expected from the Tripartite Pact still eluded Japan. German pressure had not brought Chiang Kai-shek to heel nor had Ribbentrop been able to smooth the way for a Russo-Japanese accord. And far from intimidating the United States into abandoning China, precisely the reverse had happened; as the American commitment to Chiang Kai-shek grew, Japanese hopes of ending the China incident faded; and unless they could escape from the Chinese quagmire, a southward advance would be a risky undertaking. Finally, the United States had at last agreed to formal military conversations with Britain, 'the most eloquent and conclusive evidence' that Germany and Japan had miscalculated in supposing that the Tripartite Pact would deter the United States from supporting Britain.[16]

This is a convenient point at which to comment on these significant conversations which took place in Washington early in 1941. Ever since the outbreak of war in the Far East in 1937 American and British naval authorities had exchanged information and discussed strategic problems unofficially for it was assumed in naval circles in Washington and London that both powers would be involved in the event of war in the Far East. In August 1940 a three-man team arrived in London for the specific purpose of maintaining these informal contacts. One of the team, Rear Admiral Robert Ghormley, remained in London as special naval observer to continue the discussions into the autumn. Following the signature of the Tripartite Pact Churchill renewed a request for formal consultations, and with the presidential election behind him Roosevelt agreed.

From January to March 1941 a delegation of officers representing the British chiefs of staff conferred in secret in Washington with their American opposite numbers. Their remit was to determine how the armed forces of the United States and the British Commonwealth could defeat Germany and her allies and to co-ordinate military plans to this end. In their joint report ABC 1, on which the American plan Rainbow Five was based, Britain and the United States agreed that the main war effort must be made in the Atlantic and Mediterranean theatres. Even if war broke out in the Pacific – and it was hoped to avoid this – the Pacific theatre would still remain subordinate to the Atlantic and Mediterranean theatres. This was a victory for the Americans who successfully resisted strong British pressure for an increased American commitment in the Pacific, in particular for a reinforcement of the Asiatic Fleet or for the basing of that fleet at Singapore. The American military were simply not persuaded by the British argument that if Britain lost her south-east Asian possessions, her

[16]*Op. cit.*, p. 48.

military effort against Hitler would be seriously impaired. Nevertheless, should Britain go to war with Japan, the Americans promised to take offensive action in the Pacific to weaken Japanese economic power and would even launch a limited operation to help divert the Japanese from attacking Malaya.

The Americans compromised because a new global dimension was entering the picture in the winter of 1940-1: the belief that it was in American interests to prevent Japanese encroachments on British as well as on American possessions in the Far East. We have seen already how the United States drifted into a position where she was increasingly committed to defend China despite her limited military resources. Similarly, it became accepted doctrine in official circles in Washington that a British defeat in the Far East would be a defeat for America; if Japan seized Singapore or invaded Malaya she would be encouraged to commit fresh aggression and, most important of all, the ability of Britain to resist Hitler would be impaired – in other words, the civilians in the administration began to accept the argument rejected by the military about the vital importance of south-east Asia for the British war effort. Once again there seems to have been no serious examination of the proposition but a ready acceptance of the argument that the psychological effect of a local defeat in the Far East would be catastrophic for the British war effort. And, as American officials constantly drew the attention of their Japanese counterparts to the identity of interest between Britain and the United States, the Japanese concluded, not unreasonably, that an attack on the British would bring the Americans into the war.

Broadly speaking, Rainbow Five taken in conjunction with the Lease–Lend Agreement strengthened the ties between the Anglo-Saxon powers and drew the United States nearer to war. Precisely for that reason Roosevelt withheld his formal approval from ABC 1 and from Rainbow Five, hiding behind the argument that until the United States entered the war a joint strategy had no practical significance.[17] That did not alter the fact that consultation continued and preparations were being made for joint co-operation in wartime; 'a common-law alliance' with Britain had in effect come into being.[18]

We turn back to Europe now to consider the deterioration in Russo-German relations from the summer of 1940 onwards, a development which culminated a year later in the German attack on Russia, bringing into the hostilities one of the only two major powers with the potential to ensure that the war was fought to a finish and fascism totally destroyed.

Most historians attribute Hitler's decision to attack Russia almost entirely to his obsession with the destruction of 'Jewish bolshevism' and the acquisition of *Lebensraum* in the east. According to the neat-and-tidy interpretation all his actions from the re-occupation of the Rhineland to the attack on France were preparatory steps to the grand assault on 'Jewish bolshevik' Russia which he

[17]Roosevelt was in tune with public opinion. Although a clear majority favoured all possible aid to Britain, opinion polls in October 1941 revealed that 83 per cent were opposed to the United States entering the war.

[18]R. Sherwood, *Roosevelt and Hopkins. An Intimate History* (New York, 1948), p. 264.

had dreamed of since 1924; and all deviations from this programme, such as the Russo-German Pact, were purely tactical manoeuvres forced on him by circumstances and quickly repudiated as soon as practicable.

No one familiar with the structure of decision-making in the Third Reich would deny that Hitler's pathological hang-ups about Jewry were a major policy determinant; without the consent and active encouragement of Hitler the systematic extermination of European Jewry between 1942 and 1944 would have been quite inconceivable. Nevertheless, it is at least arguable that the evidence, such as it is, does not really permit the same degree of confidence about the primary of ideological commitment in the decision to attack Russia.

Hitler's references in the autumn of 1939 to the temporary nature of the pact and his reiterated belief that states only kept agreements as long as it suited them, though sometimes construed as evidence of long-term ambitions in the east, may have been intended only to reassure his deeply anti-bolshevik audience that he still knew what he was doing. On the other hand, his reference to eastern Poland as 'a military concentration point for the future' and his instruction that all roads and railways in the area be kept in good order is, admittedly, less easy to explain away.[19] But his remark to his commanders in November 1939 that only when Germany was free in the west could she 'oppose Russia' was less a proleptic hint of German policy than an argument *ad hominem* to overcome opposition to the impending campaign in the west for it is clear that he was perfectly satisfied with Russian behaviour at that time. And turning to the summer of 1940 one must remember that Hitler's oft-quoted remark during the western campaign to Rundstedt and General Georg von Sodenstern, chief of staff at Army Group B, that once England made peace he would concentrate on 'his real mission: the conflict with bolshevism' comes from an unreliable source.[20] Similarly, one must treat with caution Jodl's comment in 1943 that three years previously, again during the western campaign, Hitler told him of his 'fundamental decision' to take steps against this danger [i.e. from Russia] the moment our military position made it possible'.[21]

There is at least as much evidence that in the winter of 1939–40 Hitler's views on Russia were on the point of undergoing a metamorphosis as he started to revert to the opinions he expressed when he first entered politics in 1919 and before Rosenberg persuaded him that Russia in the grip of 'Jewish bolshevism' was the mortal foe of Germany. Even before the Russo-German Pact was signed there were signs that Hitler and Ribbentrop were beginning to think that Russia was abandoning her revolutionary aspirations in favour of old-style tsarist absolutism. In July Ribbentrop, in conversation with the Bulgarian minister president, remarked that changes were taking place within bolshevism

[19]*IMT* XXVI, 864-PS; cf. *KTB* Halder i, p. 107. But see also B. Stegemann, 'Hitlers Ziele im ersten Kriegsjahr 1939–1940', in *MGM* I/80, p. 96.

[20]K. Klee, *Das Unternehmen 'Seelöwe'. Die geplante Landung in England* (Göttingen, 1958), p. 189. Sodenstern did not reveal Hitler's comment until 1954 which casts doubt on its authenticity. According to another and even less reliable source 26 years after the event, Hitler is said to have remarked on 25 June that confrontation with the east was Germany's mission but this might not occur for 10 years and would probably be undertaken by his successor: H. Böhme, *Der deutsch-französische Waffenstillstand im Zweiten Weltkrieg* Teil I (Stuttgart, 1966), p. 79.

[21]*KTB OKW* IV, p. 1,540; *IMT* XXXVII, 172-L, p. 638.

the significance of which had yet to be assessed but that a normalization of relations with Russia might well be achieved. In August Hitler told the Hungarian foreign minister that Russia might be putting on 'a nationalist helmet'.[22] Her internationalism was receding into the background he told his military commanders in November. In March 1940 he assured Mussolini, who was greatly concerned about the new Russo-German friendship, that the 'Jewish international leadership' of Moscow had been the fundamental reason for Nazi opposition to Russia. If bolshevism was now changing over to a 'Russian state ideology' this was a reality which could not be ignored. And he reminded the Duce that Germany and Russia had 'often lived in peace and friendship for very long periods of time'.[23] Ribbentrop took up the same theme with the Duce two days later declaring even more emphatically that Stalin had abandoned the idea of world revolution. Since Litvinov's abrupt dismissal in May 1939 – an event which deeply impressed Hitler – there were no more Jews in Russia's central agencies; on the contrary, as Ribbentrop could confirm from personal experience, the Politburo was staffed by Muscovites with little interest in the outside world. A day later Ribbentrop told Pope Pius XII, a bitter opponent of communism, of the 'firm and lasting basis for a positive friendship' between Germany and Russia.[24] Finally, on 18 March at the Brenner meeting with Mussolini Hitler, while conceding that bitter necessity had forced Germany and Russia together and that bolshevism and National Socialism remained ideologically incompatible, still insisted that Russia was undergoing a great transformation. Jews were being forced out of the central administration and bolshevism 'had discarded its Muscovite–Jewish and international character and had assumed a Slavic–Muscovite character'.[25] Of course, one cannot overlook the distinct possibility that Hitler and Ribbentrop were deliberately concealing from the Italians their intention of escalating the war in the near future. On the other hand, at the very end of his days, with the Third Reich crashing about his ears in February 1945, a moment of truth if ever there was one, Hitler still maintained that for a year he had hoped that a durable 'if not unreservedly friendly' entente with Russia confined to economic collaboration would have been possible because he believed that Stalin 'would have rid himself of the nebulous Marxist ideology' largely because he had dealt so ruthlessly with the Jewish intelligentsia.[26] Whether this process of ideological reassessment would have continued had it not been for the dramatic events of the summer of 1940 we will never know. But the episode does at least cast some doubt on the belief that Hitler pursued the same old ideological objective relentlessly and without equivocation from 1939 to 1941.

On the whole it is quite likely that the initial impetus for the decision arose out of the changing Balkan situation. This is not to deny that Hitler's dream of *Lebensraum* at the expense of 'Jewish-bolshevik' Russia – possibly fading in the spring of 1940 – revived in the afterglow of victory in the west and quickly became intertwined with strategic necessity. But it is an odd coincidence, to say

[22]*DGFP* D V, no. 784, 8 August 1939.
[23]*DGEP* D VIII, no. 663, 8 March 1940.
[24]*Op. cit.*, no. 668, 11 March 1940.
[25]*DGFP* D IX, no. 1, 18 March 1940.
[26]F. Genoud, ed., *The Testament of Adolf Hitler* (London, 1959), p. 99.

the least, that Hitler began to think seriously of attacking Russia precisely when that power was bullying the Baltic states and forcing Rumania to hand over Bessarabia and north Bukowina.

It is not necessary to rely on the suspect testimony of Ribbentrop to arrive at this conclusion.[27] At the end of June Secretary of State Baron Ernst von Weizsäcker told Halder that Hitler, while expressing satisfaction that Russia had abandoned her claim to southern Bukowina, went on to say: 'Britain will probably need a further demonstration of strength before giving up and leaving our rear free for the east' – not necessarily evidence of a firm intention to seize *Lebensraum* but more likely an *ad hoc* response to a new situation which threatened Germany's strategic and economic interests in the Balkans.[28]

It is significant that army command, quite independently of Hitler, was concerned about the build-up of Soviet forces in southern Russia and was taking steps to deal with the situation: on 25 June Brauchitsch and Halder decided to increase the forces earmarked 10 days earlier for transfer to the east from 15 to 24 divisions with the addition of six armoured and three motorized divisions. Already on 3 July Halder instructed the operational planners at Army High Command to examine the problem of how best to deliver a blow at Russia to force her to recognize the dominant role of Germany in Europe.

By mid July a new factor entered the picture. On 19 July Roosevelt's speech convinced Hitler that by 1941 Britain would be receiving massive aid from the United States. And British radio broadcasts rejecting Hitler's peace offer on the same day confirmed him in his belief that she would not capitulate without further military action being taken. During the next two days he conferred with Keitel, Jodl and Brauchitsch, all of whom were deeply worried by Russian troop movements. On 21 July Hitler took the first step towards Operation Otto (as Barbarossa was originally called) when he ordered preliminary studies of the feasibility of an attack. The army was, of course, one step ahead of the Fúhrer this time, and when Brauchitsch informed Halder on 22 July the latter ordered his staff to begin work at once on an operational plan. If we are to believe Jodl, by the end of July Hitler's old sense of mission had surfaced again for on 29 July Jodl told his colleagues that Hitler had decided 'to rid the world of the danger of bolshevism by a surprise attack on the Soviet Union at the earliest possible moment'.[29]

All the more surprising, therefore, that when Hitler revealed his intention to a wider circle of senior officers at the Berghof on 31 July he defended his decision not in terms of ideological commitment but of global strategy. Possibly his knowledge that some officers had reservations explains his careful avoidance of ideological terminology. Yet his standing with the generals was at its zenith and he had no need to fear that a deeply anti-bolshevik officer corps would find his own fanaticism repugnant. This does suggest that global strategy was still the consideration uppermost in his mind.

At all events, his starting-point was the perverse refusal of Britain to admit

[27] Joachim von Ribbentrop, *The Ribbentrop Memoirs* (London, 1954), pp. 145–6.
[28] *KTB* Halder I, p. 375, 30 June 1940.
[29] W. Warlimont, *Im Hauptquartier der deutschen Wehrmacht. Grundlagen. Formen. Gestalten* (Frankfurt a.M., 1964), p. 216.

that the war was virtually over. To invade England – he had signed the order for Operation Sealion on 16 July – would be difficult. There was a less risky way of attaining the objective. Britain was still hoping to win over Russia as an ally and in addition would one day have the United States on her side so that, once again, time was not on Germany's side. But if Germany struck a sudden blow at Russia, all Britain's hopes would be dashed. Not only would she lose her last possible continental ally but the United States would then be less likely to intervene in Europe because she would have her hands full fending off an aggressive Japan which would not fear to advance southwards once Russia was neutralized. Those officers who had concluded on 30 July on the basis of more accurate information about Russian strength that, after all, it would be best to remain friends with Russia for the time being rather than risk a two-front war with Britain still undefeated, did not contradict Hitler. Now under the spell of 'the greatest commander of all time', as Keitel had dubbed him, and convinced that Russia was a long-term threat, they set to work with enthusiasm on the details of the operational plan to attack Russia in May 1941.

Before Hitler finally approved Operation Barbarossa in December 1940 he gave his support to the so-called peripheral strategy. As an attack on Russia had been ruled out as impracticable in 1940 and as it became clear that Britain would not surrender nor could she be invaded – by early September the *Luftwaffe* had lost the Battle of Britain – a strategic deadlock loomed up robbing Hitler of the political initiative. This gave Ribbentrop and Raeder an opportunity to advocate other strategies for bringing Britain to heel. Ribbentrop revived his old dream of a bloc stretching from Madrid to Yokohama which Russia would be invited to join; this would, he hoped, neutralize America leaving an isolated Britain with no choice but to come to terms with Germany. Raeder, on the other hand, pressed Hitler to agree to military action in the Mediterranean, Near East and North Africa to force Britain to surrender even at the risk of bringing America into the war.

That Hitler gave his support to the peripheral strategy and indeed played a prominent part in attempting to implement it from September to November 1940 raises an important question: did he believe it was a genuine alternative to the attack on Russia? Historians who believe in the primacy of Hitler's ideological obsessions maintain that he never wavered in his determination to destroy 'Jewish bolshevism' and could not, therefore, have had any faith in the alternative strategy. A minority believe just as strongly that he only decided finally to go ahead with Barbarossa when the peripheral strategy failed. More likely, Hitler simply kept his options open as long as possible. While keeping a watchful eye on the development of the military planning for Barbarossa, he went along with another strategy which if it succeeded against the odds in forcing Britain to her knees would have achieved one of his objectives.

It was the impact of the victory in the west on Japan that enabled Ribbentrop to win Hitler's support for the continental bloc project. Japan had swallowed her resentment of the Russo-German Pact and approached Germany to ascertain her attitude to the disposal of the French and Dutch colonial empires. Ribbentrop seized with alacrity this new opportunity of working for a Tripartite Pact. As explained earlier, once Hitler realized by September that a British surrender was unlikely he supported his foreign minister's efforts and at the end of the month the Tripartite Pact was signed.

Meanwhile Raeder had secured Hitler's approval for ambitious military measures to secure complete Axis control of the Mediterranean and drive the British out of the Near East. Gibraltar and Suez, the keys to the Mediterranean, would be seized, the former with Spanish assistance and the latter through a joint German–Italian offensive against Egypt. Germany would secure bases at Dakar, Casablanca and in the Azores from which to intensify the war in the Atlantic. And once in possession of Egypt the Germans would link up with the Italians in East Africa and also sweep through Palestine and Syria to the Turkish frontier. Britain could not, it was confidently supposed, survive these heavy blows and would have to sue for peace. By this time Germany would be in such a strong strategic position that she would have no need to fear American intervention in the war. To succeed, this strategy required the active co-operation of Spain, Vichy France and Italy.

In practice it proved impossible to secure their help. Fascist Spain had shown partiality for Nazi Germany long before the outbreak of war. When Italy plucked up courage to stab France in the back in June 1940, General Francisco Franco also overcame lingering doubts; he changed Spain's status to that of non-belligerent, made known in Berlin Spanish demands for Gibraltar and Morocco and promised to join in the war (with German equipment and supplies) if Britain continued to fight after the fall of France. At this stage Hitler remained non-commital having no desire to offend France by handing away her colonial empire, especially when the German foreign office and naval command were busily formulating – with Hitler's approval – extensive claims for colonial possessions in Africa. By mid September Goering's failure to establish air supremacy over the British Isles compelled Hitler to postpone Sealion until May 1941. Following this Hitler changed his mind. In October he sounded out Italy, Spain and Vichy France – for it now made strategic sense to seek to protect Germany's southern flank and forestall possible British action against French and Italian colonial territories. There was soon another reason; once Italy embarked upon her ill-timed attack on Greece at the end of October it was more necessary than ever to take all practicable steps to drive the British out of the Mediterranean and prevent them sending aid to the Greeks.

However, by the time Hitler approached Franco he found the Caudillo had grown circumspect; now that Britain was clearly determined to continue the war it occurred to him that intervention might well have disastrous consequences for his small and weak country. Hitler, too, had become cautious; having no high regard for Spanish military capabilities, he now felt that to promise specific French territories to Spain would only encourage more Frenchmen to rally to the standard raised by General Charles de Gaulle, leader of the Free French. The negotiations dragged on without much success until in December Franco finally refused to budge from his non-belligerent status and German plans for the seizure of Gibraltar (Operation Felix) effectively lapsed.

With France Hitler was no more successful. The Vichy government had to be handled with some care as it controlled the French fleet and as Morocco, Algeria and Tunisia had resisted the blandishment of de Gaulle and remained loyal to the metropolitan government. For a time Hitler and his advisers actually toyed with the idea of an alliance with Vichy France. But apart from a small group around Foreign Minister Pierre Laval, there was scant support for such a policy. Nor could Hitler help matters along with concessions to Vichy for fear of offending Italy and Spain. Conversations with Marshal Pétain on 24 October revealed that the head of state was not averse to collaboration with Germany but, as befitted an octogenarian, he was unwilling to take any positive steps. He, too, appreciated the significance of continued British resistance and had secretly promised London that he would not allow the Germans to have bases on French colonial soil.

Finally, once Mussolini was embroiled in Greece upsetting the status quo Hitler had been so anxious to preserve, the Führer lost what little interest he had in helping the Italians consolidate their colonial empire in North Africa. At a conference on 4 November the peripheral strategy was greatly modified. To help Mussolini whose troops were retreating ignominiously before the Greek forces, Hitler was obliged to order an attack on Greece to take place in the spring. Germany's military efforts would now be concentrated on this objective. For the time being the proposal to send an armoured division to Libya to join with the Italians in attacking Egypt and thrusting towards Suez and the Turkish frontier was shelved. And although Operation Felix was confirmed, it could not be carried out without Spanish aid which, as Hitler knew, was not forthcoming though he pretended that Franco would soon join in the war.

By now the Balkan situation was moving into the foreground. In a directive issued on 12 November Hitler referred to the Russian problem: 'Political discussions for the purpose of clarifying Russia's attitude in the immediate future have already begun. Regardless of the outcome of these conversations, all preparations for the east . . . . will be continued'.[30] What persuaded Hitler to make this approach to the Soviet Union which led to the famous confrontation with Molotov in Berlin in November?

Relations between Germany and Russia had been deteriorating since the high summer. Once Hitler made the provisional decision to attack Russia, the aim of German diplomacy was to give positive assistance to strategically important powers such as Rumania and Finland both for the prosecution of the war in general and to secure their military collaboration in the event of an attack on Russia.

After Rumania was forced to cede Bessarabia and northern Bukowina she sought frantically to ingratiate herself with Germany as insurance against the wrath to come from Hungary and Bulgaria, both eager to enforce claims for the return of their irredenta. But before Hitler would protect Rumania he insisted that she settle these claims fearing that otherwise Russia would begin to fish in troubled waters. Under pressure from Germany and Italy, thinly disguised as mediation, Rumania accepted the Second Vienna Award which obliged her to hand over half of Transylvania to Hungary and southern Dobruja to Bulgaria. In return the Axis powers guaranteed Rumania's new frontiers. When the strongly pro-German General Jon Antonescu, who ousted King Carol from power early in September with the aid of the Iron Guard, the indigenous fascist party, asked Hitler to send a military mission to Bucharest, he complied. Not only was it essential to protect the oil-fields on which Germany was increasingly

[30]H.R. Trevor-Roper, *Hitler's War Directives 1939–1945* (London, 1964), p. 86.

dependent, but Hitler hoped to secure Rumanian assistance for the attack on Russia.

Molotov protested at once about the Vienna Award on the grounds that Russia had not been consulted on a matter of common concern in accordance with the Russo-German Pact and that, as Russia had an interest in southern Bukowina, no guarantee ought to have been given in respect of Rumania's new frontiers. To this charge Ribbentrop replied sharply that Russian claims in the Balkans had been finally settled with the cessions made by Rumania in June, and that her protest was, therefore, invalid. On 21 September Molotov returned to the attack reiterating that Russia had considerable Balkan interests and still regarded the Vienna Award as a violation of the 1939 Pact. On hearing this, Ciano commented with *Schadenfreude* that 'the dream of an understanding with Russia has vanished for ever in the rooms of the Belvedere at Vienna'.[31] The *rapprochement* with Rumania continued despite the Soviet attitude. Ostensibly to assist the German military mission in Bucharest in its task of re-organizing the Rumanian army – but in reality to protect the Ploesti oil-fields and prepare the ground for the attack on Russia – German airforce units, a motorized and later an armoured division were sent to Rumania in the autumn. Late in November Rumania aligned herself firmly on the German side by joining the Tripartite Pact.

In the case of Finland all attempts by the Helsinki government in the spring and early summer of 1940 to obtain German help for the eventual revision of the peace treaty imposed on the Finns met with no success. Then at the end of July the German attitude changed abruptly. Arms deliveries to Finland were resumed; and in September Finland signed agreements with Germany granting her the right to send troops through the country *en route* for Norway and to station troops in Finland to guard these transit routes. Again the Soviet Union protested and again this did not prevent the ties between Germany and her new client state deepening in the months that followed.

From the summer of 1940 onwards there was growing uneasiness in German military circles about the Soviet military build-up along her southern frontier. From June onwards the number of German units in the east had been increasing, and by the autumn some 30 divisions were stationed there. Since the war with Finland Russia, too, had been overhauling her army. It was a measure of the effect of the Five Year Plans that whereas Russia had 1,500,000 men under arms in 1937, by the beginning of 1941 this had risen to 4,200,000 and by May to 5,000,000 with the call-up of 800,000 reservists. It would be quite wrong to imply that there is any truth in later German allegations that the German attack in June 1941 was a preventive strike. The Germans were perfectly capable of dealing with what they believed was the extremely unlikely eventuality of a Russian attack. Nevertheless, they felt what their predecessors had felt in 1914: that in a few years the Russian armies would become a formidable fighting force; all the more reason to strike Russia down while she was still relatively weak.

Against this darkening international background Germany took the

---

[31]M. Muggeridge, ed., *Ciano's Diary 1939–1943* (London, 1947), p. 291. The award was signed in Vienna's Belvedere Palace.

initiative. On 13 October Ribbentrop invited Molotov to Berlin for discussions. This invitation, which preceded Hitler's conversations with Laval, Pétain and Franco, was the work of Ribbentrop. Encouraged by his success in bringing about the Russo-German Pact in 1939, he flattered himself that he could draw her into a continental bloc and force Britain to surrender. Hitler was clearly more sceptical than Ribbentrop but was prepared to give his foreign minister his head; at the lowest estimate it might help break up the log-jam in the negotiations for the 1941 economic treaty with Russia currently causing concern in Berlin. In a conciliatory letter to Molotov Ribbentrop did his best to explain away German policy. The transit arrangement for German troops through Finland was no threat to Russia but simply a move to strengthen German defences in Norway against possible British attack. Similarly, military aid to Rumania was necessary to prevent British attacks on the Ploesti oilfields. Finally the Tripartite Pact, which alarmed Russia, was not directed against her but against the British and American 'warmongers'. The reality, as Ribbentrop saw it, was that Russia, Italy, Japan and Germany were now at last in a position to establish a long-term relationship by delimiting their respective spheres of influence on a world-wide scale. To facilitate this process he proposed a meeting of the four interested powers.

The Russian response was positive. If Germany was prepared to relieve Russia of her fears and, more to the point, to make further concessions – a distinct possibility to view of continued British resistance and growing American involvement – then Russia was prepared to negotiate as she had been in 1939. But Stalin insisted on bilateral negotiations excluding Italy and Japan in the first instance. This condition was accepted by Ribbentrop. On 12 November Molotov arrived in Berlin for two days of discussions with Hitler and Ribbentrop. Both assured Molotov that the war was virtually over and the time ripe for a definition of the spheres of influence of the four powers; Japan would look to the south Pacific, Italy to north and east Africa, Germany to central Africa and Russia could move towards the Persian Gulf and the Arabian Sea to secure the ice-free ports she needed.

Molotov showed scant interest in Hitler's world-historical perspective but much to the latter's surprise and displeasure turned to his brief from Stalin which was to clarify German attitudes towards Russian interests in the Balkans and Black Sea. Hitler was subjected to a hail of questions about German intentions in Finland, the meaning of the Tripartite Pact, the significance of the Nazi New Order in Europe with particular reference to Russian interests in Bulgaria, Rumania and Turkey, and the objectives behind Japan's Greater Asia Co-Prosperity Sphere. The next day Molotov brushed aside Hitler's offer of a share in the impending auction of the bankrupt British Empire – an offer which was hardly genuine in view of Hitler's continuing admiration for that edifice – and stuck doggedly to his catechism about the Balkans. Hitler's explanation that German interest in the Balkans was temporary in nature and due to a need for raw materials did not satisfy Molotov. German troops must leave Finland, he insisted, hinting very plainly, when questioned by Hitler, that Russia intended to annex that state; and in view of Russia's claim to southern Bukowina the guarantee of Rumania's frontiers should be withdrawn. On the evening of 13 November during an air-raid which forced

Ribbentrop and Molotov from a banquet into the Reich chancellery shelter, the German foreign minister made a final ill-timed attempt to capture his Russian guest for a grandiose four-power division of the world, producing from his pocket a draft agreement in which each power pledged itself to respect the other's sphere of influence. Molotov again refused to take the bait and reiterated that Russia was interested in the Balkans and Baltic not the Indian Ocean. Back in Moscow he sent a formal reply. Russia would agree to a Four Power Pact but only on condition that German troops were withdrawn from Finland; Bulgaria was recognized as being in the Russian sphere of influence and signed a mutual assistance treaty with Russia; Russia was given bases for land and naval forces within range of the Bosphorus and Dardanelles and if Turkey objected to this the four powers would peremptorily compel her to comply with the Russian demand; the area south of Batum and Baku in the direction of the Persian Gulf was recognized as a Russian sphere of influence; and, finally, Japan ceded to Russia her concessions for the exploitation of the oil and coal resources in north Sakhalin.

If Hitler ever had any doubts what the next step should be this comprehensive and unambiguous statement of Russia's ultimate objectives in Europe removed them for good. And by the end of 1940 the deepening ties between the United States and Britain also convinced him, as he said on 17 December, that all continental problems must be solved in 1941 for by 1942 America would be able to intervene in the war. He now hoped to resolve all these mounting problems by smashing Russia and placing Germany in an impregnable position to meet the challenge of the Anglo-Saxon powers. On 18 December he signed the directive for the operation against Russia which he renamed Barbarossa. Once more he pinned his faith to the well-tried blitzkrieg technique: in a rapid campaign the Russian airforce would be destroyed on the ground and armoured spearheads, supported by the *Luftwaffe*, would race into Russia, destroy the bulk of the Russian armies and erect a barrier against Asiatic Russia on the line of the Volga river and Archangel. All preparations were to be completed by May 1941.

Difficult though it is to establish the exact relationship between ideological conviction and strategic necessity in explaining the attack on Russia, it is certain that both factors were closely interlocked in Hitler's mind by the end of 1940. The same is true of economic factors which also played a significant part in this decision. For the *Lebensraum* concept which Hitler added to his political stock-in-trade in the mid 1920s was an amalgam of various elements: racial fanaticism, anti-bolshevik and anti-semitic prejudice, power-political ambition, strategic necessity and the doctrine of economic self-sufficiency. The alleged racial superiority of the Aryans supposedly justified their eastward expansion to displace the racially inferior Slavs; the destruction of 'Jewish bolshevism' was an ideological imperative for fanatical Nazis; the establishment of a huge land mass stretching from the Atlantic coast to the Ural mountains would also give Germany a militarily secure base from which to make a bid for world power; and, last but not least, the economic resources of this vast empire would make it self-sufficient, capable of surviving global war because it would no longer be dependent on overseas sources of supply easily cut off by wartime blockade.

When war broke out in 1939 German economic experts were confident that Germany could survive a blockade in the short-term so far as food was concerned without Russian assistance. Only in respect of manganese ore, raw phosphates and naptha products were there critical shortages which could be made good by purchases from Russia; under the economic agreement signed in August 1939 Germany had offered Russia a two-year credit of 200 million RM for the purchase of machinery from Germany in return for deliveries of raw materials. But as the war dragged on through the winter of 1939–40 and as the blockade cut German imports by over 60 per cent by December 1939, Germany became much more dependent than she had expected on Russian supplies. In a new treaty signed in February 1940 Russia promised to deliver raw materials and food worth 640 million RM over the next 12 months. In all 1,000,000 tons of oil, 1,000,000 tons of grain, 800,000 tons of scrap metal and iron ore, 500,000 tons of phosphates, 100,000 tons of cotton and 100,000 tons of chrome ore were delivered to Germany in return for capital goods. Of equal importance was the Russian promise to keep the trans-Siberian route open for that enabled Germany to beat the British blockade and continue to purchase rubber and tin from the Far East. Under a second agreement signed in January 1941 Germany did even better; by May 1942 Russia promised to delivery 2,500,000 tons of grain and 1,000,000 tons of oil whereas German capital goods deliveries were to begin early in the summer of 1941, a very considerable advantage in view of the decision to attack Russia in May.

While there can be little doubt about the value of this trade for Germany, nevertheless, the course of Russo-German trade relations was never smooth. Each side was naturally anxious to have the best of the bargain. As Russia struggled to become a major industrial power under the stimulus of the Five Year Plans internal demand for food and raw materials grew as did her need for capital goods – including armaments, for Stalin insisted on very high priority for the latest military technology in his bid for great power status for Russia. The Germans, on the other hand, were anxious to obtain the maximum possible out of Russia in terms of raw materials and food while delaying as long as possible capital goods payments. There was a natural imbalance in the exchange of goods in as much as food and raw materials when harvested or extracted from the ground can be delivered immediately whereas capital goods have to be manufactured – and the overstretched German wartime economy found it extremely difficult to meet delivery dates. True, the Germans persuaded the Russians to agree that while Russia would deliver her food and raw material quotas within 18 months, the Germans would be allowed 27 months for the delivery of capital goods. To minimize this concession, the Russians insisted on three-monthly reviews to check the proportional relationship between German and Russian deliveries; if dissatisfied, the Russians reserved the right to stop further deliveries until the imbalance was rectified. This the Russians did in March 1940, compelling Germany to divert armaments intended for their armed forces to Russia, so urgently needed were Russian raw materials. Only in the early days of the western campaign did deliveries recommence. Again in September 1940 Russian threats of further suspensions obliged the hard-pressed Germans to accelerate deliveries to Russia. Therefore, after the decisive victory in the west when official circles in Berlin were busy planning the shape of the *Grossraumwirtschaft* which would underpin German political domination of Europe it did not escape their notice that Russia would not fit into their neat-and-tidy schemes. She would not be content to remain a primary producer supplying Germany on a indefinite basis with the food and raw materials her new empire would require, but would continue to build up her industrial potential and look to eastern Europe for the markets which formerly belonged to Germany. It was also significance that Soviet Russia had insisted on maintaining her trading links with the west and with the United States. In the short term that was fortunate for Germany because to meet deliveries to her Russia has been obliged to divert 50 per cent of her own imports. But it also indicated very clearly that Russia had no intention of becoming an economic dependent of the Third Reich. So by the summer of 1940 the basic incompatibility between the two economies was patently obvious.

Germany was by this time facing mounting economic problems. Shortages of skilled labour and the use of old machinery were holding back production below pre-war levels; the Four Year Plan Office anticipated serious raw material shortages from the summer of 1941; and the harvest shortfall in 1940 amounted to three million tons with prospects of only a moderate harvest the next year, a situation which resulted in drastic ration cuts on the eve of the attack on Russia. Furthermore, although considerable stocks had been looted from occupied territories in the west in 1940, there were limits to the amount of food and raw materials that could be taken if the peoples in the west were to be reconciled to German rule and play their part in the war effort. These economic difficulties pointed up the German dilemma. The longer Britain held out, the more likely it was that Germany would have to prepare to fight a long war, in which case she would became increasingly dependent on Russia. Thus the temptation to dispense with further arduous bargaining with the Russians when the present treaty expired in 1942 and to seize Russian stocks on the ground grew greater as time passed.

Simple arithmetic deluded many experts into the belief that a war of exploitation could solve their economic problems permanently. For example, pre-war Europe (excluding Russia) consumed 142.5 million tons of grain of which she produced 132 million tons. The shortfall was made up with 10.5 million tons of imported grain, not available in wartime. Russia produced about 100 million tons of grain of which she exported only 2.5 million tons. Goering's economic experts planned to seize between 8 and 10 million tons of this grain to make up for the shortfall without any regard for the effect this would have on the Russian people. The Nazi leadership felt no sense of moral responsibility for the fate of 'racial inferiors' in the east; they were only statistics to be crossed off the ledger to maintain the living standards of the 'higher' races. Goering's Economic Staff East, an office created in April 1941 to deal specifically with the exploitation of the Russian economy in the short-term interest of the Third Reich, spelt it out in all its stark brutality in a directive in May 1941: 'Many tens of millions of people will become redundant and will either die or have to emigrate to Siberia. Any attempt to save the population there from death by starvation by importing surpluses from the black soil zone would be at the expense of supplies to Europe. It would reduce Germany's staying power in the war, and would undermine Germany's and Europe's power to resist the blockade. This must be clearly and absolutely understood'.[32] Another attraction for the planners was control of Russia's oil reserves. The Axis powers used 1.5 million tons of oil a month; by August it was estimated that only 800,000 tons would be available; the missing 300,000 tons could easily be supplied from the Caucasian oil-fields with their annual production of 27 million tons.

Of course, one cannot say with certainty how far economic considerations influenced Hitler or indeed whether he simply used them to justify before men a course of action he had decided upon for a mixture of ideological and strategic reasons. All one can say is that he had been kept informed of the vicissitudes of the German–Russian trade saga and had intervened on occasions to keep it flowing smoothly; he was aware of Germany's mounting economic difficulties; and he did express the belief from time to time that these could all be solved by seizing the oil and grain of Russia.

Hitler's interest in the Ukraine, the 'wheat chamber' of Russia, was of long standing as a few examples will illustrate. As early as 1923 he described the seizure of the 'wheat lands of Poland and the Ukraine as the most important task in the next war'.[33] Speaking at the Nuremberg Rally of 1936 he declared: 'If we had at our disposal the incalculable wealth and stores of raw material of the Ural mountains and the unending fertile plains of the Ukraine . . . . our German people would swim in plenty'.[34] On the eve of war in conversation with Carl Burckhardt, the League of Nations High Commissioner for Danzig, he denounced the stupidity of the west in refusing him a free hand in the east and went on to say that after coming to terms with Russia to defeat the west he would then turn east for: 'I need the Ukraine so that we cannot be starved out as in the last war'.[35] It is not without significance that during the planning stages of Barbarossa he disagreed with Halder who wanted to give a high priority to the seizure of Moscow. That city had no significance, argued Hitler, who insisted that the campaign plan be extended to take in the Baltic states in order to safeguard the Swedish ore supplies and in the south to seize the Donetz industrial basin, the wheat of the Ukraine and the oil of the Caucasus. Only when these objectives had been reached should the attack on Moscow proceed. During the campaign in August 1941 when Guderian tried to persuade Hitler to allow the attack on Moscow to go ahead Hitler explained patiently to a favourite general why this could not be; according to Guderian Hitler went on: 'the raw materials and agriculture of the Ukraine were vitally necessary for the future prosecution of the war. He [Hitler] spoke once again of the need of neutralizing the Crimea "that Soviet aircraft carrier for attacking the Rumanian oil-fields". For the first time I heard him use the phrase: "My generals know nothing about the economic aspects of war" '.[36]

As Germany's economic difficulties increased in the winter of 1940–1 Hitler

---

[32]*Nazi Conspiracy and Aggression* VII, EC-126, p. 300.

[33]E. Hanfstaengl, *Zwischen Weissem Haus und Braunem Haus* (München, 1969), p. 78.

[34]M. Domarus, ed., *Hitlers Reden und Proklamation 1932–1945* (Würzburg, 1962-3) I, pp. 642-3.

[35]C.J. Burckhardt, *Meine Danziger Missioin 1937–1939* (München, 1960), p. 348.

[36]Heinz Guderian, *Panzer Leader* (London, 1974), p. 200.

relied more and more on the coming economic exploitation of Russia to solve them. Early in January 1941 reviewing the details of Barbarossa he emphasized to his top military advisers on several occasions the importance of the 'corn and timber' of Russia and concluded by saying that the land of Russia 'conceals immeasurable riches. Germany must dominate [this area] economically and politically without annexing it. Then we will have all we need to be able to fight whole continents in the future'.[37]

He also showed concern about the repercussions of Soviet advances, recent and threatened, upon Germany's precarious economic situation. Later in January he pointed out that Molotov's threat to annex Finland would deprive Germany of the 60 per cent of her nickel supplies which came from the Petsamo mines; and it would enable Russia to cut off vital Swedish ore as well. Early in September 1940 he had authorized the formation of a task force to seize Petsamo in the event of Russian moves against Finland. Imports of Rumanian oil, which at one million tons represented 50 per cent of German oil imports, were also at risk. In an era of air power Russia could turn the Ploesti oilfields into 'an expanse of smoking debris . . . . and the life of the Axis depends on those oil fields'.[38] In August 1940 when Bulgaria and Hungary were pressing their claims against Rumania Hitler, worried by the possibility of Russian action, had ordered an army corps to stand by in Vienna to seize the oilfields. Finally, two days before the attack on Russia he admitted that Germany had gone too far in her attempts to achieve autarky within existing frontiers; 'We must follow another course and conquer what we need . . . . so that the aim must be to secure by conquest all areas which are of special significance to our war industry'.[39]

Not only in the economic field did the Germans intend to exploit Russia whatever the cost to the population. From the spring of 1941 onwards Hitler made it abundantly clear that the war in the east would be conducted on very different lines from the western campaign. Early in March he set the tone for Barbarossa when he sent back to Armed Forces High Command their draft campaign instructions with the comment, *inter alia*, that: 'this coming campaign is more than a clash of arms; it is a confrontation between two philosophies of life . . . . the Jewish-bolshevik intelligentsia, the oppressor up to now, must be removed'.[40] Fourteen days later he spelt it out more clearly to Halder, Quartermaster General Eduard Wagner and Colonel Adolf Heusinger, chief of army operations section: 'the intelligentsia installed by Stalin must be annihilated. The leadership structure of the Russian state must be smashed to pieces. In Great Russia application of the most brutal force necessary. Ideological ties do not yet bind the Russian people together firmly. These will be severed once Soviet officials are removed'.[41] Finally, on 30 March he addressed a wider circle of commanding officers on the coming campaign. Halder jotted down the essentials of the message in his diary: 'Confrontation between two philosophies of life. Devastating critique of bolshevism; is equated with anti-social

[37]*KTB OKW* I p. 258, 9 January 1941.
[38]*IMT* XXXIV, 134-C, 20 January 1941.
[39]*IMT* XXXVII, 1456-PS.
[40]*KTB OKW* I, p. 341, 3 March 1941.
[41]*KTB* Halder II, p. 320, 17 March 1941.

criminality. Communism immense danger for the future. We must depart from the attitude of soldierly comradeship. The communist never had been or ever would be a comrade. We are talking about a war of annihilation. If we don't realize this, then we will still defeat the enemy but 30 years later we will face the communist enemy again. We are not waging war to preserve the enemy . . . . annihilation of bolshevik commissars and communist intelligentsia . . . . commissars and members of the GPU (Russian secret police) are criminals and must be dealt with as such . . . . in the east severity is kindness for future generations'.[42]

Hitler's rabid racialism comes as no surprise. What should not be overlooked is the ready acceptance of Hitler's murderous plans by most of the officer corps. This was not done out of cowardice or because Hitler's advisers had drifted away from the high standards of the old Prussian officer corps and degenerated into unthinking military automatons indifferent to moral issues. On the contrary, it was a measure of the deep-seated hostility to 'Russian bolshevism' which permeated the officer corps throughout the Weimar period. That is why the military were prepared to translate Hitler's bloodthirsty instructions into precise military orders.

Already on 13 March discussions commenced between Wagner and Reinhard Heydrich, Himmler's deputy and head of the Reich Security Head Office, to work out details of an unholy partnership between the army and four specially-recruited murder squads composed of Gestapo, criminal police and security police officers. These squads were to operate independently in the rear of the advancing armies but would liaise with army commanders who would be responsible for supplies. In June Heydrich informed the four murder squad commanders that on Hitler's orders they were to execute communists, Jews and radical elements. On 13 May on Hitler's express orders Armed Forces High Command issued an order to senior commanders that partisans were not to be court-martialled but shot summarily. On 6 June the notorious 'Commissar Order' was issued informing these commanders that commissars captured in battle were to be shot forthwith. Meanwhile those in charge of army propaganda had not neglected the vital task of preparing the common soldiers emotionally for flagrant breaches of international law. By May guidelines had been drawn up with the approval of Army High Command. Commanding officers were to depict bolshevism as the deadly enemy of the National Socialist German people; soldiers were exhorted to take ruthless and energetic action against 'bolshevik agitators, partisans, saboteurs, and Jews and to crush absolutely any active and passive resistance'; they were warned to handle members of the Red Army, including prisoners, with the greatest reserve and to remain constantly on their guard as they were likely to be treacherous fighters: 'the Asiatic soldiers of the Red Army are especially unfathomable, incalculable, cunning and without feeling'.[43] Because it was so thoroughly indoctrinated into fighting a war of annihilation, Hitler could rely on the German army to

---

[42] *Op. cit.*, p. 337, 30 March 1941; see Halder's affidavit at Nuremberg, 22 November 1945 *Nazi Conspiracy* III, 873-PS for a more colourful version.

[43] *Das Deutsche Reich und der Zweite Weltkrieg IV Der Angriff auf die Sowjetunion* (Stuttgart, 1983), p. 441.

co-operate willingly in his grand design for destroying the fabric of Soviet society and realizing the old dream of *Lebensraum* in the east. Six months later when the German armies ground to a halt in the winter of 1941–2 it became only too apparent how utterly wrong Hitler and the officer corps had been in their understanding of Russia. Terroristic methods only served to weld the Russian people together more strongly in defending their homeland against fascist aggression.

5

The Superpowers Enter the War

The power of myth in history had been alluded to once before in this book in connection with the Anti-Comintern Pact. It was argued that despite the surface appearance of solidarity, Germany, Italy and Japan had little in common; this did not prevent American policy-makers assuming when Japan made threatening moves towards the' Pacific that this must be part of a carefully orchestrated world conspiracy for Axis domination of the world.[1] Much the same can be said of the Rome–Berlin Axis itself.

The façade of ideological solidarity barely concealed serious differences of interest. Mussolini threw in his lot with Hitler not out of any spiritual affinity with National Socialism but because he felt that only by working closely with the Germans could Italy achieve her territorial ambitions in the Mediterranean and north Africa at the expense of France. Furthermore, the line to Berlin would, he supposed, enable Italy to establish herself as the equal partner of the Third Reich. The sober truth was that as Germany grew in strength, Italy was reduced to the role of junior partner of the German dictator. Mussolini bitterly resented this turn of events and tried vainly to stop the rot. Thus, when Hitler seized Rump Czechoslovakia in March 1939 without informing the Italians in advance, Mussolini, intent on keeping his end up, occupied Albania on Good Friday of that year. Another disappointment awaited him in the summer of 1940. As France collapsed and Mussolini moved in for the kill, he found his German friend disinclined to dismantle the French colonial empire in north Africa. That was not all; Mussolini noted with alarm the signs of growing German influence in the Balkans. The movement of German troops into Rumania and German attempts to win over Bulgaria to the Tripartite Pact made it plain that Hitler did not regard the Balkans as an Italian sphere of influence. Mussolini's mounting frustration exploded at last in October 1940. Though warned several times by the Germans not to upset the status quo in the Balkans, Mussolini decided to demonstrate his independence of Germany. The standard 'frontier incident' was manufactured on the Albanian–Greek frontier and an ultimatum dispatched to Greece demanding bases on Greek soil. When she rejected it, Mussolini launched an attack from Albania.

[1]For example, Roosevelt told the Senate Military Affairs Committee in January 1939 that 'about three years ago we got the pretty definite information that there was in the making a policy of world domination between Germany, Italy and Japan. That was when the first Anti-Comintern Pact was signed. . . . There exists today, without any question whatsoever – if I were asked to prove it, I could not prove it, of course – what amounts to an offensive and defensive alliance': Donald B. Schewe, ed., *Franklin D. Roosevelt and Foreign Affairs January 1937–August 1939* second series (New York, 1979) VIII, no. 1,565, 31 January 1939.

Whether Hitler was greatly annoyed or not by Italy's act of disobedience has been disputed.[2] Possibly he assumed that as Italy was a large country and Greece a small one, the outcome could not be in doubt and the damage to his own plans would be minimal. But when the Greeks repulsed the Italians and carried the war into Albania the situation changed dramatically. Even if Hitler had toyed with the idea of leaving the Italians to flounder on their own, he knew that he dare not remain inactive. For a prolonged war in the Balkans would give the British a golden opportunity to re-enact the Salonika landing of the First World War. Small British forces had already landed on the islands of Crete and Lemnos on 31 October and near Athens early in November. If a considerable force landed on the Greek mainland British bombers could easily attack the Ploesti oilfields. And in any case it was essential to re-establish peace in the Balkans before the attack on Russia began. German military intervention was, therefore, unavoidable. The plan of campaign for Operation Marita, finally approved by Hitler in December 1940, followed the well-established blitzkrieg pattern; 17 divisions, three armoured and one motorized, would be assembled in Rumania and would cross into Bulgaria. Six divisions would guard the Turkish frontier while the remainder launched an attack on Greece when the weather improved in the spring of 1941.

Throughout the winter of 1940–1 Italy's plight worsened. When France fell British power in the Mediterranean had been put in jeopardy; Italy's entry into the war endangered Britain's lines of communication with her forces in the Middle East and exposed the beleagured garrisons to the prospect of attack with no hope of early reinforcements. In Egypt 36,000 British troops faced 215,000 Italian troops in Cyrenaica and Tripolitania while in the Sudan 9,000 British and colonial troops faced 200,000 Italians in Eritrea and Ethiopia. Already in September Italian troops had advanced 50 miles into Egypt and built a series of entrenched camps near Sidi Barrani.

By the beginning of 1941 the balance of military advantage had swung dramatically in Britain's favour. In November British torpedo planes struck a heavy blow at the Italian fleet anchored in Taranto harbour putting three battleships and two cruisers out of action for several months. In December General Sir Archibald Wavell, Commander-in-Chief Middle East, defying the heavy odds against success, launched what was originally intended to be only a large-scale raid against the Italians in western Egypt. After initial successes the raid developed into a major offensive. Wavell swept the Italians out of Egypt and in the weeks that followed Bardia, Tobruk and Benghazi fell into British hands. By February the Italians had been driven out of Cyrenaica and 133,000 prisoners had been taken, including four generals. Similar success was enjoyed by a smaller British force in northeast Africa which by May 1941 had forced the Italians to capitulate. Had Wavell been allowed to continue his advance into Tripolitania the likelihood is that Italian forces would have been driven completely out of Africa. But at this crucial point the Greeks asked for British military assistance, assuming correctly that the German forces concentrated in Rumania were soon to be unleashed against them. Wavell was ordered by

[2]Martin van Creveld, *Hitler's Strategy 1940–1941. The Balkan Clue* (Cambridge, 1973), pp. 49–50.

Churchill to send an expeditionary force of 60,000 men which landed in Greece early in March.

Meanwhile, at the end of February the German divisions assigned to Marita had crossed into Bulgaria after King Boris finally decided to throw in his lot with the Germans. Still, an operation conducted hundreds of miles from base and dependent on communications running through Hungary, Rumania and Bulgaria was a hazardous undertaking unless Germany could rely on at least the neutrality of Yugoslavia. Though Yugoslavia, an important producer of raw materials, was tied economically to Germany, she had hitherto avoided binding political commitments. Subjected to heavy German pressure at the beginning of 1941, Yugoslavia finally capitulated. On 25 March the Yugoslav prime minister and foreign minister signed the Tripartite Pact; in return the Axis powers guaranteed Yugoslavia's territorial integrity and promised her the Greek harbour of Salonika. Then, suddenly, Germany's war plans were upset by a palace revolution in Belgrade. The pro-German ministry and the pro-German regent, Prince Paul, were replaced by a pro-Allied ministry. As a hostile Yugoslavia in Germany's rear would endanger Barbarossa, a furious Hitler ordered an attack on Yugoslavia as well as Greece. The four-week delay which this entailed does not account for the failure of the Russian campaign as was once believed.

The attack on Greece and Yugoslavia was the last in the series of successful blitzkriegs which placed Germany in a position of dominance in western and central Europe. The ill-equipped armies of Greece and Yugoslavia were no match for the armoured divisions which, despite formidable natural obstacles in the mountainous terrain, swiftly overwhelmed both countries in April 1941. The Yugoslavs were demoralized by the savage aerial bombardment of Belgrade on 6 April which reduced the city to smoking ruins. Attacked from the north and east, the disorganized and disoriented Yugoslav forces surrendered on 17 April.

On 21 April the Greeks did likewise. Tactical mistakes hastened their collapse. Fourteen of their 20 divisions were fighting in Albania. The remainder were divided; some were guarding the Metaxas Line, a complex of fortifications behind the Bulgarian–Greek frontier, whilst others were deployed to the west in the region of the Vadar valley and supported by the British forces. All these forces depended for the protection of their flank and rear on one Yugoslav division. The German Twelfth Army commanded by General Sigmund Wilhelm List raced down the Struma valley and quickly reached Salonika cutting off the Greek forces in Thrace. Other German units rushed through the Monastir Gap forcing the British to fall back on the sea. While the Greeks negotiated their surrender British forces were being evacuated in the last days of April. Those who went to Crete had short respite. On 20 May 7,000 German paratroopers landed on the island and by 27 May, after half of the 28,000 British troops had been evacuated to Egypt, the island fell to the Germans.

Meanwhile disaster had struck in Egypt. Already in February whilst the Italians were surrendering in their thousands in Cyrenaica Hitler had sent General Erwin Rommel to North Africa with a mechanized force of two divisions, the nucleus of the famous Afrika Korps. Hitler's hope was that a diversion by Rommel in the desert would deter the British from sending substantial forces to Greece. By a mixture of bluff and mobility Rommel persuaded the British that he was far stronger than his two divisions. Helped also by the fact that the victorious troops of the first Libyan campaign had been replaced by less experienced units, he succeeded in driving the British out of Cyrenaica as swiftly as they had conquered it in the first place.

The first of the two momentous events which transformed the European war into a truly global confrontation occurred in June when Germany attacked Russia. Six months later German army command realized that the blitzkrieg had failed and that Germany was committed to at least another 12 months of fighting in the east. And when the campaign of 1942 failed to achieve its objectives, then at last it dawned on the Germans that they were trapped in a life-and-death struggle in the east. For the first time since September 1939 the prospect of defeat opened up for Hitler's Thousand Year Reich.

But at first all went smoothly. With the defeat and occupation of Greece and Yugoslavia the last obstacles to Barbarossa were removed. By the middle of June 157 infantry divisions, 13 motorized and 17 armoured divisions were in position, an army of three million men supported by 2,500 aircraft. In addition Rumania and Finland provided 600,000 men. The attack was to be launched in three directions. Von Leeb's Army Group North was to attack from East Prussia and thrust through the Baltic states towards Leningrad. The main thrust would be made by von Bock's Army Group Centre, the strongest with eight armoured and four motorized divisions; he was to advance from Warsaw towards Minsk and Smolensk and on to Moscow but only after von Leeb had captured the Baltic states and taken Leningrad. Von Rundstedt's Army Group South would deliver the third thrust south of the Pripet marshes and drive towards the river Dnieper and the ancient city of Kiev. The object was to encircle and destroy the Soviet forces west of the rivers Dnieper and Dvina before they could retreat into the interior luring the Germans after them. They were confident that they could break the back of Soviet resistance within five weeks. Then Germany would dominate Europe from the Atlantic to a line running from the river Volga to Archangel.

Historians have long ago exposed the glib alibis of German generals who rushed into print after the war and blamed the Russian debâcle on Hitler's insane racism. The truth is that the generals were every bit as culpable as their Führer. Filled with a boundless optimism in the efficacy of the blitzkrieg they had fashioned, they assumed it must succeed despite vastly different geographical and climatic conditions. Not until the high summer of 1941 did it dawn on them that they faced for the first time a foe capable of waging total war. It had been widely believed that Russia would fall like a pack of cards under the initial impact of the blitzkrieg. The reality was very different. Though there were initially some serious signs of disaffection, the Soviet people, tightly controlled by the communist leadership and moved by a mixture of patriotism, fear and idealism, quickly rallied and offered fierce resistance to the invader.

The Germans soon discovered their mistake in supposing the size of Russia and the absence of good communications would count for little. Even in a

German armoured division only 300 of the 3,000 wheeled vehicles were tracked which meant that as the tanks raced ahead across country huge gaps opened up between them and the supporting infantry and supplies which had to stay on the few roads Russia possessed. Adverse weather conditions greatly accentuated the problem; when it rained heavily in July the soft-surfaced roads turned into seas of mud and a large part of the German army was bogged down for several days at a vital stage in the operation. When winter set in early the appalling climatic conditions added enormously to German difficulties. The fixation on a short campaign had other disastrous consequences. Little account was taken of the industrial potential Russia was known to have beyond the Urals or of the immense reserves of manpower she could draw on in a long campaign. Once the blitzkrieg failed it was the manpower and industrial potential of Soviet Russia that turned the tide against the Germans – for the *Luftwaffe* with only 2,500 planes at its disposal was quite unable in a country the size of Russia to deal the devastating blows at industrial plant, communications and troop concentrations which had guaranteed the success of the blitzkrieg in previous campaigns.

Even for a short campaign the Germans had grossly underestimated Russian strength. In part this was due to the extreme difficulty of obtaining reliable information about the state of Soviet Russia's defences. Moreover the purges of 1937, which decimated the higher echelons of the Red Army, and the initial reverses in the Finnish war led most military experts in western Europe to underrate very seriously the Red Army's potential. What compounded the error in the German case was that even when more reliable information received in the spring and summer of 1941 forced the planners to revise their estimates upwards, they remained quite confident of success. Superior German tactics and battle experience would surely, it was supposed, outweigh the fact that Russia had 226 divisions west of the Urals in June 1941 not 141 as intelligence believed a year before. It was also thought that Russia had some 10,000 tanks compared with 3,700 German tanks but that many of the former were of poor quality. In fact, Russia had around 24,000 tanks and many of them were vastly superior to German models as was quickly apparent on the battlefield.

The essence of the German plan was to destroy Soviet forces by swiftly executed enveloping movements trapping them before they had time to withdraw. Despite spectacular advances in the last days of June which carried the German armies 100 miles into Russia, the enveloping movements were only partially successful. At Slonim two Russian armies were encircled but over half the Russian soldiers managed to evade capture before the undermechanized German infantry could seal off the escape routes. It was a similar tale at Belostok and Minsk where 324,000 Russians were captured but another 300,000 escaped. A further enveloping movement at Smolensk also failed despite the capture of another 310,000 Russians. The overall result was that the path to Moscow 200 miles ahead was still blocked by substantial Soviet forces which had eluded the Germans and withdrawn behind the Dnieper and Dvina rivers and were being steadily reinforced from beyond the Urals.

At this point when it was beginning to dawn on army command that it had grossly underestimated its opponents, Hitler clashed sharply with his military advisers. Convinced that Moscow was of little significance, he wanted to switch part of von Bock's armour northwards to help von Leeb capture Leningrad where Russian resistance in the besieged city was stiffening, and the other armour southwards to help von Rundstedt's encircling movements. The argument swayed back and forth from mid July to mid August, the pros and cons nicely balanced. While Brauchitsch and Halder believed that an encircling movement to capture the troops in front of Moscow and then the city itself would end the campaign and vindicate the blitzkrieg strategy, Hitler was already moving to the view that it was too late for final victory in 1941. The objective should be to gain absolute control of the Baltic, the Ukraine and the Crimea in order to lay a sound foundation for victory in 1942. Hitler got his way in the end. The advance on Moscow was halted on 18 August. With the aid of Guderian's armour von Rundstedt's encircling movement at Kiev ended in the capture of the city and added 650,000 prisoners to the mounting total, which by October had reached three million. But at Kiev, as earlier at Slonim, Bialostok, Minsk and Smolensk the fierce resistance of the encircled Russians delayed the German advance. And although von Rundstedt overran the Donetz basin and by November reached Rostov on the Don he could not reach the Caucasus with its oil, for at the end of September Guderian's armour had been switched back to von Bock's army group.

With Leningrad under heavy bombardment and presumably on the point of surrender and with the Ukraine under German control Hitler agreed that the advance on Moscow could be resumed. On 2 October von Bock, his armour restored to him, began to advance. At Vjas'ma another encircling movement added 600,000 prisoners to the bag despite the fall of the first snow. But by mid October von Bock's troops were bogged down in a sea of slush. Only on 15 November was the drive on Moscow resumed but finally came to a halt 20 miles south of the city. On 2 December a fresh offensive carried forward units into the suburbs of Moscow but not into the heart of the city.

Then disaster struck the Germans. On 5 December Marshal Grigorii Zukov launched a counter-offensive with 100 divisions. Subjected to the most appalling weather conditions which froze guns and tanks and demoralized the fighting men, Army Group Centre reeled back under the initial impact of the attack. At this critical point when a rout might easily have developed Hitler stepped into the breach, dismissed Brauchitsch, assumed personal command of the army and ordered a stand-fast along the entire front. No doubt his action averted a grave disaster, and enabled Army Group Centre to check the offensive and live to fight another day in 1942. But for the purpose of this book it is enough to reiterate the point already made: the blitzkrieg had failed. The truth had dawned on Hitler and his generals that 'Beyond the striving claws of German pincer movements there were always more miles of forest, marsh and steppe, more Soviet units, more war industries, and more loyal Russians to prove that the German leaders had committed a monstrous error in believing their blitzkrieg was capable of defeating the Soviet Union'.[3] The consequences for Germany were grave in the extreme: Russia would still be fighting in 1942, Britain remained undefeated and in December the United States entered the

[3]B. A. Leach, *German Strategy against Russia 1939–1941* (Oxford, 1973), p. 240.

war bringing into being a formidable coalition dooming Germany inevitably to defeat. That Hitler was determined to fight on was due less to a realistic calculation that his enemies would not make peace with him than to his fanatical Social Darwinistic belief that in a struggle to the finish for world mastery the superior race must win in the end.

In the remainder of this chapter we shall be looking at the events leading to the direct involvement of the United States in the Second World War. The point has been made already that the destroyers deal in September 1940 signified a decisive departure from her neutral status. Much as Roosevelt refused to accept that an element of inevitability was creeping into America's deteriorating relations with Germany, it is clear enough retrospectively that the United States was now on a slippery slope. Actions taken by the administration in the winter of 1940–1 to honour Roosevelt's commitment to give all possible material aid to the western democracies drew the United States appreciably nearer war with Germany.

In October 1940 Britain placed massive orders in the United States totalling $5,000 million for military equipment and aircraft. As America's productive capacity was insufficient to enable her to put her own defences in order and simultaneously complete British orders, Roosevelt's readiness to allow the latter to be placed with American manufacturers raised a number of fundamental questions about the future direction of the American economy. When the economy was mobilized should first priority be given to building up America's defences or to producing war material for Britain? And if British orders were given the highest priority must not America's productive capacity be vastly increased to produce these weapons without delay? This raised further questions: had the time come to place the American economy on a war footing? Was it not essential to curtail consumer production, lengthen hours of work and impose central controls on the economy – all of which would arouse the wrath of consumers, trade unionists and the business community? Furthermore, should not the myriad of legal restrictions which impeded the export of much needed war material to Britain be swept away by executive action or more likely by an appeal to Congress? And if the president had to go to 'the Hill' must he not admit frankly that fulfilment of British orders would have a serious impact on the American people and carried with it a risk of war? In short, were not pressures building up which would force the president to give a clear lead to the people? With the election campaign moving to a climax Roosevelt was disinclined to take any action on sensitive issues about which the electorate was still muddled; the people might have willed the sending of material aid to Britain by a clear majority but judging by the pollsters they had not willed the means. What is surprising is that Roosevelt still refused to face up to these issues even after his re-election by a margin of five million votes in November 1940.

He was finally forced off the fence and made to face up to this whole complex of problems by the distress signals from London; soon, it was alleged, Britain would be unable to pay for the equipment she needed for survival. Hints to this effect were dropped as early as July 1941 without eliciting any clear response from the White House. Then in late November Lord Lothian informed an American press conference that Britain faced urgent financial problems and that a Treasury official was on his way to Washington with precise figures. On 8 December Churchill wrote formally to Roosevelt stating bluntly that if Britain was to survive she had dire need of shipping, munitions and finance. At last the president was driven to action. Fearing that if he asked Congress to repeal the Neutrality and Johnson Acts to allow war material and loans to be given to Britain, he might well be rebuffed, he came up with a novel thought for by-passing Congress for the time being. On 17 December he outlined to the press an idea which was soon turned into Lease–Lend. Pouring scorn on traditional methods of financing war, he insisted that the time had come to be rid of the 'silly foolish old dollar sign'; when British assets, which were sufficient to pay for current orders were used up, America must give war material to Britain on the understanding that repayment would be 'in kind' after the war. Choosing a homely simile, he spoke of a neighbour's home catching fire; if one had a garden hose, one did not demand from the neighbour the $15 it cost but connected it up to the hydrant, helped put out the fire and recovered the hose later. However, in answer to a press question he insisted that the scheme would not bring the United States nearer to war but was simply designed to safeguard the security of the western hemisphere.

Twelve days later on 29 December in a fireside chat to the American people, the so-called 'Arsenal of Democracy' speech, he moved someway towards an admission that there were dangers in the new undertaking: 'If we are to be completely honest with ourselves, we must admit that there is risk in any course we may take'. It seems likely that the overwhelmingly favourable response to the speech was due not so much to this note of realism cautiously concealed within but to his uncanny ability for articulating the mood of the people; while most Americans were at last awakened to the unpleasant fact that their country faced an emergency 'as serious as war itself', one calling for real sacrifice if Britain was to survive, they still clung to the hope that the course the president advocated involved 'the least risk now and the greatest hope for the future'. And they were reassured by his comment that they could 'nail any lie about sending armies to Europe as deliberate untruth'.[4] These remarks enabled them to fudge the issue and overlook the plain fact that the Lease–Lend Act passed on 11 March 1941 was an act verging on war which transformed the status of the United States from that of a non-belligerent to that of a quasi-belligerent. It was, as Stimson observed, 'a declaration of economic war'.[5]

Lease–Lend served another important function. It enabled Roosevelt to mobilize the American economy for war at British expense. Already in 1939–41 British and French orders for aircraft gave the aircraft industry a welcome injection of capital; advance payments – totalling $605 million in Britain's case – enabled the capacity of industry to expand fourfold. After the fall of France, as British dependence on American production increased, she

[4]S. Rosenman, ed., *The Public Papers and Private Addresses of Franklin D. Roosevelt* (New York, 1938–50) IX, p. 640.

[5]Henry L. Stimson and McGeorge Bundy, *On Active Service in Peace and War* (New York, 1947–8), p. 360.

had to allow the Americans access to British development projects and to use British patents, thus enabling American industry to catch up technologically in areas such as aircraft motors where Britain had been well ahead of America. Lease–Lend credits, the administration of which remained firmly in American hands, were a further assurance of continuing American prosperity and a justification for industrial mobilization.

That Washington would use her power over Britain to advance American imperial interests after the war was made painfully obvious in the summer of 1941 when during negotiations for the Lease–Lend treaty the State Department demanded that Britain realize all her assets in the United States before any credits were given and that as part of the post-war repayment she should abandon Imperial Preference as a step towards the multilateral trading world the Americans were committed to. However, reverses at the hands of the Japanese early in 1942 put a stop for the time being to plans which would have treated Britain worse than she ever 'thought proper to treat the humblest and least responsible Balkan country'.[6] The Mutual Aid Agreement was a compromise: Britain accepted the desirability of eliminating all forms of discrimination but Roosevelt conceded that these matters would be decided after the war and that Britain was not obliged to abandon Imperial Preference as a condition of receiving Lease–Lend.

The implications of the new relationship between America and Britain for the struggle with Hitler was spelt out clearly over the problem of British shipping losses in the Atlantic in the winter of 1940-1. Already in December 1940 Churchill painted sombre pictures of losses so heavy that despite the victory in the Battle of Britain defeat could not be discounted; he pleaded for a revision of the Neutrality Act to allow the United States to trade with all countries with the important corollary – of vital importance to Britain – that American shipping be protected by American naval vessels and aircraft.

With the Lease–Lend bill going through both Houses of Congress in February and March by substantial majorities a basic issue which had the gravest implications for the status of the United States had sooner or later to be faced squarely: what was the logic of agreeing to appropriations of $7,000 million, part of it for war material for Britain, if German submarines and raiders were sinking ships carrying these goods simply because British resources were too strained to allow her to protect them? This issue Roosevelt steadfastly refused to face up to. He remained silent when Stimson, Morgenthau, Knox and Stark bluntly informed him in January 1941 that his policy of all aid short of war would probably not save Britain and that, therefore, the time had surely come to take all necessary steps to secure the vital life line across the Atlantic regardless of the consequences.

The issue refused to go away. By the early spring of 1941 with German wolf packs sinking 500,000 tons of shipping a month Britain was manifestly fighting for her very existence in the Atlantic. Both in Berlin and Washington the heads of state came under intense pressure to escalate the crisis further. Raeder, who never missed an opportunity to draw Hitler's attention to each and every

---

[6]D. Moggeridge, *The Collected Works of John Maynard Keynes* (Cambridge, 1979) XXIII, p. 46. J.M. Keynes to Nigel Ronald, 11 March 1941.

American violation of her neutrality, redoubled his efforts over the Lease–
Lend Act; Germany should reply to this hostile act by refusing to respect the
American Neutrality Zone or at the very least insist it be restricted to 300 miles
from the coast of the western hemisphere. Hitler, however, was anxious to
avoid all steps likely to offend the United States and bring her into the war
before Germany had defeated Russia. He resisted Raeder's pressure and
settled on 25 March 1941 for a more modest proposal extending the German
combat zone in the Atlantic westwards to include all Iceland and the ocean up
to the three-mile limit of Greenland. In this area all neutral merchantmen as
well as belligerents could be sunk on sight.

In April it was the president's turn to come under pressure. Stimson, Knox
and Morgenthau renewed their plea for a clear-cut answer while there was still
time to save Britain. At first Roosevelt leaned towards prompt action. On 2
April, encouraged by Stimson and Knox, he approved Stark's plans for
escorting British vessels and agreed that a sizeable contingent of three battleships, one aircraft carrier, four cruisers and supporting destroyers be transferred from the Pacific to the Atlantic Fleet for escort duties. A week later he had
second thoughts. On 8 April an opinion poll claimed that only 41 per cent
approved of escorts and 50 per cent were still opposed to them. Meanwhile
inside and outside Congress isolationists were making their opposition known;
on 31 March Senator Charles W. Tobey and Congressman Harry Sauthoff
introduced a bill into Congress which sought to prohibit escorts. But what
finally decided Roosevelt against escorts was news of the Russo-Japanese
Neutrality Pact which by freeing Japan in the north exposed America to greater
danger in the Pacific.

In the end he rescinded the proposed transfer of warships for convoy duties
but in a typical Rooseveltian compromise to help the hard-pressed British he
extended the Neutrality Zone eastwards to line of longitude 26° west which
included the whole of Greenland and the Azores. This vast area overlapped the
German combat zone (extended by Hitler a month before) and thus increased
enormously the chances of an incident in these waters. British convoys would
be encouraged to sail within this zone as far as possible. The United States
undertook to patrol the extended area and by broadcasting openly on radio the
location of German raiders and submarines notify the British of their presence
so that their convoys might take evasive action. American naval vessels would
not, however, escort convoys nor would they be allowed to hunt and destroy
raiders – that task must be left to the British.

Within the limits of the compromise Roosevelt did his best to make patrol
arrangements as effective as possible. First of all, by agreement with the Danish
minister in Washington Greenland was taken under American protection. The
objective was to forestall any German attempt to establish a base on an island
occupying a key strategic position on the flank of the Newfoundland–Britain
Lease–Lend route. Secondly, Axis and Danish merchant vessels in American
ports were requisitioned with Congressional authority and pressed into service
in the Atlantic. Thirdly, as the British had now conquered north-east Africa,
the Red Sea was removed from the list of combat areas forbidden to American
shipping, enabling supplies to be conveyed by American merchantmen to the
British forces in the Middle East. But cautious as ever, Roosevelt avoided

personal involvement in the public announcement of the new measures, leaving that task to Hull and Knox. And at his press conference on 25 April, the day after their speeches, he went out of his way to emphasize that extended patrolling represented no new departure and was not equivalent to the escorting of British vessels.

The onward march of events undermined the compromise almost as soon as the president had sought refuge behind it. In the spring of 1941 Hitler's war machine was rolling again. As indicated earlier, in April and May Greece and Yugoslavia were invaded and the British driven out of Greece, Crete and Cyrenaica. Following these victories Nazi pressure on Spain and Portugal increased. Despite mounting evidence that an attack on Russia was imminent, the possibility could not be discounted that the Germans might still seize Gibraltar and take possession of the Azores, Madeira and the Cape Verde islands. If that happened, the British position in the Atlantic, already critical in the spring of 1941, would be truly desperate and the safety of the western hemisphere would also be called into question. Meanwhile the German bombing offensive over England intensified and shipping losses continued to increase. American doubts about the ability of Britain to survive began to surface again for the first time since the summer of 1940. As the crisis deepened, Churchill pressed Roosevelt on 3 May to abandon the status of quasibelligerency and intervene openly in the war.

Yet Roosevelt remained as determined as ever to avoid any major commitment likely to result in war. Temperamentally he was always happier following rather than leading public opinion. And in resisting those such as Stimson, Knox and Morgenthau who wanted a clear-cut decision for war, Roosevelt found an ally of sorts in the opinion polls. The views of ordinary Americans, neatly tabulated at frequent intervals by the pollsters, seemed to indicate that the public mood was still ambivalent though clearly edging towards intervention if the worst came to the worst. By May 1941 there was overwhelming support for material aid to Britain and an awareness that the United States would probably be dragged into the war in the end. A very substantial majority believed that Britain must be assisted even at the risk of war although at the same time only a small majority favoured the escorting of British merchantmen. Nevertheless, an overwhelming majority still wanted to stay out of the war, whilst a large majority felt that the president had gone far enough already.[7] Far from acting as a brake on presidential action these rather confused findings probably coincided with his own fading hope that material aid might even at this late hour be sufficient on its own to tip the balance against the Axis powers. Indeed, his own scepticism about the value of polls strongly suggests that they were a convenient alibi rather than a reason for avoiding further action.

Meanwhile to keep the 'war party' at bay Roosevelt relied on rousing speeches of which that delivered on 27 May 1941 is a classic example of

---

[7]In May 76 per cent thought that Britain should be helped even at the risk of war; but only 55 per cent favoured escorting, though 73 per cent favoured it if the alternative was a British defeat. Yet in June 76-9 per cent thought the United States should not enter the war: H. Cantril and M. Stunk, *Public Opinion 1935-1946* (Princeton, 1951), pp. 972, 1, 128.

enthusiasm without commitment. He did not mince his words. The Axis powers, he declared, were bent on world domination; the safety of the United States would be undermined if they succeeded in occupying Greenland or Iceland or the Azores or the Cape Verde islands. Thanks to British resistance they had failed to do so. But if Britain fell, the Germans would 'close in relentlessly on this hemisphere'. Furthermore, the heavy shipping losses Britain was suffering, twice the size of combined British and American production, made it imperative to send all possible material aid to Britain and, equally crucial, to ensure by patrolling the high seas that the aid reached its destination. 'All additional measures necessary to deliver the goods will be taken' he added ominously.[8] He concluded with a rousing declaration that an 'unlimited national emergency' would be proclaimed to ensure that the maximum effort was made to handle this critical situation.

The overwhelmingly favourable response to his speech delighted him and far exceeded his expectations. Then inexplicably the next day at his press conference he dashed cold water on any hopes of bold 'additional measures'. Nothing had changed; he had no intention of asking Congress to repeal the neutrality legislation or to authorize the escorting of merchantmen. Incredibly, he disclaimed any intention of issuing the necessary executive orders to make the 'state of emergency' effective. The best that can be said for Roosevelt's speech is that in his own tortuous way he was giving due warning to Congress and people that further action was imminent.

Why, then, did his attitude change three months later when he ordered escorts for all shipping in the Neutrality Zone, a step which might well land the United States in war? There is no easy answer to this question; all one can say is that a number of circumstances came together to point him in this direction.

The American reaction to the German attack on Russia was certainly one of them. It was widely felt in official circles in Washington that the war in the east could last no more than 12 weeks at most. Stimson, Knox and Stark urged Roosevelt to seize a unique chance while Hitler was fully engaged in Russia to dispatch all possible aid to Britain and to begin to convoy British ships. The president was impressed by this argument and promised to turn his mind to the problem. In parentheses it is interesting to observe how long it was before America gave substantial aid to Russia. The steady retreat of the Russians – and regard for the strong anti-communist sentiments of the American public after the Finnish war – made Roosevelt as cautious as he had been a year earlier in the British case. Although he unfroze Russian assets at once, not until August did he agree to supply Russia with war material for cash on the nail; not until early November was she granted $1,000 million credit under Lease–Lend.

A second factor in the equation was the occupation of Iceland in July 1941. During the staff conversations in Washington in March it was agreed that the United States should take over from the British division occupying Iceland by September in order to relieve it for service elsewhere. The take-over came earlier than expected because of reports that German submarines had been sighted in Icelandic territorial waters and that German aircraft were flying over

[8]Rosenman, *Public Papers* X, p. 190.

the country – which had, incidentally, declared its independence from Denmark in May. To forestall a possible German landing, Roosevelt ordered 4,000 marines to land in Iceland by agreement with the Icelandic government. Churchill welcomed the move, declaring in the House of Commons that, as American merchantmen supplying American forces in Iceland would have to be escorted by the United States navy, no doubt co-operation between the two navies would increase. But although pressed by Stimson to announce that as the United States was now in control of Iceland it would begin to escort British convoys across the Atlantic, in his message to Congress on 7 July Roosevelt merely stated that the occupation was necessary to protect the western hemisphere against hostile attack. Had the Germans taken over Iceland supplies to Britain would certainly have been at risk, as he admitted, but there he left the matter.

However, favourable public reaction encouraged him to go further. On 11 July Roosevelt reached a momentous decision; he would offer to escort ships of any nationality which chose to join convoys of American and Icelandic vessels bound for Iceland; in effect the shipping would have American naval protection for over half the voyage across the Atlantic. A week later in his usual vacillating manner he suspended that part of the arrangement offering protection to non-American shipping. Nevertheless, the role of the American navy had undergone an important change; it was now under orders not only to escort American and Icelandic shipping to Iceland but also to destroy hostile forces threatening those vessels, a step clearly edging the United States nearer to war.

Thirdly, although the position in the Atlantic had eased in July and August as a result of the American occupation of Iceland, in September there was a sharp deterioration. As the Joint Army–Navy Board pointed out to Roosevelt on 11 September, unless British shipping losses were reduced Britain could not hold out indefinitely. If she was to remain in the war, not only must America produce more ships than ever before but she must be prepared to use American vessels and aircraft to protect British merchantmen. Now that Russia, contrary to expectations, was likely to continue resisting the Germans aid to this new opponent of Nazism assumed a high priority. And as British merchantmen carrying supplies to Russia had to be escorted along the Norwegian coast to Murmansk and Archangel, a new burden had fallen on the British navy which made American assistance in the Atlantic a categorical imperative.

Fourthly, forward action in the Atlantic might be the last chance of avoiding American involvement in an invasion of Europe, a likely prospect in the opinion of army and navy chiefs. During the Washington conversations in the spring of 1941 the British, anxious to conserve their forces in order to defend their imperial possessions and avoid bloody battles in Europe, remembering the experiences of the Somme and Paschendaele, had argued that the blockade plus aerial bombardment would be sufficient to bring the Germans to their knees. Their American counterparts had registered sharp disagreement, although the British view appealed to Roosevelt. In April and May the War Department worked out new strategic estimates based on Rainbow Five. Early in July army and navy agreed on the need for a threefold increase in war production. Faced with this request Roosevelt, long conscious of the inadequacy of American production but loathe to do anything about it, initiated steps which led to the 'Victory Program', the first attempt to estimate the level of production needed to defeat the Axis powers. To justify this step a clear statement of America's strategic objectives was called for. The Joint Army–Navy Board statement, handed formally to the president late in September, pulled no punches. It stated unequivocally that the Axis could not be defeated unless the United States entered the war and took offensive action in Europe and Africa. Should Britain and Russia be defeated, the United States must continue the war. For the time being the United States must do all it could to help Britain and would intervene in the war only when it had built up a huge land army capable of delivering the *coup de grâce* to Hitler. If this most unwelcome course of action committing American troops to war overseas could be avoided by doing more to help the British on the high seas, then Roosevelt was ready to agree to naval escorts for British merchantmen. Such a step would in all probability not lead to retaliation because Hitler, now committed to a longer campaign in Russia than he had bargained for, would be unlikely to challenge the Americans.

It looks as if Roosevelt had changed his mind even earlier and that by the time he met Churchill at the historic Atlantic Conference between 9 and 12 August he was already coming to the conclusion that material aid alone would not be enough to save Britain but that naval escorts were now essential. The three days spent in Churchill's company discussing grand strategy and the principles on which a future peace settlement would be based – always a subject of absorbing interest to Roosevelt – probably strengthened him in his half-formulated decision. American naval representatives in attendance at the conference quickly worked out arrangements with their British colleagues for the escorting of British as well as American merchantmen as far as Iceland with effect from 1 September. It is indicative of the new mood of resolution on his part that he did not seek to wriggle out of the commitment after the event but when an external event – the USS *Greer* incident – cleared the way for a public announcement of the new policy he seized the opportunity with alacrity.

Roosevelt's response marked a new departure in American policy. On 4 September 1941 an American destroyer was taking passengers and mail to Iceland when a British patrol aircraft radioed to it the location of a German submarine some miles ahead. The USS *Greer* trailed the submarine for three hours and having located its position precisely, radioed back to the aircraft. The plane dropped a few depth charges and departed. Not surprisingly, as this was a German combat zone, the submarine fired two torpedoes which missed the USS *Greer*. The destroyer retaliated with depth charges which also missed. Honour satisfied, the submarine departed and the USS *Greer* continued on its way.

In a press statement the next day Roosevelt emphasized the deliberate nature of the attack on the destroyer. On 11 September in a nationwide broadcast he went much further. With a blatant disregard for the facts, he declared that the submarine in a wanton act of piracy had fired without warning upon the destroyer with the intention of sinking it. That was no isolated incident, he warned his audience, but part of a grand design to create 'a permanent world system based on force, terror and murder' – that, too, was blatantly untrue for despite Raeder's pleas, after news of the speech reached Berlin, that Hitler authorize attacks on American ships, the Führer insisted that U-boat commanders avoid incidents until mid October, by which time he hoped the Russian campaign would be over. Roosevelt went on to say that if the Nazis were to attain their objective of dominating the western hemisphere, they would have to abolish the traditional freedom of the seas. Americans must cease to delude themselves that the United States could survive in a Nazi-dominated world. The time for action had come. 'We have sought no shooting war even with Hitler. We do not seek it now . . . . But when you see a rattlesnake poised to strike you do not wait until he has struck before you crush him. These Nazi submarines and raiders are the rattlesnakes of the Atlantic. They are a menace to the free pathways of the high seas. They are a challenge to our sovereignty'.[9] From now on American naval vessels and aircraft would not wait for Nazi submarines and raiders to strike the first blow but would act in defence of all merchantmen sailing in the Neutrality Zone. All the same, with an eye on the 80 per cent of Americans whom pollsters climbed were against participation in the war, he denied that this new policy amounted to an act of war.[10]

The logic of events was drawing the United States nearer and nearer the brink of war with Germany. The escort policy led inevitably to a further step: revision of the Neutrality Act.[11] For it made no sense for the American navy to escort and defend merchantmen who were forbidden by law from defending themselves. Repeal of section VI of the Neutrality Act was imperative to permit the arming of merchantmen carrying cargoes to Iceland. It was even more essential to repeal sections II and III to enable American merchantmen to enter combat zones and to carry war material directly to friendly ports, thus eliminating the time-consuming transfer of American cargoes to British ships at Icelandic ports. Public opinion was moving in favour of repeal. Difficulties were likely to arise in Congress; conversations with leading Democrats convinced Roosevelt that, while Senate was likely to repeal all three sections, the House of Representatives would probably refuse to do so. In the end Roosevelt decided to ask the House for the repeal of only section VI, which it was likely to approve, and then request Senate to repeal all three sections; his calculation was that the House would then agree to repeal the other two sections.

Another naval incident smoothed the president's path. On the night of 16–17 October, before the debate on the repeal of section VI was over in the House, the USS *Kearney* was struck by a German torpedo and 11 lives were lost. The sober facts were that this destroyer, in company with three other American destroyers, had been sent from Iceland to help a convoy under attack from German submarines. In the ensuing battle the *Kearney* was hit. But the American people did not see it in this detached light. Their anger, whipped up by the

---

[9]*Op. cit.*, p. 390.

[10]The difficulty of adhering slavishly to the opinions elicited by pollsters is revealed in a Gallup Poll in early October showing that 70 per cent responded positively when asked the more precise question whether it was more important to defeat Hitler than to stay out of the war.

[11]When Churchill asked in September for transport ships to ferry troops to the Middle East Roosevelt actually offered American naval transports manned by navy crews. Then his political instincts reasserted themselves; he suspended the offer and decided to seek Congressional approval first.

press, may well have helped to secure a larger than anticipated majority when the House repealed section VI by 259 votes to 138.

Contrary to expectation the going was tougher in the Senate where Roosevelt was asking for repeal of sections II and III as well as VI. To influence the vote he delivered a blistering speech on Navy Day, 27 October, in which he denounced the 'attack' on the *Kearney* as an attempt to force the Americans off the high seas. Conjuring up the ghost of the Zimmermann Telegram, he alleged that according to secret documents in his possession the Nazis were planning the division of South and part of Central America into five vassal states.[12] Another document 'proved' Hitler's intention to abolish all religions and impose a Nazi church on the whole world. The American people may well have been roused by these 'revelations' but their anger did not rub off onto the Senate. Only by 50 votes to 37 did that body repeal the three sections on 7 November. When the bill was referred to the House of Representatives, it only supported repeal of sections II and III by 212 votes to 194 and then only because the president in a letter to Congress declared that failure to pass the amendments would seriously damage the security of the United States. Not that the closeness of the votes in Congress meant that it did not want to do all that was possible to aid Britain. Many senators and congressmen, like other Americans, found it difficult to reconcile steps bringing the United States closer to war with the desire of the people, if pollsters were to be believed, to avoid war. That raises the question whether Roosevelt should have acted more positively to force the public to accept the inexorable logic of the situation.

Whether one is inclined to praise Roosevelt's caution as an act of political prudence or condemn it as woeful lack of leadership, the fact remains that the United States was now on the brink of war with Germany. The policy of escorting British merchantmen had already eased Britain's position enabling her to switch 50 destroyers from the Atlantic. For the time being Hitler was prepared to tolerate American escorts for British ships in the Neutrality Zone. But after the revision of the Neutrality Act it is difficult to see how war with Germany could have been avoided. If the Germans had sat back and made no attempt to stop American merchantmen laden with war material sailing to the British Isles through the German combat zone, this would have amounted to an admission that Germany had lost the Battle of the Atlantic. Attacks on American merchantmen in the near future were as certain as anything could be whatever Hitler said in Munich on 18 October about German vessels not firing the first shot but being ready to defend themselves if attacked.

The intriguing question is whether Roosevelt thought that war was absolutely inevitable. Even at this late stage it is possible that he shared the feeling of many Americans that, whilst more aid than ever before must be given to Britain in order to defeat Hitler, the country must stay out of direct involvement in the war. Asked by a reporter at a press conference on 3 November whether the time had not come to end diplomatic relations with Germany he summed up his position frankly in these off-the-record remarks: 'We don't

[12]British intelligence operators in the United States were responsible for this forgery: D. Reynolds, *The Creation of the Anglo-American Alliance 1937–1941. A Study in Comparative Co-operation* (London, 1981), p. 219.

want a declared war with Germany because we are acting in defense – self-defense – every action. And to break off diplomatic relations – why, that won't do any good, I really frankly don't know that it would do any good. It might be more useful to keep them [relations] the way they are'.[13]

It was the situation in the Far East not the deepening crisis in the Atlantic that brought the United States into the war in December 1941.

By the end of 1940 Japanese foreign policy was trapped in a cul-de-sac. The Tripartite Pact had failed to deliver the anticipated benefits. On the contrary, relations between Japan and America had deteriorated quite sharply, an outcome which exercised the mind of the Konoe cabinet though it in no way weakened its resolve to exploit the developing situation in south-east Asia.

There were differences of opinion about the correct tactics to adopt towards the United States. On the basis of his experiences as a student in America, Foreign Minister Matsuoka firmly believed that whatever threatening noises emanated from Washington, the United States would surely back down if Japan was seen to be pursuing a forward policy with determination. To enable her to do so, closer relations with Germany and an understanding with Soviet Russia were essential. But other cabinet members, notably Konoe and Navy Minister Yoshida Zengo, fearing that bad relations with the United States could lead to a war which it was not in Japan's interests to risk, favoured conciliatory tactics to achieve the same goal. Their fears were shared by business and financial circles all too well aware of Japanese dependence on American oil and scrap metal. The clash between 'moderates' and 'extremists' inside the Konoe cabinet explains why conflicting signals emanated from Tokyo in the winter of 1940–1.

The appointment of Nomura as ambassador to Washington in November 1940 was clearly a victory for the moderates. As Nomura had been military attaché in Washington for several years, knew Roosevelt personally when the latter was secretary of state for the navy, and was believed to favour closer ties with the Anglo-Saxon powers, his appointment to the post was welcomed by the American administration.

Another sign that influential circles in Japan wanted to avoid war with America were feelers for an understanding put out in the winter of 1940–1 by private citizens who enjoyed in varying degrees the support of Konoe and some of his colleagues. Late in 1940 Toda Teikichi, a prominent member of the Japanese Economic Federation, informed Ambassador Grew that Hashimoto Telsuma, head of the powerful Black Dragon Society, intended to visit America on a fact-finding mission. Toda succeeded in convincing Grew that Hashimoto's efforts to improve American–Japanese relations had the support of Konoe and Zengo, both of whom were strongly opposed to Matsuoka's pro-Axis policy likely in their opinion to lead to war. Hull arranged for

---

[13]Rosenman *Public Papers* X, p. 463. One is reminded of the novel idea he patented in 1937 for a blockade of Japan involving America in hostilities but not in war; he told the cabinet at that time: 'We want to develop a technique which will not lead to war. We want to be as smart as Japan and Italy. We want to do it in a modern way': John Morton Blum, *From the Morgenthau Diaries: Years of Urgency 1938–1941* (Boston, 1965) I, p. 489.

Hashimoto to meet State Department officials informally in January and February 1941. Nothing came of the conversations once it emerged that Hashimoto was only offering changes in Japanese policy on condition that the United States recognized the 'Japanese mission in east Asia', concluded a new trade treaty with her, gave her a loan and induced Chiang Kai-shek to make peace.

Simultaneously another set of private negotiations was under way. In December 1940 Bishop James E. Walsh, superior general of the Catholic Foreign Missionary Society, accompanied by a Father James M. Drought, were in Tokyo on missionary business. Through a friendly bank official they secured an interview with Matsuoka. In view of his anti-American stance it can only be assumed that under pressure from Konoe he asked the two priests to take secret proposals to Washington. There they contacted Postmaster General Frank C. Walker, a prominent Catholic layman. Through the intervention of Hull they were able to see Roosevelt and indicate to him that Japan was willing to abandon the Tripartite Pact and withdraw her troops from China in return for the restoration of trading relations with the United States. Whilst the president, like the secretary of state, remained profoundly sceptical of proposals emanating from Tokyo, he was playing a waiting game in the Far East, trying to maintain a delicate balance between coercion and appeasement of Japan. It was expedient to allow the priests to maintain contact with the Japanese embassy. In March the bank official and Colonel Iwakuro Hideo representing the ministry of war turned up in New York. In consultation with Bishop Walsh and Father Drought they produced a document which Hull received on 9 April 1941. Essentially, it reiterated the proposals the priests had brought back from Tokyo: Japan, though unwilling to abandon the Tripartite Pact, pointed out that she was only obligated to come to the aid of Germany if the Americans were the aggressors. In return for this 'promise' the United States was to arrange peace between Japan and Nationalist China on the basis of the withdrawal of most (but not all) Japanese troops from China, recognition of the Open Door Policy, the merger of the Chungking and Nanking regimes and the recognition of Manchukuo by China. If Chiang Kai-shek refused these terms, the United States would withdraw aid from him. Furthermore, the United States was to restore commercial relations with Japan, grant her a loan and assure her of free access to the raw materials she so urgently needed. Then a spectacular conference in Honolulu with Roosevelt and Konoe as the star turns would symbolize the dawn of a new era in American–Japanese relations.

In conversation with Nomura on 16 April a highly sceptical Hull insisted that these proposals would only be acceptable to the United States as a basis for negotiation if accompanied by a real change of heart in Tokyo, and sincere acceptance of his well-known Four Principles: respect for the sovereignty and independence of all nations, non-interference in their internal affairs, equality of economic opportunity for all and the maintenance of the status quo in the Pacific. Only on that strict understanding did Hull ask Nomura to inquire of his government whether it would be willing to give official approval to the informal proposals.

These peaceful gestures were accompanied by signs of a quite different policy certain to exacerbate relations with the United States still further.

Matsuoka, who made no secret of his faith in the Tripartite Pact as the sheet-anchor of Japanese policy, won the support of the Liaison Conference on 30 January 1941 for renewed efforts to strengthen ties with the Axis powers and to negotiate an agreement with Russia. On 3 February another conference decided that Matsuoka should visit Berlin and Moscow. The 'war scare' early that month made approaches to Germany and Russia seem a matter of some urgency. Reports of an impending Japanese attack on Indo-China or on the Dutch East Indies produced a sharp reaction from Britain. The foreign secretary, Anthony Eden, warned the Japanese ambassador that if Japan attacked British possessions Britain would fight. Roosevelt, it is true, backed away from the crisis vetoing Hull's proposals for sending warships to the Far East; instead he warned American citizens to return home and tried to persuade Nomura (unsuccessfully) that public indignation might one day force a reluctant administration into war. However, Roosevelt's characteristically weak riposte was, for once, offset by the effect of remarks made by a counsellor at the American embassy in Tokyo who, in a remarkably outspoken interview with the Japanese vice-minister for foreign affairs, warned the latter that if Japan attacked Singapore war with the United States could not be ruled out. These and other warnings evidently impressed Matsuoka. He backed away very quickly, made reassuring noises about Japanese policy, repudiated all thought of violence and went on his travels all the more determined to return home with a big stick in his hand.

In Berlin Matsuoka was well received for German policy towards Japan was changing in the spring of 1941, basically for three reasons. In the first place Berlin had realized that the calling into existence of the Tripartite Pact had failed to deter the United States. There was now a distinct possibility that Japan, trapped in China and beset with mounting economic problems, might beat a retreat before she found herself at war with America. Was not Nomura's appointment a sign that Japan was ready for an accommodation with the United States? And if Japan did succeed in coming to terms with the Americans, the latter would then be able to concentrate on the Battle of the Atlantic, which would further exacerbate the situation from a German point of view. Secondly, Britain remained undefeated. And, thirdly, with the attack on Russia due to start in June it was essential that the attention of Britain and the United States be deflected to the Far East.

For all these reasons the Germans decided that the time had come to bring Japan into the war. If she could be persuaded to attack Singapore, Britain would be obliged to divide her forces at a critical stage in the Battle of the Atlantic; that could only advantage Germany who had to win the grim struggle on the high seas if she was to drive Britain out of the war. It was, of course, quite possible that the United States would not intervene in the Far East if Britain and Japan went to war. But hostilities between them would most certainly put an end to the possibility of an American–Japanese *rapprochement*. And if the United States did intervene in the war, that would still benefit Germany because public opinion would oblige the administration to keep the fleet in the Pacific, which could only weaken Britain in the Atlantic. And as the United States was in no position to wage war at this time, she would risk defeat if she did fight.

Hitler and Ribbentrop urged Matsuoka to seize a 'unique' opportunity of expanding southwards and delivering the *coup de grâce* to Britain – whom they hastened to assure their Japanese guest was at her last gasp – before American aid could be of much use to her. America was unlikely to intervene. But if she did, Germany would declare war on her, a promise Hitler honoured in December 1941. Nor need Japan fear a Russian attack in her rear; 160 German divisions would deter the Russians though, again, if Soviet Russia attacked Japan, Germany would declare war on her.

The Germans did their level best to draw Japan into the war. But, as Hitler explained later to Mussolini, Matsuoka combined 'the hypocrisy of an American bible missionary with all the wiles of a Japanese oriental'.[14] While the Japanese foreign minister was quite prepared to agree with his hosts that Japan could only attain her goals by force, he remained extremely evasive about the timing of an attack on Singapore, and repeatedly stressed the difficulties he faced in Japan from those opposed to war. The truth was that at bottom he had no more desire than Konoe to fight Britain or the United States. The whole point of Matsuoka's strategy was to intimidate, not to fight, the Anglo-Saxon powers.

The hints Matsuoka picked up in Berlin about the state of Russo-German relations were of great assistance to him. Originally his aims were extremely ambitious; he had supposed on the basis of the Russo-German Pact that he could negotiate a general settlement of the differences between Japan and Russia and align that power with the Tripartite Pact powers in a grand Quadruple Alliance – a revealing insight into the ignorance in Tokyo about the European situation. Although Hitler was not prepared to reveal the secret of Barbarossa to Japan – and incredibly did not seek Japanese military help until later – Ribbentrop did at least admit that relations with Russia had deteriorated to a point where war was possible. Armed with this intelligence, Matsuoka went on to Moscow for what was clearly the most crucial stage in his European tour. It was a simple matter of geography; unless Russia was neutralized, Japan dare not move southwards and take over the colonial possessions of the white powers. An agreement with Russia was as essential for Japan as the Russo-German Pact had been to Hitler in 1939; both were triggers enabling one partner to launch a war of aggression.[15] What Matsuoka took to Moscow was the certain knowledge that it was pointless to waste time trying to persuade Russia to associate closely with the Tripartite Powers as he had done previously during conversations with Stalin and Molotov when he stopped off in Moscow *en route* for Berlin. All that could be obtained in Moscow was a bilateral agreement. At first even this modest objective was difficult to accomplish. Negotiations deadlocked over Sakhalin island; Russia wanted to buy south Sakhalin from Japan and Japan north Sakhalin from Russia. Although Russia and Japan eventually agreed to abandon their demands, Russia still

---

[14]D. Irving, *Hitler's War* (London, 1977), pp. 261–2.

[15]Matsuoka had no intention of respecting a pact with Russia. He told the German ambassador: 'If war should break out between Germany and the Soviet Union, no Japanese Prime Minister or Foreign Secretary would be able to keep Japan neutral. In such a case Japan would be impelled by national considerations to join Germany in attacking Russia'. *DGFP* Ott to German Foreign Office, 6 May 1941.

insisted that Japan surrender all the concessions she enjoyed in north Sakhalin. Matsuoka was on the point of returning home in despair when in a final interview with Stalin the latter suddenly waived this demand and on 13 April a neutrality pact was signed in which Japan and Russia promised to remain neutral in the event of the other partner being involved in war with one or more powers.

Stalin's attitude changed because of uncertainty about German intentions. In all probability he was greatly disappointed by the failure of the Germans to come to terms with Molotov about the Balkans in November 1940. There were ominous signs that Germany was encroaching on what the Russians regarded as their sphere of influence. At the end of February German troops entered Bulgaria and on 1 March she signed the Tripartite Pact. Early in April Hitler attacked Greece and Yugoslavia and by 16 March Yugoslavia, with whom Russia had only just signed a non-aggression pact on 5 April, was on the point of surrender. At times Stalin seems to have doubted whether peace could be preserved until 1942 when, if war came, Russia would be much better prepared. And if it did come in 1941, Russia did not wish to fight on two fronts. Therefore it made sense to have an agreement with Japan committing her to neutrality in the event of a German attack on Russia. It should be added that Stalin was not seeking or planning war with Germany. On the contrary; after the German victories in the Balkans he made every effort to appease the Germans, insisting, for example, that the terms of the commercial treaty signed in January 1941 be scrupulously observed: food and raw materials continued to be delivered to Germany right up to the moment of attack. Stalin persuaded himself that German troop movements in Poland and Rumania were intended only as a weapon of diplomatic coercion to intimidate Russia for he obviously could not bring himself to believe that Hitler would gamble on being able to defeat Soviet Russia before he had dealt with Britain and the United States.

For Matsuoka the neutrality pact was a consolation prize for what had been a disappointing mission to Europe. It did at least guarantee Japan's northern frontier in China should an advance in the Pacific lead to war with the United States. The pact might also strengthen Japan's hands in negotiations with Chiang Kai-shek even if Stalin had refused to abandon Nationalist China to please the Japanese. However, on his return to Tokyo Matsuoka discovered to his dismay that the moderates had won another victory. On 21 April the Liaison Conference had agreed to continue negotiations with the United States on the basis of the 'American plan' transmitted to Tokyo by Nomura. In cabinet Matsuoka opposed a decision which would weaken Japan's ties with the Axis powers and, as he saw it, prevent Japan attaining her objectives. Only by standing up to the Americans – so Matsuoka believed – would they back down, precisely the effect the American 'hawks' maintained their tactics would have on Japan. But a majority, fearful that a hard line would drag them into war with the United States – now a distinct possibility in the light of the deteriorating Atlantic situation – stood firm. In the end proposals, modified somewhat to meet Matsuoka's objections, were sent to Washington on 12 May.

The chances of success were slight from the outset. However sincere the

Konoe cabinet was in its desire for an agreement with the United States, it was not prepared to pay the price of abandoning its ambitions to make Japan the dominant Pacific power. And Tokyo had misunderstood the American position; Nomura, in his desperate anxiety to act as matchmaker, did not mention Hull's Four Principles to Tokyo and implied that the draft he sent home was an 'American plan' which it most certainly was not.

Why did the United States allow negotiations with Tokyo to go ahead despite extreme scepticism in official quarters about the possibility of any settlement with the Japanese?

In the first place the grave situation in the Atlantic obliged Roosevelt to reinforce the Atlantic Fleet by transferring ships from the Pacific. The fact that the Japanese were prepared to conduct negotiations at all made it marginally easier to weaken the Pacific Fleet. True, Roosevelt compromised in the end and only three battleships and one aircraft carrier were transferred leaving the Pacific Fleet 75 per cent intact. Still, by the end of May these ships were playing a vital part in the Atlantic patrol. Secondly, Ambassador Grew, an experienced diplomat, believed that in view of the widespread opposition to war he thought he detected in Japan, there was a real chance that Matsuoka's pro-Axis policy could be undermined if the United States showed willingness to negotiate with Japan. Thirdly, even if the negotiations foundered very quickly, as the administration expected, a further breathing space would have been won in the Pacific. And with persistent rumours of an impending attack on Russia reaching Washington it made good sense to do everything possible to avoid war with Japan. Finally, time was important because of a change in American strategy in respect of the Philippines. In the past the army had planned to abandon the islands in the event of attack. In the summer of 1941 the decision was taken to defend the Philippines by stationing a force of B-17 bombers there, which Stimson and Knox thought would act as a deterrent to Japanese aggression. Not until March 1942 would the build-up be completed and 165 B-17s deployed in the Philippines.

The conversations in Washington in May and June followed a predictable course. There was no meeting of minds. Though the Japanese continually assured the Americans that they genuinely wanted an agreement – which was undoubtedly true – they did not modify their position sufficiently to make this possible. They were prepared to play down the importance of the Tripartite Pact but would not promise neutrality in the event of war between Germany and the United States arising out of America's 'defensive' measures to help Britain. Nor would they promise categorically to expand in south-east Asia by peaceful means only. And whilst ready to have the United States acting as mediator in the China war, they were unwilling to withdraw their troops from Manchukuo, Inner Mongolia or north China in the near future. The Americans were equally inflexible, being convinced that only if they insisted on the maximum could they deter the Japanese from war. And the more the Japanese twisted and wriggled to get the best of both worlds, the more the Americans accused them of duplicity.

The German attack on Russia both surprised and displeased the Japanese. Despite Hitler's refusal to inform Tokyo of his plans, Japan's representatives in Berlin constantly warned Tokyo of German intentions from mid April onwards. After seeing Ribbentrop on 5 June Ōshima cabled home that war was inevitable, a view confirmed by the military attaché a few days later. Curiously enough the Liaison Conference discounted the rumours feeling that if they were genuine Stalin would avoid war by making whatever concessions were necessary to appease the Germans; more likely if Hitler intended to launch a new campaign it would be against Britain.[16] But resentment at Germany's highhandedness was quickly superseded by eagerness to exploit the opportunities suddenly opening up for Japan.

Matsuoka was all for joining in the attack on Russia at once. In this he was encouraged by Ribbentrop but not by Hitler who believed that Germany could win without the assistance of the 'yellows'. In fact Matsuoka was virtually isolated in the corridors of power where he was being criticized for his promise to Stalin that he would persuade Tokyo to abandon the Japanese concessions in north Sakhalin. After intense discussion army command decided, notwithstanding its long anti-communist tradition, not to risk war with Russia. The reverses suffered by the Japanese in 1938–9 had inculcated into army command a healthy respect for the Russian Far Eastern Army which was currently 700,000 strong compared with the 350,000 strong Kwantung Army. Army command was not convinced that Germany would win easily against Russia, another good reason for not getting trapped in a second protracted war. The strategy of the 'ripe persimmon' had everything to commend it, i.e. to build up the Kwantung Army and intervene in Russia only when the Germans had virtually defeated her. This decision was important for Russia, too, because when the spy Richard Sorge informed Moscow of it, 200,000 men were at once switched westwards to stem the German advance. The Japanese navy, initially hostile even to the build-up of forces in the north, finally acquiesced in the new strategy on condition that the navy's own plans for southward expansion were no longer opposed by the army. A start would now be made in this direction by occupying southern Indo-China. Although resistance was not anticipated from either Britain or the United States, nevertheless military preparations would be put in hand to deal with this eventuality. After much animated discussion the Liaison Conference endorsed this strategy on 30 June and the Imperial Conference on 2 July.[17]

Economic necessity was already impelling the Japanese towards precipitate action in the Pacific. Japan produced only 2.3 million barrels of oil annually; she was, therefore, massively dependent on imports to the tune of 33.5 million barrels; 27.2 million barrels from the United States, 4.8 million barrels from the Dutch East Indies and Borneo and 1.5 million barrels from other sources. Whilst the Dutch East Indies exported 48.4 million barrels of refined products annually, only 2.3 million barrels went to Japan. To rectify the position Japan opened negotiations with the Dutch East Indies in September 1940 in the expectation of a fivefold increase in oil imports and substantial increases in tin

[16]Matsuoka commented to the emperor on 6 June that 'the outlook for German–Soviet relations was 60 per cent for the conclusion of an agreement and 40 per cent for war': J.W. Morley, *The Fateful Choice. Japan's advance into South-east Asia 1939–1941* (New York, 1981), p. 82.

[17]The Imperial Conference, like the Liaison Conference, was an unofficial body. It had broadly the same composition but met in the emperor's presence. Like the Liaison Conference it was dominated by the military.

and rubber imports. On 17 June 1941 the negotiations ended in complete failure much to the annoyance of the Japanese who blamed it on British and American encouragement of Dutch resistance to Japanese pressure. Then on 20 June the United States struck another blow at Japanese oil supplies when she prohibited the export of oil from Atlantic and Gulf Coast ports to countries other than Britain and the Latin' American states. As Japan had reserves of crude and refined oil products of only 48.9 million barrels, sufficient for a mere 18 months, the Dutch and American decisions in effect set a time limit to the realization of Japanese ambitions in south-east Asia.

As the temptation to seize the oil and mineral wealth of the Dutch East Indies grew in Tokyo, the signs multiplied that Britain and the United States would offer resistance if she did so. Immediately after the signature of the Russian–Japanese neutrality agreement Britain renewed her pressure on the United States for a meeting of military representatives to discuss the joint defence of south-east Asia against Japanese aggression. Although the United States was committed to a defensive strategy in the event of a Pacific war, she had agreed at the Washington Conference to collaborate with the British and Dutch in the preparation of joint plans for the area. At the Singapore Conference, held between 22 and 26 April, officers from the United States, Britain, Australia, New Zealand, India and the Dutch East Indies attempted to work out a common strategy, the so-called ADB Agreement. In practice little progress was made because of the stumbling block of Singapore. Britain was anxious to defend it, America was not. In the end all that emerged was an agreement that all the interested parties including the United States would declare war on Japan if she attacked British, Dutch or American territory, or moved into Siam or Timor or the Loyalty islands off New Caledonia. Although these measures in no way committed the United States automatically to war with Japan, Tokyo saw in the conference another proof that the American attitude was becoming much more belligerent.[18] By the spring of 1941 the policy-makers in Tokyo, military and civilian alike, were convinced that the Americans, British and Dutch were attempting to encircle Japan and prevent her by force from achieving what she regarded as her rightful place in east Asia. Western aid to Chiang Kai-shek, American rearmament, the continued stationing of the American fleet at Hawaii, the refusal of the Dutch East Indies to sell more oil to Japan and Roosevelt's freezing order were seen not as an inevitable reaction to their own ill-advised moves taken with little thought of their consequences, but as deliberate steps in a sinister plot to force Japan to surrender.

The arrival of the American note on 21 June confirmed this belief. Summing up the American position, Washington insisted that a *sine qua non* for all subsequent negotiation would be a declaration by Japan that she would not go to war if the United States went to war with Germany. On China Japan must agree to make peace on the basis of respect for the sovereignty of that country before the United States would consent to act as mediator. The illusion that the United States might be willing to compromise on the abstract principles constantly invoked by Hull was dispelled by the blunt statement the secretary of state read

---

[18]In July 1941 Admiral Stark and General Marshall refused to endorse the ADB Agreement on the grounds that it covered too vast an area, the United States fleet could find itself operating in areas of no strategic interest to America and the plan still pivoted on the defence of Singapore.

out to Nomura when handing over the note. Because Nomura had misled Tokyo in the first place into supposing that the United States had taken the initiative in the negotiations, the note was inevitably interpreted as a hardening of the American position when, in fact, it was no more than a reiteration of an established attitude. This latest evidence of American intransigence deepened Tokyo's paranoid suspicion of the white powers and strengthened the conviction of the policy-makers that time was running out for Japan. The conclusion was inescapable: the quicker she moved towards her goals the better, even if it meant war with Britain and the United States. That was the essence of the decision taken by the Imperial Conference on 2 July 1941.

But with an ambivalence characteristic of Japanese policy a majority of the cabinet still hoped to square the circle and wanted to continue the conversations with the United States as long as possible. That Germany opposed further talks did not in the least dismay them; Japanese interests guided their policy, then as in the past, not loyalty to the Germans. Significantly, army and navy command supported this policy, being just as reluctant as the civilians to resort to force if there was still a chance of negotiations succeeding; at the very least these should continue until southern Indo-China had been occupied. To all this Matsuoka was violently opposed. Obliged by military pressure to agree to new conversations, he sought to frustrate them by going over Konoe's head and instructing Nomura to reject Hull's oral statement and hand over the latest Japanese note several days later, not simultaneously as Konoe wished. This proved Matsuoka's undoing. The military policy-makers were already exasperated by his attempts to interfere with their monopoly in foreign affairs as well as by his habit of leaking plans to the Germans. Konoe and his colleagues felt strong enough to get rid of an uncongenial colleague. Frightened to drop him outright lest it was thought they were deferring to American pressure, they covered their tracks by resigning en bloc on 16 July. In the third Konoe cabinet the new foreign minister was Vice Admiral Toyada Teijirō, a 'dove' reputedly well-disposed towards the Anglo-Saxon powers. That army and navy still had the upper hand is evident from the fact that half of the 14 cabinet members were military men.

The fall of Matsuoka and the extensive changes in foreign office personnel that followed were not interpreted in Washington as evidence of an impending change in Japanese policy. Ominous news of the call-up of reservists and the clamour of the strident and viciously anti-British and anti-American press in Tokyo pointed in the opposite direction. Most important of all this pessimistic diagnosis was confirmed by American naval intelligence, which in the autumn of 1940 had broken some of the Japanese diplomatic codes and was now deciphering all dispatches between the Tokyo foreign office and the Washington embassy. The material uncovered by the so-called Magic operation left no doubt in the minds of the American administration that the objectives of the new cabinet were unchanged.

It came as no surprise when on 14 July Japan demanded that the French allow Japanese troops to occupy southern Indo-China and establish several naval and air bases in that area. Failing a positive answer within the month, Japan threatened to send her troops into Indo-China in any case. With no hope of support from the United States or Britain, Vichy France gave in on 21 July.

By the end of the month 50,000 Japanese troops had entered Indo-China and established bases. Strategically Japan was now in a position to close the Burma Road, the most important supply route to Chiang Kai-shek; more alarming still, she could attack the Dutch East Indies and obtain by force the oil she had failed to secure by negotiation.

Reprisals followed swiftly. Roosevelt and Hull had always opposed a total ban on the export of oil and oil products, arguing, with considerable force, that if the Japanese were deprived of their oil, they were more likely to seize the Dutch East Indies. Up to the summer of 1941 they had been able to hold the hardliners – Stimson, Morgenthau and Ickes – at bay. Once it became clear by mid July that Japan intended to expand southwards whatever the consequences, the president and his secretary of state accepted the inevitability of further sanctions. On 23 July Hull informed Nomura that in view of the Japanese decision to pursue a policy of 'totalitarian expansion', he was terminating the long-running conversations. On 26 July all Japanese funds and assets in the United States were frozen and the cabinet agreed to impose tighter controls on the export of fuel to Japan.

This was not a total ban, however, for Roosevelt was still convinced, as were Hull and Welles, that to deprive Japan of all fuel would simply precipitate a conflict in the Pacific. Therefore the new regulations issued on 9 August still permitted the export of fuel products provided they did not exceed in volume the quantities exported in 1935–6 and that oils suitable for aircraft were excluded. The president clearly envisaged a temporary interruption of trade with Japan to be followed by a resumption of this trade at a reduced level equal to that of 1935–6. But the issue was, in fact, decided not by the president but by two newly-formed government agencies: the Economic Defence Board, headed by a 'hawk', Vice President Henry Wallace, on which Stimson, Morgenthau and Knox sat, and by the three-man Interdepartmental Committee headed by another 'hawk', Dean Acheson. By refusing to allow the release of funds even for the purchase of inferior grades of fuel they imposed in effect a total embargo so that after 1 August virtually no oil was shipped to Japan. When Roosevelt realized early in September what had happened, it was too late; a reversal of policy would have been misconstrued in Tokyo and London and by the American public. So with great reluctance Roosevelt acquiesced in the total embargo he had never planned. Middle-echelon officials in Washington, like their Japanese counterparts, had been able to give a decisive twist to American policy. For looking back over the events of 1941 it could well be argued that the Japanese decision to start military preparations for southward expansion and the American riposte in the form of a total oil embargo set the United States and Japan on a collision course which made war well-nigh unavoidable. All the same, war did not appear to be imminent in the summer of 1941 because both sides were anxious to delay a confrontation for sound military reasons.

Japan's leaders were completely taken aback by the oil embargo. The consequences for Japan were extremely grave. Britain and the Dominions had followed the American lead by impounding Japanese assets and terminating trade with her. In August the Dutch East Indies did the same. This left Japan with less than two years' oil reserves which she was using up at the rate of

12,000 tons daily. 'From now on the oil gauge and the clock stood side by side. Each fall in the level brought the hour of decision nearer'.[19] Unless Japan seized the oil and raw materials she needed in the near future she would be quite powerless to resist American pressure for the abandonment of her plans to dominate east Asia.

Yet it was also recognized not only by moderates but by extremists as well that in any trial by battle the odds would be very heavily weighted against Japan. To get to the Dutch East Indies the Japanese would first have to seize Singapore and the Philippines, which would in all probability mean war with Britain and America; and by then the Dutch would have blown up their oil installations; before production was restored the reserves would have run out and Japan would face certain defeat. The only viable alternative was to try to negotiate with Washington in the faint hope of escaping from a military cul-de-sac. With Britain reeling back in the Middle East and the tension between the United States and Germany moving inexorably towards crisis-point in the Atlantic, perhaps the Americans might after all be ready to recognize the new power realities in the Pacific. So it was agreed that Konoe should approach the United States. But while the navy wholeheartedly endorsed Konoe's efforts, the army insisted that if no progress was made Konoe must promise to fight the Americans.

On 6 August new proposals approved by the Liaison Conference were put to Washington. Japan promised not to send troops into territories other than Indo-China; her troops would be withdrawn from that territory as soon as the China incident was terminated; in return the United States would be expected to recognize Japan's special position in Indo-China and urge Chiang Kai-shek to negotiate with Japan; Japan would also guarantee the neutrality of the Philippines; in return Japan would expect the United States to suspend the build-up of military forces in the south-west Pacific and request the British and Dutch to do the same; finally, Japan would expect the United States to co-operate with her in ensuring access to raw materials in south-east Asia. Konoe, who doubted whether anything less than a Japanese withdrawal from China would move the Americans, seems to have hoped to short-circuit the military – who would certainly not accept what he had in mind – by proposing an immediate summit meeting with Roosevelt where the differences between the two countries could be resolved with the emperor's approval but without further reference to Tokyo. The conference proposal was eagerly endorsed by Ambassador Grew who felt that time was running out quickly for the moderates as American economic pressure began to bite.

Fortified by the knowledge from Magic intercepts that the Japanese military had not the slightest intention of abandoning their expansionist plans, the Americans regarded the new proposals as nothing but a subterfuge. Hull was profoundly disillusioned by the Japanese move into Indo-China, and returned from the Atlantic Conference convinced that further appeasement of Japan was quite useless. To him there were no moderates or extremists in Tokyo, only militant aggressors. As he put it succinctly on 2 August: 'Nothing will stop

---

[19]H. Feis, *The Road to Pearl Harbor. The Coming of War between the United States and Japan* (Princeton, 1950), p. 244.

them except force. Unless we figure that they are going to turn back, we should not figure that they are going to be satisfied to stop where they are. The point is how long we can maneuver the situation until the military matter in Europe is brought to a conclusion . . . . there is naturally going to continue to be an element of risk and danger in our course, if it is sufficiently firm and extensive to checkmate them. I just don't want us to take for granted a single word they say but appear to do so to whatever extent it may satisfy our purpose to delay further action by them'.[20] Accordingly he responded coolly to the Japanese proposals and held out little hope that the president would agree to a summit meeting.

The president did indeed take an equally pessimistic view of the situation. When he discussed Japan with Churchill at the Atlantic Conference in early August the British prime minister urged Roosevelt to agree to an ultimatum to Japan following her occupation of southern Indo-China. Churchill, in his turn, was under pressure from Australia and from the Dutch who, fearing an imminent attack on the Dutch East Indies, wanted the United States to commit herself to offer military resistance to Japan. Churchill favoured a joint warning by the United States, Britain and Soviet Russia leaving the Japanese in no doubt about the consequences if they moved into the Dutch East Indies or Malaya. Roosevelt refused, preferring to continue the conversations with Japan. Not that he trusted her an inch; nor did he intend to ease the economic sanctions or allow her to use Indo-China as a base for attacking China. The overriding purpose of American policy, he told Churchill, was to gain time – even a bare month would be useful. This he believed was best done by going through the motions of negotiating with the Japanese. In the end Roosevelt agreed to deliver a stern warning to Nomura making it clear that if Japan made further advances, the United States would take steps likely to lead to war, and would give assistance to any territory attacked by Japan. Back in Washington Roosevelt agreed with Hull that it might be wiser to tone down the warning simply to ensure the continuation of the discussions with Japan.

At his meeting with Nomura on 17 August Roosevelt did his best to minimize the significance of the warning he gave the Japanese ambassador. In an expansive mood he indicated a willingness to consider resuming the conversations suspended a month before provided the Japanese suspended 'their expansionist activities' and were genuinely ready to 'embark upon a peaceful program for the Pacific'. In advance of this he was ready to meet Konoe at a summit conference in October in Alaska if Japan would state unambiguously what her intentions and plans were. This statement the Japanese promptly supplied. As always, Japan's actions were depicted as being purely 'defensive in nature' whilst American counter-measures were always a 'serious threat' to Japan; still, she repeated her offer to withdraw troops from Indo-China when the China incident was over; she declared that her activities in Indo-China were not a prelude to further military advances; and, finally, she promised not to attack Russia provided that that power respected the neutrality pact.

When he received this reply from Nomura on 28 August Roosevelt was still outwardly genial and friendly, and amenable to Japanese suggestions that a

[20]*FRUS* IV, p. 359. Memorandum by Cecil W. Gray, 2 August 1941.

summit conference be held as early as September. A few days later the president's scepticism had reasserted itself. Strong opposition to summitry was being expressed not only by Hull but by the Far Eastern Division in the State Department and in the Treasury. Under this pressure Roosevelt had second thoughts. When Nomura was received by the president and secretary of state on 3 September he discovered that the American position had suddenly hardened. They now insisted that proof of a change of heart on Japan's part must precede a summit meeting; specifically, Japan must detach herself from the Tripartite Pact, withdraw her forces from China and practise non-discrimination in economic matters. Whatever slender hopes Konoe had pinned to a meeting with Roosevelt were dashed by these impossible terms. The irony of the situation was that when some Japanese were at least holding out a slim possibility that the expansionist drive into south-east Asia might be halted, the American administration had moved onto the offensive.

Was this a lost opportunity to avoid a tragic war in the Pacific? Should the president have met Konoe? And might not a summit meeting have discovered a *modus vivendi* between the two powers even at this late stage? Few would disagree that 'jaw jaw' is better than 'war war'. But it is an inescapable fact of international life that negotiations can only reach a successful conclusion when both parties are prepared to make significant concessions to the other's point of view. The sad truth is that by the summer of 1941 the respective positions of the United States and Japan had moved too far apart for any accommodation to emerge. There is much force in the contention that whatever Konoe might say and even genuinely have believed, his credibility was reduced by the pressure of economic reality, the power of an inflamed and chauvinist-minded public opinion and the determination of the Japanese military not to miss the bus in south-east Asia. A withdrawal of troops from China would certainly have impressed the 'hawks' in Washington but such a concession was quite inconceivable on the part of a government driven into a cul-de-sac by its own ambitions. Had Konoe made the offer even with the emperor's approval and probably with the support of naval command, it is difficult to imagine that the course of Japanese foreign policy would have been altered; more likely Konoe would have fallen victim to an assassin's bullet.

On the American side the 'hawks', now fully in control of policy in the summer of 1941, never wavered in their stern belief in the perfidy of the wily orientals, a belief fed continually by knowledge of the diplomatic correspondence between Tokyo and Washington. Nothing short of a complete withdrawal from China and from Indo-China as well would now convince the administration and a fiercely anti-Japanese public opinion that Japan had at last seen the error of her ways and was prepared to retrace her steps.

The stumbling blocks standing in the way of better relations between Japan and America were not the Tripartite Pact nor the issue of economic discrimination. Had the United States gone to war with Germany, Japan had virtually promised to remain neutral despite the pact. Nor in view of the small amount of trade the Americans conducted with China need the monopoly practices of the Japanese have proved an insuperable obstacle in negotiation. But about the future of China there were formidable differences of opinion.

For Japan only a resounding defeat for Chiang Kai-shek could justify the years of strenuous effort in China; anything less than a peace favourable to Japan would be a humiliation intolerable to bear; that was a political reality which Japan expected the United States to accept. But for America the victory of Chiang Kai-shek was now considered an essential requirement if a free, independent and democratic China was to emerge as a stabilizing factor in the politics of the Far East; and the victory of Nationalist China was equated by American policy-makers with the defence of American imperial interests and with the realization of her long-term economic objectives in the Far East. Ties with the Chinese were growing throughout 1941. Chiang Kai-shek was allocated a $166 million share of Lease–Lend, and American army and airforce pilots were allowed to volunteer for service in China. Relatively little material aid was reaching China because priority was given to Britain and later to Russia and also because of the sheer physical difficulty of getting supplies through to Chungking. As a moral gesture to placate Chiang Kai-shek for the lack of material assistance, the United States announced on 26 August that a military mission was being sent to China, a step hotly denounced in the Tokyo press as one more proof of American hostility.

A heretical thought may occur to the reader at this point. Might there not have been considerable short-term advantages for the United States in achieving a *modus vivendi* with Japan and in effect turning her back on the Far East? Why did the Americans not leave China to fight on alone so that they could concentrate all their efforts on the defeat of Germany? Certainly Japan would in all probability have conquered all south-east Asia to obtain the raw materials she so desperately needed. But arguably the United States – and Britain too – might have obtained the oil, tin and rubber they needed from alternative sources of supply had they put their minds to it. Nor need the contribution of Australia and New Zealand to the war effort in the Middle East have been too seriously impaired by a temporary Japanese victory in the Far East for Japan had no intention of attacking either nor could she have controlled the Indian Ocean across which troop transports from the Dominions travelled. And once Germany was defeated the constellation of world power would change. Japan, surrounded by a coalition of victorious powers, would then have little choice but to capitulate in the face of diplomatic and economic pressure and surrender her conquests as she had done in 1894 and again in 1921, probably without any American blood being spilt.

Machiavellian calculations of this sort do not, however, fit easily into the American scene in the summer of 1941. No American president, especially one as sensitive to public opinion as Roosevelt, could possibly have carried through a *volte-face* on this scale in the teeth of an outraged public taught by the press magnates and by vociferous pressure groups to regard the Japanese as the Devil Incarnate and to equate appeasement with moral turpitude. A Far Eastern Munich made excellent strategic sense but it would have spelt political suicide. Also, any hint of surrender to Japan would have had a demoralizing effect on the enemies of the Axis. For if Japan was encouraged to occupy southeast Asia what hope could there be of the imperialist powers restoring the old colonial order after the war? Thirdly, the 'hawks' were in the ascendancy in Washington and it was their unwavering belief that appeasement only encouraged the Japanese as it had encouraged Hitler in Europe. Some 'hawks' still thought a firm line would bring Japan to heel even at this late hour. But even if tough measures drove Japan to war, as many others in the administration thought likely, she would be defeated quickly – an astonishing overestimation of American power in the Pacific, which the military knew was a nonsense. Finally, the problem of Japan was seen not in isolation but in a global context; far from freeing the United States to concentrate on the defeat of Germany, appeasement would encourage the Germans to believe America was wavering in her resolution to destroy fascism.

Thus, for one reason or another, the American attitude to Japan showed no sign of weakening. But it must be emphasized once more that whilst Americans had maintained a constant interest in China and had always thought of a stable China as the sheet-anchor for a future era of peace and order in the Far East, the United States had not been willing in the past to risk an armed conflict with Japan on behalf of the Chinese; neither in 1931 nor in 1937 had military action in support of China commended itself to Washington. Only in 1941, precisely when informed military opinion was strongly opposed to armed intervention, did the administration decide to take its stand on the sovereignty and independence of China. The economic pressure being applied to Japan was not intended simply to deter further Japanese advances whilst allowing them to hold on to the gains made in the last decade; the Americans made it absolutely clear that they would not be satisfied until they had turned back the clock and forced Japan out of China, a quite unrealistic objective which would in all probability end in the very war which both president and secretary of state were as anxious as the military to avoid.

In Tokyo the count-down to war commenced on 6 September when the Imperial Conference approved plans for action. Even before the intransigent American note of 3 September arrived, the military leaders were demanding action in the near future. It was decided on 6 September that preparations for war with the United States, Britain and the Netherlands should be put in hand forthwith. As early November was the best time for a successful landing in the Dutch East Indies and December the last possible date before the arrival of the monsoons delayed military operations until the spring of 1942, all preparations for action must be completed by the end of October. Negotiations with the United States would continue because Tokyo still believed the United States did not want war with Japan and would pay a high price to avoid it. Resolutely ignoring the size of the gap separating them from the American position, the Japanese acted as if redoubled efforts by Nomura and Kurusu must persuade the Americans of the justice of Japan's case. But if the negotiations had not succeeded by early October the final decision to commence hostilities would be taken. Operational imperatives in the shape of declining oil reserves and the approach of bad weather were decisive for the army and navy. The Japanese made exactly the same mistake as the Germans in dismissing the immense industrial potential of their opponents as a factor of little significance because both Axis powers assumed that they could win in a short swift campaign. A heavy responsibility rested on naval command at this point for army command – knowing full well that military success depended on the navy – forced naval command to declare its hand without equivocation. Senior naval officers such as Navy Minister Oikawa Koshirō were acutely aware of the heavy odds against Japan and accordingly reluctant to fight. But in the navy, as in the army, middle-echelon officers carried the day with their wildly optimistic assertions that swift Japanese victories in the early stages of a war plus a possible German victory over Britain and Russia would throw the United States onto the defensive and lead to the conclusion of peace within a matter of months. Furthermore, if Japan waited until 1942 her present naval superiority over the British, Americans and Dutch in the Pacific would disappear. So they persuaded their superior officers that Japan could seize and hold a vast area in south-east Asia even though Japan lacked transport to ship the oil of the Dutch East Indies to the homeland and the airpower to defend the new empire they would conquer. The casual assumption that the United State would lost heart and capitulate rather than mobilize her vast potential was a product of short-term military responses to the situation they were in. What they steadfastly refused to face up to – despite the accurate information they possessed about American potential – was the certainty of defeat in a long war. Of course, the atmosphere in September 1941 did not encourage doubts; ultra-nationalist organizations were clamouring for action and threatening the lives of those who wavered.

The short-term strategy the Japanese pursued after the freezing order was imposed was not even a calculated though foolhardy risk but a mad decision certain to end in disaster. Admiral Nagano Osami, chief of naval staff, expressed the curious mixture of despair and defiance which filled many of his colleagues when he commented gloomily: 'if there is a war, the country may be ruined. Nevertheless, a nation which does not fight in this plight has lost its spirit and is already a doomed country. Only if we fight to the last soldier will it be possible to find a way out of this fatal situation'.[21] Driven into a corner by their enemies and haemorrhaging fatally, Japan's leaders fell back on the old samurai traditions: it is better to face certain death than surrender; the spiritual power of an indomitable will is certain to give Japan victory over superior military force, and the Almighty will stand by his people in time of crisis – much the same qualities Hitler invoked when Germany was trapped in a life-or-death struggle she could not win by human reckoning. This attitude was poles apart from that of Washington officials who believed in their neat and rational manner that each turn of the screw would force Japan to surrender – a view which completely ignored the mounting sense of desperation in Tokyo as the man-trap closed. And if she did fight, the Americans reasoned, why she would lose very quickly and must surely realize that.

The sheer inability of the Japanese to offer terms that stood the remotest chance of acceptance doomed all negotiation to inevitable failure. On China they simply re-stated the old proposal that America and Britain leave the ring clear for Japan to settle the China incident by closing the Burma Road and terminating all aid to Chiang Kai-shek. A few days later the Liaison Conference reduced the chances of agreement still further by revealing that Japan intended to keep her forces in northern China and Inner Mongolia after peace had been arranged with the Nationalists, and that Chiang Kai-shek was

[21]Quoted in James B. Crowley, ed., *Modern East Asia: Essays in Interpretation* (New York, 1970), p. 261.

expected to recognize Manchukuo and merge his government with the satellite regime of Wang Ching-wei. Japan also expected Britain and the United States to freeze their forces at present levels, take no military action considered hostile by Japan, co-operate with her in ensuring access to raw materials and finally restore normal trading relations. In return Japan offered not to use Indo-China as a base for military action against other territories, to withdraw troops eventually from Indo-China and to guarantee the neutrality of the Philippines.

It is hardly surprising in view of the intransigent American attitude that no progress was made in the exchanges between Tokyo and Washington in September and October. Each accused the other of hiding behind general principles and refusing to specify in detail what concrete steps it expected the other to take. By mid October Konoe, under heavy pressure from an impatient army, was forced out of office. He had pleaded in vain with Tōjō to withdraw the army from China, the only concession likely to impress the Americans. Tōjō was adamant in his refusal; the prestige of the army and the national security of Japan were at stake; nor did he think the United States would be satisfied with one concession; other demands would surely follow, for was America not seeking hegemony in the Far East at the expense of Japan? Although the navy ministry was sympathetic to Konoe's views, it was too frightened of the middle-echelon officers, who dominated the naval general staff and were in favour of immediate action, to come out clearly on his side. To resolve the deadlock Konoe resigned on 16 October. The next day a cabinet was formed under General Tōjō.

In America the appointment of Tōjō, later tried and condemned to death at the Tokyo War Crimes Trials, was regarded as a sure sign that the military were in complete control and that war was imminent. In fact, Tōjō was prepared to give Konoe's conciliatory policy a last chance, this because the emperor informed Tōjō that in view of the differences between army and navy, he should look afresh at the situation 'with a clean slate' and not feel bound absolutely by the decision of 6 September. Strong opposition to further negotiation was expressed by the army and – to a lesser extent – by the navy general staff who wanted an immediate decision for war. But Tōjō, mindful of the imperial mandate, supported a final attempt at negotiation – on Japan's terms of course – before the decision for war was taken. On 1–2 November a consensus strategy emerged and was approved by the Imperial Conference on 5 November.

A final attempt at negotiation would be made. Two plans would be presented to the Americans: Plan A which raised yet again the fundamental issues on which past negotiations had deadlocked: non-discrimination in trade; Japan's membership of the Tripartite Pact; the vexed question of the withdrawal of Japanese troops from China. In the virtually certain event of this plan being rejected the Japanese negotiators would fall back on Plan B for a *modus vivendi* with the United States. Japan would promise to make no fresh military advances in south-east Asia – with the exception of Indo-China – provided the United States gave a similar undertaking. The United States must promise not to oppose Japan's attempts to make peace with Chiang Kai-shek. When she succeeded in this she would withdraw her troops from Indo-China. But in advance of a peace settlement – and provided she could reach an agreement with the United States – Japan was now prepared to withdraw her troops from southern Indo-China into the north of that country. Finally, the United States was expected to co-operate with Japan to obtain the raw materials both needed from the Dutch East Indies, to restore normal trading relations and to supply Japan with one million tons of aviation fuel. But if agreement with the Americans had not been reached by 30 November the final decision for war would be taken. Meanwhile preparations for military action went ahead. On 3 November Nagano approved the plan for the attack on Pearl Harbor which navy staff had been working on since January. On 5 November the navy was orderd to be ready for action by early December. And on 20 November orders were issued for offensive operations against Malaya and the Philippines.

Nor were there any illusions left in Washington about the future of American–Japanese relations. That war was imminent was apparent to both Roosevelt and Hull. Already on 7 November the president asked members of the cabinet whether the American people would support him if the United States went to war following a Japanese attack on Malaya or the Dutch East Indies. He was assured by colleagues that he would have popular support for even that step. Still, he was determined to gain as much time as possible before the inevitable confrontation occurred. In this he was strengthened by his military advisers. At the very moment when the authorities in Tokyo were trying to decide whether it was worth making one final effort to negotiate, the American administration was in the midst of a crisis over China. The appointment of Tōjō aroused great alarm both in Chungking and in London, where it was feared that Japan would launch an immediate offensive from Indo-China through Yunnan province to cut the Burma Road, capture Kunming and squeeze the life out of Nationalist China, a distinct possibility in view of the desperate shortages in Chungking. London applied pressure to Roosevelt to issue a ringing declaration in support of China; if it did not scare off Japan, it would at least commit the Americans to military action. Momentarily the president wavered but was reminded sharply by the military of the need for the old defensive strategy in the Far East.

The advice of the Joint Army–Navy Board was unequvocal. The overriding priority was the defeat of Germany. Therefore everything possible must be done to avoid war with Japan. The hard fact was that the American navy was too weak to take on Japan and would have to be reinforced in the event of a Pacific war at the expense of the Atlantic Fleet; in all probability that would spell defeat for Britain in the crucial Battle of the Atlantic. However, the military thought the position would improve in a few months. By December American air and naval power in the Philippines would be strong enough to deter Japan from any offensive action south-west of the Philippines. It was conceded by the Joint Board that if Japan attacked British or American territory or the Dutch East Indies, the United States would have to go to war even though she would be obliged to stay on the defensive in the Pacific. But if the Japanese launched a new offensive in China – or attacked Russia – the United States should not take military action. It was argued that an attack through Yunnan province would be a difficult operation and that the Chinese stood a good chance of repelling it. To soften the blow the military asked that more aid be given to China and that economic pressure on Japan be maintained. But no ultimatum should be sent to Japan nor should military forces be committed to help Chiang Kai-shek.

A sharp dichotomy was revealed here between Washington's diplomatic and military priorities. While the administration gave top priority to the total evacuation of China – undoubtedly the major stumbling block in negotiations with Tokyo – the military were willing to live (temporarily at least) with the possibility of the complete collapse of the Chungking government. The fact that Roosevelt and Hull accepted this advice without further discussion and gave no warning to Japan in respect of China placed them in an untenable position; at one and the same time they agreed that China could be forgotten and that war in the Far East must be avoided at all costs yet on the diplomatic front they still insisted on the total evacuation of Japanese troops from China, a demand which brought war nearer.

'Around and around the same circle' – Hull's own phrase – cannot be bettered as a description of the negotiations between the United States and Japan resumed in November 1941 against a sky heavy with storm clouds and with the press on both sides of the Pacific adopting a hysterically belligerent and hectoring tone.[22] There was not the slightest chance of agreement on Plan A. Although Japan did not reject the principle of non-discrimination in trade outright, she would only accept it if it was adopted across the board by all nations, a condition impossible of fulfilment. Similarly, while Japan was very ready to suggest that her membership of the Tripartite Pact would take second place in her scheme of things once she had landed an American agreement, she was unwilling to abandon the pact completely. But on this point of principle Hull was adamant; if Japan would not renounce the pact this was proof positive to him of aggressive intent; and as he knew from intercepts that Japan had every intention of renewing it for another five years – though only for the sake of appearances, in fact – he felt justified in his suspicions. On China the intercepts proved that Japan had no intention of withdrawing all her forces but, as Hull saw matters, was trying to dispel American fears through verbal gymnastics and cosmetic changes in troop dispositions.

By the time Nomura and Kurusu had abandoned Plan A and turned on 20 November to the interim proposals in Plan B, they discovered to their surprise that the United States was also interested in a *modus vivendi*. Behind the change in American tactics lay strategic considerations. As the Joint Army–Navy Board report on 5 November anticipated that the Americans would soon have sufficient force concentrated in the Philippines to deter aggression, Roosevelt decided that it made good political sense to try to secure this valuable breathing space by heading off an imminent Japanese attack. With this in mind he floated the idea of a cooling-off period or armed truce during which the United States and Japan would make no military advances in the Pacific area. There was a flurry of activity in the State Department and by 22 November a package

[22]Contemporary writers sum up the differences between the negotiators succinctly: Hull's approach was that of the 'orderly nineteenth century when imperial ambitions could be satisfied without provoking war . . . and the powers professed regard for the law of nations'. Nomura's outlook 'stretched back to the Emperor Jimmu, traversing centuries of samurai militarism, unmodified by Christian idealism and scarcely touched by democratic individualism': Forrest K. Davis and Ernest K. Lindley, *How War Came* (New York, 1942), p. 210.

emerged bearing more than an accidental resemblance to Plan B.

Whilst the Americans did not retreat in the slightest from their oft-proclaimed general principles as the only basis for a final settlement, they were now offering to unfreeze Japanese assets in the United States, supply petroleum on a monthly basis for civilian needs, ask the British and Dutch to do likewise and, finally, were prepared to encourage the Chinese to commence armistice or peace talks with the Japanese. In return for these concessions Japan must withdraw from southern Indo-China – which she had already offered to do – and limit her forces in Northern Indo-China to 25,000 men. This *modus vivendi* would last 90 days during which period the United States and Japan were supposed to move towards a general settlement. Admiral Stark and General Leonard T. Gerow (Marshall's deputy) strongly approved of this arrangement, which would enable them to complete defensive preparations in the Philippines.

Whether these refreshingly realistic proposals would have led to fruitful discussions with Japan remains extremely doubtful. In any case, the proposals were never handed over to the Japanese negotiators but quietly interred in the State Department. There were several reasons for this change of position.

In the first place a Magic intercept to Nomura on 22 November revealed that, while Tokyo had extended the deadline for negotiations from 25 to 29 November, 'the deadline absolutely cannot be changed. After that things are automatically going to happen', a comment which so infuriated official circles in Washington that all hopes of a *modus vivendi* were virtually abandoned.[23] Two days later Admiral Stark advised all naval commanders that a surprise attack on the Philippines was a possibility. Secondly, on 25 November Stimson received a report, originating with British intelligence, that 30 to 50 Japanese transports carrying five divisions (bound, in fact, for Malaya) had been sighted south-east of Formosa. When Roosevelt was informed of this the next day he bitterly denounced this fresh evidence of Japanese bad faith. Thirdly, American public opinion was reacting indignantly to rumours – circulated by Chinese Nationalist agents – about the proposed *modus vivendi* which the press rejected at once as a piece of ill-timed appeasement. Finally, although the British, Australian and Dutch envoys reacted favourably to it, their governments were at best lukewarm while the Chinese Nationalists were outspoken in their condemnation; Chinese opposition, according to Hull, was the decisive factor. On 26 November Roosevelt agreed with Hull that the proposals must be shelved to dispel any suspicion that they were planning a Far Eastern Munich.

Meanwhile the State Department had been working on another document, originating in the Treasury Department, which contained terms for a final settlement with Japan and had been intended to accompany the *modus vivendi* proposals. On 26 November Hull handed this memorandum to the Japanese negotiators as a possible basis for a long-term discussion. This uncompromising statement, the so-called Ten Point Program, reiterated those lofty general principles from which the United States refused to deviate. It called for the withdrawal of all Japanese troops from China and Indo-China, recognition of

---

[23] *The 'Magic' Background to Pearl Harbor* (Washington, 1977) IV, appendix no. 162, Tokyo to Washington 22 November 1941.

Chiang Kai-shek, and in effect the abandonment by Japan of the Tripartite Pact; in return the United States would unfreeze Japanese assets and negotiate a new trade agreement allowing Japanese silk to enter the United States duty free. In substance though not in form this was an ultimatum. True, no time limit was attached to the offer, nor did the United States threaten to resort to force in the event of a Japanese rejection of the terms. But, as always, the Americans utterly refused to recognize the changing balance of power in east Asia over the previous 10 years. No accommodation was possible on the basis of the Ten Point Program as Roosevelt and Hull were well aware. This was the end of the line. In effect they had abandoned all pretence that war could be avoided, and now awaited impassively the inevitable attack.[24] On 27 November Stark and Marshall sent messages to the commanders of the American forces in Hawaii and the Philippines warning them that negotiations had broken down and an agggressive move by Japan was expected in the next few days.

The intransigent American memorandum simply confirmed the Japanese in their decision taken on 5 November and reaffirmed on 22 November to stake all on war. Even before news of the Ten Points reached Tokyo the task force for the attack on Pearl Harbor had left the Kurile islands on 26 November. On 27 November the Liaison Conference decided on war, a decision confirmed by the Imperial Conference on 1 December. The operational plans were now activated; on 2 December the Pearl Harbor task force was informed that D Day would be 8 December.

In the United States a very heated controversy has raged over the Pearl Harbor disaster. A school of revisionist historians has argued that Roosevelt deliberately manoeuvred the United States into war in the Pacific. Some even alleged that by omitting to take the necessary military precautions he encouraged the Japanese attack on the American fleet confident that such a blow would unite American public opinion against Japan and enable him to bring the United States into the European war through the Far Eastern back door. Behind this emotive thesis lay vestiges of the old isolationism, the conviction that the United States faced no external threat from either Germany or Japan in 1941 so that her entry into the war must have been the result of a deliberate conspiracy against the national interest on the part of the president and his associates. This interpretation does not, however, stand up to detailed investigation.

That war in the Pacific was now virtually unavoidable was understood in Washington. Where the blow would fall the Americans did not know for Magic intercepts revealed nothing about Japanese military planning. It was assumed

---

[24]On 25 November according to the Stimson Diary Roosevelt in discussion with Stimson, Knox, Marshall and Stark 'brought up the event that we were likely to be attacked perhaps [as soon as] next Monday [1 December] for the Japanese are notorious for making an attack without warning, and the question was what we should do. The question was how we should maneuver them into a position of firing the first shot without allowing too much damage to ourselves': *Joint Committee on the Investigation of the Pearl Harbor Attack*, part II, p. 5,433. All the controversial last sentence meant was that the United States must minimize the risk to herself while awaiting the inevitable Japanese attack somewhere in south-east Asia. On 27 November Hull told Stimson: 'I have washed my hands of it and it is now in the hands of you and Knox – the Army and the Navy': *op. cit.*, pp. 5,384–5. But Hull denies the remark in C. Hull, *The Memoirs of Cordell Hull* (New York, 1948) II, pp. 1,079–80.

from reports received on 28 November of large Japanese troop movements in Indo-China that Japan intended to attack Siam, or Malaya or the Dutch East Indies but not the Philippines. On 1 December Roosevelt asked the State Department to request Japan to state her intentions in view of these troop concentrations. On the same day the British ambassador, Lord Halifax, called on Roosevelt and informed him that Britain expected an attack on Siam and was prepared to fight on this issue. Roosevelt replied that if Japan attacked British or Dutch territory 'we should obviously all be together'.[25] The British government, surprised that the president had given this momentous commitment in so casual a manner and anxious to pin him down, requested Halifax to see Roosevelt again on 3 December. Again the president replied that if Japan attacked British colonial possessions, America would give 'armed support'.[26] This was in reality a voyage into uncharted waters; whatever he said to Halifax, he was by no means certain that Congress – which alone had the power to declare war – would commit America to war to keep the Japanese out of Dutch or even British territory.

The crisis deepened still further. On 5 December in reply to the American inquiry of 1 December Japan blandly stated that the build-up of forces in Indo-China was directed exclusively at China. But a day later reports come in of three large Japanese convoys, accompanied by naval vessels, sailing round the tip of Cape Cambodia apparently bound for Siam. At this point the president made a personal appeal to the emperor – a step which the cabinet contemplated some days before – to do all he could to avert war. This message was, in fact, deliberately delayed by the Japanese military to make sure – unnecessarily – that it would have no effect on the situation. For in the face of the unanimous decision of army, navy and civilians to fight, there was nothing the emperor could have done to avert war.

On the evening of 6 December the Japanese reply to the Ten Points started to arrive in code at the Japanese embassy in Washington. Thirteen parts of the 14-part reply were translated in the embassy and simultaneously by American naval intelligence. Not only did the *résumé* of relations between the two countries leave no doubt that Japan totally rejected the thought of further negotiations but the accompanying instruction from Tokyo to the effect that Nomura was not to present the reply until part 14 arrived on 7 December seemed to indicate that military action was imminent. When Roosevelt received this message at 21.30 he turned to Harry Hopkins and remarked that this meant war, although whether he envisaged war between Britain and Japan or America and Japan is uncertain.

On 7 December part 14 arrived. It stated quite bluntly that the Americans and British were conspiring together to prevent Japan establishing her New Order in east Asia, that the United States was 'always holding fast to theories in disregard of realities, and refusing to yield an inch on its impractical principles' so that it was impossible to reach agreement with her.[27] By 10.00 Roosevelt had

[25]Quoted in Deborah N. Miner, *United States Policy towards Japan 1941: The Assumption that Southeast Asia was Vital to the British War Effort* DISS (Columbia, 1976), p. 390.

[26]*Op. cit.*, p. 392.

[27]*The 'Magic' Background to Pearl Harbor* IV, appendix no. 32.

this message in his hands. Another intercept from Tokyo ordered Nomura and Kurusu to hand over the reply at 13.00 Eastern Standard Time. On receiving this message Marshall sent another warning to all army commanders informing them that the Japanese were presenting what would amount to an ultimatum at 13.00 and ordering them to remain on the alert. The Japanese were slower at decoding than their American opposite numbers and the meeting with Hull was postponed at Japanese request until 13.45. In fact, Nomura and Kurusu appeared in front of Hull at 14.00. Half an hour before at 07.55 Hawaii time the American fleet had been attacked – an unfortunate piece of mistiming for Tōjō had intended the message to be in American hands before hostilities commenced thus complying (more or less) with the requirements of international law. Armed with knowledge of the attack, Hull blasted the embarrassed Japanese out of his room with withering comments on the 'infamous falsehoods and distortions' in their reply to the Ten Points. A meeting of the president's advisers was called at once and quickly agreed on war. On 8 December Roosevelt delivered a message to Congress denouncing the treachery of Japan and asking for a declaration of war. This was agreed in the House of Representatives by 388 votes to one and carried in Senate by 82 votes. On the same day Britain declared war on Japan followed by the governments of the British Commonwealth. Although several of Roosevelt's advisers urged him to include Germany in the declaration of war on the ground that she was the real enemy, Roosevelt refused being unwilling to run ahead of public opinion. The Germans rescued the administration from its dilemma by declaring war on the United States on 11 December.

All this does not mean that the attack of Pearl Harbor was anticipated by the Americans. On the contrary; American naval command both underestimated the capacity of the enemy and overestimated his intelligence while senior officers in Hawaii compounded these errors through their own relative inaction. In the early months of 1941 there had been a flurry of concern about the possibility of an air attack on Hawaii. By the autumn this anxiety had abated because few officers supposed that the Japanese were capable of mounting more than one amphibious operation; it was assumed that reports of troop movements in the South China Sea indicated an amphibious operation against either the Philippines or Siam or the Kra Isthmus or Borneo. And as Japanese aircraft carriers and aircraft seemed to be fully engaged in guarding these convoys, another operation seemed most unlikely.

At the same time American naval command assumed that their Japanese counterparts would act rationally and realize that the American fleet could not possibly prevent Japanese landings; a fleet operating 4,000 miles from base and without reinforcements would place itself in mortal danger if it tried to intervene – and the fates of the British battle cruiser *Repulse* and the battleship *Prince of Wales*, both sunk at Singapore just after the Pearl Harbor attack, confirmed this. There can be no doubt that the Japanese attack was an act of strategic madness. The Japanese failed to bomb the permanent installations and the oil tanks at Pearl Harbor. Most of the vessels they damaged were eventually repaired and used later against the Japanese. Psychologically it was a colossal blunder; by striking a humiliating blow at American national pride Japan made it easy for Roosevelt to unite the people in going to war whereas an attack on the Dutch East Indies or even the Philippines might not have achieved that.

At local level some mistakes were undoubtedly made. Certainly Marshall's message on 7 December warning army commanders to be on the alert only reached Honolulu at 07.33, minutes before the attack – not for any sinister reason but because he sent it by the Western Union office instead of by scrambler telephone. General Walter Short, the local commander, only received it seven hours later. But on the basis of previous warnings received by them Admiral Husband E. Kimmel and General Short might have been better prepared for an emergency. Technical deficiences, shortage of personnel, inadequate training and a lamentable lack of close liaison between navy and army were all to blame. Equally to blame were unclear signals from Washington where those interpreting intelligence reports could not see the wood for the trees – though this is always easier after the event. But most potent of all in the situation was the assumption that Pearl Harbor would not be atttacked. The result is history; the fleet was taken completely by surprise in an attack in which 2,403 soldiers, sailors and civilians were killed, five battleships sunk, three more damaged and 188 aircraft destroyed.

Japan did not stand alone for long. On 11 December Hitler delivered a blistering attack on Roosevelt to an estatic Reichstag and ended his speech amidst tumultous applause with the announcement that the American *chargé d'affaires*, Leland Morris, was to be handed his passport. The same afternoon Ribbentrop read out the declaration of war to Morris. In the evening Germany, Italy and Japan signed a tripartite agreement declaring their intention of waging war to the bitter end against the United States.

The German decision to support Japan calls for some explanation. As we have seen earlier, Hitler and Ribbentrop had encouraged Japan in the spring of 1941 to attack British possessions in the Far East without delay, calculating that this would keep Britain and the United States fully occupied while Germany finished off Russia. But neither Hitler nor his generals were anxious to have Japan participate in the attack on Russia. However, Japan had avoided all commitment to military action in the Pacific in the near future in the belief that she could attain her objectives without war.

In the summer of 1941 the German attitude changed. Ribbentrop, always more anxious than Hitler to involve Japan in the Russian war, asked Ambassador Ott on 28 June and again on 10 July to try to draw Japan into the conflict. More surprisingly, on 14 July Hitler in conversation with the Japanese ambassador Ōshima urged Japan to join in and help liquidate the assets of the Soviet Union before joining with Germany in an attack on the United States whose imperialism constituted a threat both to Europe and to east Asia. Hitler's motives are far from clear. It is unlikely that he was seeking confrontation with the United States even if the announcement in Washington that American forces were replacing British forces in Iceland angered him. Perhaps he was genuinely anxious to bring Japan in as an occupying power east of the Urals now that Russia was – so he thought – on the point of collapse, and as a sop to the Japanese he promised to underwrite their Pacific ambitions in the future.

The desire to prevent any *modus vivendi* between Japan and the United States was probably another consideration in his mind, for though Japan was highly secretive about her negotiations with the Americans, the German Foreign Office feared – rightly – that Japan was quite prepared to jettison the Tripartite Pact if it suited her interests to do so. Although it looked as if the Japanese army might throw caution to the winds and intervene in Russia in the second half of July, by August the general staff had concluded that Germany faced a long struggle and that discretion was the better part of valour in that direction. Once it was clear that Soviet Russia was not going to collapse in the near future, Hitler back-tracked and began to refer to the confrontation with the United States as a task his successor would have to face.[28]

By the late autumn the picture had changed dramatically. With war in the Pacific a near certainty, Japan turned to Germany for reassurance. On 15 November Ambassador Ott and the German military attaché were informed by a member of the Japanese army general staff that war with the United States was likely and that while Japan did not expect military co-operation, she wanted an assurance that Germany would not sign a separate agreement with the United States. When Ribbentrop replied cautiously but positively on 21 November it was apparent that the German attitude to America had also hardened. Early in the month it dawned on Hitler that Germany could not win in Russia before the winter set in; on 19 November he expressed his first doubts about the progress of the campaign to Halder.[29] It was also clear by mid November that he was losing patience with the Americans and accepted at last the inevitability of conflict with them. A Japanese attack on the United States now seemed to make sound strategic sense; it would distract the Americans from the Battle of the Atlantic which Germany must win if she was to defeat Britain. And if Japan could tie the Americans down in the Pacific in 1942 this would give Germany the breathing-space she now needed to finish off Russia. Then Germany could concentrate all her energies on the defeat of the Anglo-Saxon powers. Hitler's only regret was that this strategy entailed the abandonment of east Asia to non-whites but that was a price he was willing to pay for world mastery.

On 28 November Ribbentrop took the offensive and urged Japan to declare war on the United States as well as on Britain. Pressed on this point by Ōshima, Ribbentrop promised that if Japan went to war Germany would join in at once. Oddly enough the Japanese, who would have cheerfully jettisoned the Tripartite Pact if it suited their interests to do so, were concerned to have the Germans promise in writing to stand by them, and instructed Ōshima to press for a formal agreement. As Hitler was visiting the front in southern Russia, Ribbentrop did not feel able to commit Germany on his own. Meanwhile Japan approached Italy. Mussolini readily agreed to declare war on the United States as soon as conflict broke out in the Pacific for this would relieve pressure on Italy in the Mediterranean theatre of war. On Hitler's return from the

---

[28]*Hitler's Table Talk 1941–1944. His Private Conversations*, 10 September 1941; A. Hillgruber, *Staatsmänner und Diplomaten bei Hitler. Vertrauliche Aufzeichnungen über die Unterredungen mit Vertretern des Auslandes 1939–1941* (München, 1969), p. 632, 25 October 1941.

[29]*KTB* Halder III, p. 295.

Wolfsschanze on 4 December he, too, readily agreed to a formal treaty in which Germany and Italy promised to aid Japan if war broke out in the Pacific. In return Japan promised to join in if war broke out between Germany, Italy and the United States. Much to the relief of Tokyo, Hitler did not insist on a quid pro quo in the shape of Japanese participation in the Russian campaign. Hitler had, in fact, reverted to his original position that Germany could defeat Russia without Japanese help. And, as he told Ōshima in January 1942, it was important that Japan should not weaken her forces by taking on the United States, Britain and Russia at the same time. Only in January 1943 after the fall of Stalingrad did Hitler seek active Japanese assistance in Russia but by then Japan had her hands full in the Pacific.

Although Japan had not revealed her operational plans to the Germans and Italians, neither of whom were aware that a task force was steaming towards Hawaii, it cannot be doubted that both knew an attack to be imminent. When news of Pearl Harbor reached Hitler on the afternoon of 7 December he rushed with glee to inform Keitel and Jodl, and remarked to his adjutant that it was impossible for Germany to lose the war: 'we now have a partner who had not been defeated in 3,000 years'.[30] The reassurance was timely for on the same day he had been drafting a directive announcing the abandonment of all major operations on the eastern front; Germany was forced onto the defensive for the first time through bad weather and supply problems.

When Hitler returned to Berlin on 9 December Ribbentrop greeted him with the news that Ōshima had requested an immediate declaration of war by Germany. Assailed by last-minute doubts, Ribbentrop pointed out that Germany was not required under the Tripartite Pact to declare war unless Japan was the victim of attack by another power. Hitler brushed this argument aside but not so much because it would kill the pact stone dead. 'The chief reason', he remarked, 'is that the United States is shooting at our ships. They have been a forceful factor in this war and through their actions have already created a situation of war'.[31] The same day he ordered German submarines to begin an all-out attack on American ships.

The historical parallel with 1917 springs to mind at once. In that year Imperial Germany decided to wage unrestricted submarine warfare against Britain, an action almost certain to draw the Americans into the war as the Germans were well aware. The calculation in Berlin had been that Britain could – and indeed must – be beaten to her knees within six months before the Americans could arrive in force in Europe. Similarly in 1941 time was working against Germany. As Ribbentrop put it succinctly to Hitler: 'We have just one year to cut off Russia from the American supplies arriving via Murmansk and the Persian Gulf: Japan must take care of Vladivostok. If we don't succeed and the munitions potential of the United States joins up with the manpower potential of the Russians, the war will enter a phase in which we shall only be able to win with difficulty'.[32] That proved a masterly understatement.

[30]Irving, *Hitler's War*, p. 352.
[31]Quoted in J. Toland, *Adolf Hitler* (New York, 1976), p. 952.
[32]Irving, *Hitler's War*, p. 352.

Bibliography

General Works

The most detailed and authoritative diplomatic history of·the origins of the European war is G.L. Weinberg, *The Foreign Policy of Hitler's Germany: Starting World War II 1937–1939* (Chicago, 1980). Useful symposia are W. Benz and H. Graml, eds., *Sommer 1939. Die Grossmächte und der Europäische Krieg* (Stuttgart, 1979) and O. Hauser, ed., *Weltpolitik 1933–1939 13 Vorträge* (Göttingen, 1973) and *Weltpolitik II 1939–1945* (Göttingen, 1975). Also useful are G.L. Weinberg, *World in the Balance. Behind the Scenes of World War II* (Hanover, 1981) and A. Toynbee and Veronica M. Toynbee, eds., *Survey of International Affairs 1939–1946. The Initial Triumph of the Axis* (Oxford, 1958).

An indispensable if controversial book on the attempts to end the war is Bernd Martin, *Friedensinitiativen und Machtpolitik im Zweiten Weltkrieg 1939–1942* (Düsseldorf, 1974).

Two good military histories of the Second World War are B.H. Liddell-Hart, *A History of the Second World War* (London, 1970) and H. Michel, *The Second World War* (London, 1974). A. Preston, ed., *General Staffs and Diplomacy before the Second World War* (London, 1978) has useful essays by D.C. Watt, G.L. Weinberg and Robert Young. See also D.C. Watt, *Too Serious a Business. European Armed Forces and the Approach of the Second World War* (London, 1975).

The United States of America

R.D. Burns, *Guide to American Foreign Relations since 1700* (Society for Historians of American Foreign Relations, 1982) is invaluable. An immense amount of primary material on foreign affairs has been published. Of fundamental importance are the State Department publications: *Foreign Relations of the United States. Diplomatic Papers 1861 –; Papers relating to the Foreign Relations of the United States: Japan 1931–1941* (Washington, 1943), 2 vols.; and *Peace and War. United States Foreign Policy 1931–1941* (Washington, 1943), 2 vols.

Excellent text-books are Julius W. Pratt, *A History of United States Foreign Policy* (Eaglewood Cliffs, N.J., 1972) and A. Deconde, *A History of American Foreign Policy* (New York, 1971).

Still indispensable are William L. Langer and S. Everett Gleason, *The Challenge to Isolation 1937–1940* (New York, 1952) and *The Undeclared War 1940–1941* (New York, 1953). Also Herbert Feis, *The Road to Pearl Harbor: The Coming of the War between the United States and Japan* (Princeton, 1950).

Most of Franklin D. Roosevelt's papers have been published. Samuel Rosenman edited *The Public Papers and Private Addresses of Franklin D. Roosevelt* (New

York, 1938–50), 13 vols. Presidential papers on foreign policy are in the Harvard Belknap series: Edgar B. Nixon, ed., *Franklin D. Roosevelt and Foreign Affairs First Series 1933–1937* (Cambridge, Mass., 1969), 3 vols.; *Second Series 1937–1939* (Clearwater, 1972), 14 vols., edited by Donald B. Schewe. His press conferences are in *Complete Presidential Press Conferences of Franklin Delano Roosevelt*, edited by Samuel Rosenman (New York, 1972), 25 vols. Personal correspondence is in E. Roosevelt, ed., *The Roosevelt Letters 1928–1945* (New York, 1949–52), 3 vols. There is a vast secondary literature on Roosevelt. A useful assessment of American scholarship on him as a foreign policy leader is R. Dallek, 'Franklin Roosevelt as World Leader: A Review Article', in *AHR* (1971). Uncritically partisan is B. Rauch, *Roosevelt: From Munich to Pearl Harbor* (New York, 1950). The first serious biography by an admirer and still useful is James M. Burns, *Roosevelt: The Lion and the Fox* (New York, 1956); *Roosevelt: The Soldier of Freedom* (New York, 1970). The latest biography by R. Dallek, *Franklin D. Roosevelt and American Foreign Policy 1932–1945* (New York, 1979) is also sympathetic. More critical is Robert Divine, *The Reluctant Belligerent: American Entry into World War II* (New York, 1963) and *Roosevelt and World War II* (Baltimore, 1969).

On the secretary of state *Memoirs of Cordell Hull* (New York, 1948), 2 vols., tend to exaggerate his role and should be read in conjunction with the important biography by James W. Pratt, *Cordell Hull* (New York, 1964), 2 vols. On Henry L. Stimson, his personal account with McGeorge Bundy *On Active Service in Peace and War* (New York, 1948) is important. A sympathetic biography is Elting E. Morison, *Turmoil and Tradition. A Study of the Life and Times of Henry L. Stimson* (Boston, 1960); a critical one, Richard N. Current, *Secretary Stimson: A Study in Statecraft* (New Brunswick, N.J., 1954). On Henry Morgenthau, John M. Blum, *From the Morgenthau Diaries* (Boston, 1959–67), 3 vols. The substance in one volume is his *Roosevelt and Morgenthau. A Revision and Condensation* (Boston, 1970). On Harold L. Ickes there is *The Secret Diary of Harold L. Ickes* (New York, 1953–4), 3 vols. On William C. Bullitt see Orville H. Bullitt, *For the President: Personal and Secret Correspondence between Franklin D. Roosevelt and William C. Bullitt* (Boston, 1972). A particularly good biography of Ambassador Grew is Waldo H. Heinrichs, *American Ambassador: Joseph C. Grew and the Development of the United States Diplomatic Tradition* (Boston, 1966).

Relations with Germany in the 1930s are covered by Arnold A. Offner, *American Appeasement. United States Foreign Policy and Germany 1933–1938* (Cambridge, Mass., 1969). In 'Appeasement Revisited: the United States, Great Britain and Germany 1939–40', in *JAH* 62:2 (1977) Offner rejects the view that the conflict between free trade and autarky was the basic cause of the alienation of the United States from Germany.

On events leading to the outbreak of war S. Friedlander, *Prelude to Downfall. Hitler and the United States 1939–1941* (New York, 1967); James V. Compton, *The Swastika and the Eagle. Hitler, the United States and the Origins of World War II* (Boston, 1967) argues, incorrectly, that America was a negligible quantity for Hitler before 1943. A Marxist perspective in G. Hass, *Von München bis Pearl Harbor: Zur Geschichte der deutsch-amerikanischen Beziehungen 1938–1941* (Berlin, 1965).

There is no good account of American political relations with Latin America in the 1930s. Alton Frye, *Nazi Germany and the American Hemisphere 1933–1941* has much on the Nazis in the United States (New Haven, 1967).

Investigation into the relationship between foreign policy and economics is still in its infancy. Lloyd C. Gardner, *Economic Aspects of New Deal Diplomacy* (Madison, 1964), a pioneering work from a New Left standpoint, is inadequately documented and disjointed. Quite indispensable is H.J. Schroeder, *Deutschland und die Vereinigten Staaten 1933–1939. Wirtschaft und Politik in der Entwicklung des deutsch–amerikanischen Gegensatzes* (Wiesbaden, 1970). See also Detlef Junker, *Der unteilbare Weltmarkt: das ökonomische Interesse in der Aussenpolitik der USA (1933–1941)* (Stuttgart, 1975). Stimulating but overdone is Bernd Martin, 'Amerikas Durchbruch zur politischen Weltmacht. Die interventionistische Globalstrategie der Regierung Roosevelts 1933–1941', in *MGM* (1981), Heft 2, pp. 57–120.

C. Lewis, *America's Stake in International Investment* (Washington, 1938) is a mine of information. The basic facts about the Reciprocal Trade Agreements are in George L. Beckett, 'The effect of the Reciprocal Trade Agreements upon the Foreign Trade of the United States' *Quarterly Journal of Economics* (1940). Critical of RTA's effect upon the Latin American economy are Dick Stewart, *Trade and Hemisphere: the Good Neighbour Policy and the Reciprocal Trade* (Columbia, 1975); P.A. Varg, 'The Economic Side of the Good Neighbour Policy. The Reciprocal Trade Program and South America', in *Pacific Historical Review* (1976); Alan F. Repko, 'The Failure of Reciprocal Trade: the United States–German Commercial Rivalry in Brazil', in *Mid America* (1978). On the Anglo-American trade treaty of 1938 Arthur W. Schatz, 'The Anglo-American Trade Agreement and Cordell Hull's Search for Peace', *JAH* (1970). On the role of American business there is only R.N. Stromberg, 'American Business and the Approach of War', in *Journal of Economic History* (1953) which shows businessmen to be isolationist in their outlook.

On public opinion, Hadley Cantril and Mildred Stunk, *Public Opinion 1935–1946* (Princeton, 1951) is an indispensable collection of public opinion reports. M. Leigh, *Mobilizing Consent: Public Opinion and American Foreign Policy 1937–1947* (Westport, 1976) is analytical. For an analysis of the restraints of public opinion on Roosevelt Gloria J. Barrow, *Leadership in Crisis: FDR and the Path to Intervention* (Washington, 1973). On isolationism, Wayne S. Cole, *America First: the Battle against Intervention 1940–1941* (Madison, 1953) and Manfred Jones, *Isolationism in America 1935–1941* (Ithaca, N.Y., 1966). On the neutrality legislation Robert Divine, *The Illusion of Neutrality* (Chicago, 1962) is revealing on Roosevelt's attitude. For American military strategy see Mark S. Watson, *United States Army in World War II: Chief of Staff: Prewar Plans and Preparations* (Washington, 1950); S.E. Morison, *The Battle for the Atlantic September 1939–May 1943* (Boston, 1947); G. Pelz, *Race to Pearl Harbor: The Failure of the Second London Naval Conference and the Onset of World War II* (Cambridge, Mass., 1974); Holga H. Herweg, *Politics of Frustration. The United States in German Naval Planning 1889–1941* (Boston, 1976); also chapters in Dorothy Borg, *Pearl Harbor as History* (Columbia, 1973). The revision of the Neutrality Act in 1939 is covered in David L. Porter, *The Seventy-Sixth Congress and World War II* (Missouri, 1979); Lease-Lend in Warren F. Kimball, *The Most Unsordid Act; Lease Lend 1939–1941* (Baltimore, 1969); the Atlantic Conference in

Theodore A. Wilson, *The First Summit: Roosevelt and Churchill at Placentia Bay* (Boston, 1969).

On relations with Britain quite essential is D. Reynolds, *The Creation of the Anglo-American Alliance 1937–1941. A Study in Comparative Co-operation.* (London, 1981); also Callum A. MacDonald, *The United States, Britain and Appeasement 1936–1939* (London, 1981).

On Pearl Harbor the exponents of the 'revisionist' school are Charles A. Beard, *American Foreign Policy in the Making 1931–1940* (New Haven, 1946); *President Roosevelt and the Coming of the War in 1941. A Study in Appearance and Reality* (New Haven, 1948); and Charles C. Tansill, *Back Door to War. The Roosevelt Foreign Policy 1933–1941* (Chicago, 1952). The most satisfactory explanation is Roberta Wohlstetter, *Pearl Harbor: Warning and Decision* (Stanford, 1962). A mass of related primary material in *Pearl Harbor Attack. Hearings Before the Joint Committee on the Investigation of the Pearl Harbor Attack* (Washington, 1945–6), 39 parts.

Germany.

There is a mass of primary material on foreign policy in *Trials of the Major War Criminals before the International Military Tribunal*, (Nuremberg, 1947–9), 42 vols.; *Nazi Conspiracy and Aggression* (Washington, 1946–8), 10 vols., a selection of documents and affidavits used at the trial; and *Documents on German Foreign Policy 1918–1945* (Washington 1949–). Primary material on military decision-making in H.A. Jacobsen, ed., *Kriegstagebuch. Tägliche Aufzeichnungen des Chefs des Generalstabes des Heeres 1939–1942* (Stuttgart, 1962–4), 3 vols.; P.E. Schramm, ed., *Kriegstagebuch des Oberkommandos der Wehrmacht 1940–1945* (Frankfurt a.M., 1961–5), 4 vols.; *Führer Conferences on Matters dealing with the German Navy, 1939–1945* (Washington, 1946–7), 8 vols.; H.R. Trevor-Roper, *Hitlers War Directives 1939–1945* (London, 1964) based on the compilation by Walter Hubatsch; and H.A. Jacobsen, *Dokumente zur Vorgeschichte des Westfeldzuges 1939–1940* (Göttingen, 1960).

Diaries, memoirs and papers useful for foreign policy are: H. Gibson, ed., *The Ciano Diaries, 1939–1943* (Garden City, N.Y., 1946); L.E. Hill, *Die Weizsäcker Papiere 1939–1950* (Frankfurt a.M., 1974); Hildegard von Kotze, ed., *Heeresadjutant bei Hitler 1938–1943* (Stuttgart, 1974), often referred to as a diary although Engels's recollections were written down later; H. Krausnick and Harold C. Deutsch, eds., *Tagebücher eines Abwehroffiziers, 1938–1940* (Stuttgart, 1970), the diary of counter-intelligence officer Helmuth Groscurth; E. Kordt, *Wahn und Wirklichkeit: Die Aussenpolitik des Dritten Reiches* (Stuttgart, 1948); *Nicht aus den Akten. Die Wilhelmstrasse in Frieden und Krieg. Begegnungen, Eindrücke, 1928–1945* (Stuttgart, 1950), memoirs of a senior foreign office official; P. Schmidt, *Statist auf diplomatischer Bühne 1923–1945. Erlebnisse des Chefdolmetschers im Auswärtigen Amt mit den Staatsmännern Europas* (Bonn, 1954); W. Warlimont, *Im Hauptquartier der deutschen Wehrmacht 1939–1945. Grundlagen–Formen–Gestalten* (Frankfurt a.M., 1962), memoirs of Jodl's deputy at OKW.

The most detailed and authoritative account of German foreign policy is G.L. Weinberg, *The Foreign Policy of Hitler's Germany. Diplomatic Revolution in Europe 1933–1936* (Chicago, 1973); *The Foreign Policy of Hitler's Germany. Starting*

World War II 1937-1939 (Chicago, 1980). A slight account in N. Rich, *Hitler's War Aims, Ideology, the Nazi state and the Course of Expansion* (London, 1973); a more useful one in J. Hiden, *Germany and Europe 1919-1939* (London, 1977). Highly interpretative is K. Hildebrand, *The Foreign Policy of the Third Reich* (London, 1973); A. Hillgruber, *Deutschlands Rolle in der Vorgeschichte der beiden Weltkriege* (Göttingen, 1967) and *Kontinuität und Diskontinuität in der deutschen Aussenpolitik von Bismarck bis Hitler* (Düsseldorf, 1971). An attempt at integration of political, economic and military developments in W. Carr, *Arms Autarky and Aggression. German Foreign Policy 1933-1939* (London, 1979). Important symposia are M. Funke, ed., *Hitler Deutschland und die Mächte. Materialien zur Aussenpolitik des dritten Reiches* (Düsseldorf, 1976) and W. Michalka, ed., *Nationalsozialistische Aussenpolitik* (Darmstadt, 1978).

Indispensable for the Second World War is the 10-volume history *Das Deutsche Reich und der Zweite Weltkrieg* being written by a team of historians at Freiburg's *Militärgeschichtliches Forschungsamt*. To date three volumes have appeared: I *Ursachen und Voraussetzungen der deutschen Kriegspolitik* (Stuttgart, 1979); II *Die Errichtung der Hegemonie auf dem·europäischen Kontinent* (Stuttgart, 1979); IV *Der Angriff auf die Sowjetunion* (Stuttgart, 1983). Useful for the Marxist standpoint is W. Schumann, G. Hass, *Deutschland im Zweiten Weltkrieg. Vorbereitung, Entfesselung und Verlauf des Krieges bis zum 22 Juni 1941* (Köln, 1974). Monographs of importance on military strategy include A. Hillgruber's impressive *Hitlers Strategie. Politik und Kriegführung 1940-1941* (Frankfurt a.M., 1965); and Barry A. Leach, *German Strategy against Russia 1939-1941* (Oxford, 1973), who argues that army command was ahead of Hitler in planning the attack on Russia. See also R. Cecil, *Hitlers Decision to Invade Russia 1941* (London, 1975). Controversial and stimulating is M. Geyer's *Aufrüstung oder Sicherheit. Die Reichswehr an der Krise der Machtpolitik 1924-1936* (Wiesbaden, 1980), which has wider implications for foreign policy.

On Russo-German relations see G.L. Weinberg, *Germany and the Soviet Union 1939-1941* (Leiden, 2nd edn., 1972); a penetrating analysis of the Russo-German Pact in A. Hillgruber, 'Der Hitler–Stalin Pakt und die Entfesselung des Zweiten Weltkrieges – Situationsanalyse und Machtkalkül der beiden Pakt Partner' *HZ* 230 (1980).

On Hitler there is no need to list the innumerable biographies; D. Irving, *Hitler's War* (London, 1977) is wrong-headed about the Holocaust and concentrates too much on Hitler; W. Carr in *Hitler: A Study in Personality and Politics* (London, 1978) attempts to break with the traditional cradle-to-grave treatment. On Ribbentrop an important study is W. Michalka, *Ribbentrop und die deutsche Weltpolitik 1933-1940* (Münster, 1980).

Much work has been done in recent years on the economic background to the war. Indispensable symposia are F. Forstmeier and H.E. Volkmann, eds., *Wirtschaft und Rüstung am Vorabend des Zweiten Weltkrieges* (Düsseldorf, 1975) and *Kriegswirtschaft und Rüstung 1939-1945* (Düsseldorf, 1977). Tim Mason has assembled a mass of material on the late 1930s in *Arbeiterklasse und Volksgemeinschaft. Dokumente und Materialien zur deutschen Arbeiterpolitik 1936-1939* (Opladen, 1975). Important material on the involvement of German industry in the aggressive policies of the Nazis in D. Eichholtz and W. Schumann, *Anatomie der Aggression. Neue Dokumente über die Rolle des deutschen*

Monopolkapitalismus bei der Vorbereitung und Durchführung des Zweiten Weltkrieges (Berlin, 1969); *Anatomie der Aggression. Neue Dokumente zu den Kriegszielen des faschistischen deutschen Imperialismus im Zweiten Weltkrieg* (Berlin, 1972). Important monographs include B.A. Carroll, *Design for Total war. Arms and Economics in the Third Reich* (Hague, 1968); D. Eichholtz, *Geschichte der deutschen Kriegswirtschaft 1939-1941* I (Berlin, 1969) for the East German viewpoint; A.S. Milward, *The German Economy at War* (London, 1965) – his thesis that the blitzkrieg was an economic imperative has been challenged by R. J. Overy, 'Hitler's War and the German Economy', in *Economic History Quarterly* XXXV (1982) and in *Goering. The 'Iron Man'* (London, 1984); F. Neumann, *Behemoth. The Structure and Practice of National Socialism* (London, 1942) has still much that is pertinent to say; A. Schweitzer, *Big Business in the Third Reich* (London, 1964). On the general economic background to the diplomacy of the 1930s see David E. Kaiser, *Economic Diplomacy and the Origins of the Second World War* (Princeton, 1980).

On the relationship between economics and foreign policy there has been a lively controversy triggered off in part by Tim Mason's interpretation, 'Zur Funktion des Angriffkrieges', in G. Ziebura, ed., *Grundfragen der deutschen Aussenpolitik seit 1871* (Darmstadt, 1975). For a penetrating analysis see I. Kershaw's forthcoming *The Nazi Dictatorship Problems and Perspectives of interpretation* (London, 1985), chapter 3; also J. Düllfer, 'Der Beginn des Krieges 1939: Hitler, die innere Krise und das Mächtesystem', in *Geschichte und Gesellschaft* (1976).

Japan

The most important primary source is J. Pritchard and Sonia Zaide, eds., *The Tokyo War Crimes Trial* (New York, 1981), 22 vols. For the crucial 1941 Liaison Conference Ike Nobutaka, *Japan's Decision for War. Records of the 1941 Policy Conferences* (Stanford, 1967). Intercepts of messages between Tokyo and Washington in *The 'Magic' Background to Pearl Harbour* (US Department of Defense, 1977), 8 vols. Particularly important for those without Japanese are translations by J.W. Morley from a seven-volume diplomatic history of Japan published in 1962–3 and based on foreign ministry archives and military agencies: *The China Quagmire: Japan's Expansion on the Asian Continent* (New York, 1974); *Deterrent Diplomacy: Japan, Germany and the USSR 1935–1940* (New York, 1976); *The Fateful Choice. Japan's Advance into South-east Asia 1939–1941* (New York, 1980). Important, too, is the war diary of the German naval attaché in Japan 1939–43 of which vol. I has been published so far under the title *The Price of Admiralty* (Falmer, 1982).

Two good general accounts of relations with the United States are: C.E. Neu, *The Troubled Encounter: The United States and Japan 1853–1972* (New York, 1975); and Akira Iriye, *Across the Pacific: An Inner History of American-East Asian Relations* (New York, 1967). On foreign policy I. Nish, *Japanese Foreign Policy 1869–1942* (London, 1977).

After the Tokyo War Crimes Trial it was widely believed that Japan had pursued a premeditated policy of aggression from 1931 onwards much as Nazi Germany had done. This view is reflected in the works of Feis, Langer and

Gleason and R. Storry, *The Double Patriots. A Study of Japanese Militarism* (London, 1957). A corrective to this view is Robert C. Butow, *Tōjō and the Coming of War* (Princeton, 1961), which argues that Tōjō and his associates were merely 'robots of their subordinates'; B. Crowley, *Japan's Quest for Autonomy: National Security and Foreign Policy 1930–1938* (Princeton, 1966), laying equal blame on civilian leaders for Japanese aggression; F.C. Jones, *Japan's New Order in the Far East 1919–1939* (Oxford, 1971) which maintains there was no master plan; Paul W. Schroeder, *The Axis Alliance and Japanese–American Relations 1941* (Ithaca, N.Y., 1958), which goes to the other extreme and blames the Americans for their moral intransigence. An indispensable symposium is Dorothy Borg and Shumpei Okamoto, eds., *Pearl Harbor as History. Japanese–American Relations 1931–1941* (Columbia, 1973), containing the proceedings of a binational conference in 1969.

Strategic and political factors are brought together in C. Thorne, *The Limits of Foreign Policy: the West, the League and the Far Eastern Crisis of 1931–1933* (London, 1972) and *Allies of a Kind. The United States, Britain and the War against Japan 1941–1945* (London, 1978). On the Tripartite Pact a standard is T. Sommer, *Deutschland und Japan zwischen den Mächten 1935–1940. Vom Antikominternpakt zum Dreimächtepakt* (Tübingen, 1962); E. Preisseisen, *Germany and Japan. A Study in Totalitarian Diplomacy 1933–1941* (The Hague, 1958); Johanna M. Meskill, *Hitler and Japan. The Hollow Alliance* (New York, 1966). A Marxist interpretation of relations between Japan, China and Germany based on Potsdam material is K. Drechsler, *Deutschland–China–Japan 1933–1939. Das Dilemma der deutschen Fernostpolitik.* (Berlin, 1964). Also on the Far East in the 1930s is an important study by John P. Fox, *Germany and the Far Eastern Crisis 1931–1938. A Study in Diplomacy and Ideology* (Oxford, 1982).

On the Japanese navy, S.E. Morison, *The Rising Sun in the Pacific 1931–April 1942* (Boston, 1948) contains the facts. Also chapters in Borg and Okamoto, *Pearl Harbor as History*.

Useful on the structure of Japanese politics is Yale Candee Moxon, *Control of Japanese Foreign Policy. A Study of Civil–Military Rivalry 1930–1945* (Berkeley, 1957). Stimulating comments by Bernd Martin scattered over several articles: 'Japans Weltmachtstreben 1939–1941', in O. Hauser, ed., *Weltpolitik II 1939–1945* (Göttingen, 1975; 'Aggressionspolitik als Mobilisierungsfaktor: der militärische und wirtschaftliche Imperialismus Japans 1931–1941', in Forstmeier and Volkmann, *Wirtschaft und Rüstung*; and 'Die deutsch--japanischen Beziehungen während des Dritten Reiches', in Funke, *Hitler Deutschland und die Mächte.* There is also much of interest in Martin's book *Deutschland und Japan im Zweiten Weltkrieg. Von Angriff auf Pearl Harbor bis zur deutschen Kapitulation* (Göttingen, 1969). Slight and disappointing is Yoshitake Oka, *Konoe Fumimaro* (Tokyo, 1983). On economic development G.C. Allen, *A Short Economic History of Japan 1862–1937* (London, 1951).

Index